BLUE GUIDE

TRAVELS IN TRANSYLVANIA

THE GREATER TÂRNAVA VALLEY

LUCY ABEL SMITH

SOMERSET • LONDON

First edition 2016

Published by Blue Guides Limited, a Somerset Books Company
Winchester House, Deane Gate Avenue, Taunton, Somerset TA1 2UH
www.blueguides.com. 'Blue Guide' is a registered trademark.

ISBN 978–1–905131–69–3

A CIP catalogue record of this book is available from the British Library.

Distributed in the United States of America by
W.W. Norton & Company, Inc.
500 Fifth Avenue, New York, NY 10110.

The authors and the publisher have made reasonable efforts to ensure the accuracy of all
the information in *Travels in Transylvania: The Greater Târnava Valley*; however, they can accept
no responsibility for any loss, injury or inconvenience sustained by any traveller as a result of
information or advice contained in the guide.

Statement of editorial independence: Blue Guides, their authors and editors, are prohibited
from accepting any payment from any restaurant, hotel or other establishment for its inclusion
in this guide, or for a more favourable mention than would otherwise have been made.

Every effort has been made to contact the copyright owners of material reproduced in this
guide. We would be pleased to hear from any copyright owners we have been unable to reach.

Maps: Dimap Bt. © Blue Guides. The line drawings of fortified churches are taken from
The Church-Fortresses of the Transylvanian Saxons by Hermann Fabini. The author and
publisher are grateful for permission to reproduce them in this guide.
Interior images: Lucy Abel Smith (pp. 3, 49, 57, 62, 65, 78, 103, 111, 129, 133, 134, 139,
141, 150, 154, 161, 164, 169, 171, 173, 175, 176, 189, 192, 198, 199, 202, 223, 230)
David Abel Smith (p. 51); Mónika Soós (p. 53); Levente Csiszér (p. 55); Paul Billinghurst
(p. 69); Lady O'Neill of the Maine (pp. 85, 179); Richiş village archives (p. 125);
Péter Szombati (p. 136); Moşna village (p. 168); Antonia Timmerman (p. 208);
Blue Guides (pp. 24, 29, 72, 81, 88, 91, 98, 157, 204), Wikicommons (pp. 93, 195).
Cover: Stylised carnation, inspired by a design from an embroidered Saxon cloak of c. 1900.
By Hadley Kincade © Blue Guides. Title page: Ceiling boss from Mediaş.

All material prepared for press by Anikó Kuzmich.
Printed and bound in Hungary by Pauker Nyomda.

CONTENTS

PREFACE

Many guides to Transylvania, locally and nationally, focus only on the rich flora and fauna of the extraordinary valley of the Greater Târnava. Its great diversity has both incidental and accidental causes: firstly terrain; but also a history of conservative communities and centuries-old systems of agriculture, along with more recent poverty.

In the 120 or so kilometres of the valley that are covered in this short guide, there is still to be seen the stunning landscape, ancient farming methods and the extraordinary botanical variety. But there is so much more. We travel through a fraction of ancient Hungary to encounter a vast array of the peoples of Central Europe, all up until recently living together, yet in distinct communities with different customs, architecture, costumes and languages. We find the Vlachs and the Szeklers, the Hungarians, the Saxons and the Jews, the Gypsies and others, such as the Armenians, who settled here to take advantage of this tolerant and diverse land in the very heart of Europe.

There are two Târnava rivers: the Târnava Mică, the Lesser, and the Târnava Mare, the Greater. They rise in the Gurghiu Mountains in the eastern Carpathians and from there they both flow westwards through central Transylvania forming a sort of Mesopotamia in the middle. They converge at Blaj, the end of our journey. There is a nice fable about the rivers taking a bet as to which would arrive in Blaj first. The Mare was wise and flowed during the day so it could avoid any obstacles. The Mică, filled with ambition, flowed even at night and was forced to make long detours, even flowing backwards. From Blaj, the river, now known simply as the Târnava, flows on west, emptying into the Mureș at Alba Iulia.

The Târnava Mare valley is wide and fertile and seems to have provided an easy route through Transylvania for invaders and traders alike. Here, in the 1870s, the railway came too, which was of great benefit to the industries of Mediaș and Sighișoara.

In the past, the river was liable to flood. This is mentioned with reference to Dumbrăveni, where the church had to be moved and the land drained under Maria Theresa in the 1760s. Sighişoara suffered two disastrous floods in the 1970s, giving Ceauşescu an excuse to demolish a section of the old city: this was part of his grand plan to bulldoze villages and towns, destroying their, and their inhabitants', identity. The river now has a series of dams to prevent floods from recurring.

The Târnava Mare is known in German as the Große Kokel, in Hungarian as the Nagy Küküllő. The very fact that it, along with most of the towns and villages in this short guide, have three names, Romanian, Hungarian and Saxon, says it all. When I first discussed the idea of a short guide to the area, where I have bought a small village farmhouse, the journalist Beatrice Ungar, herself a Saxon, was quick to point out that I would have to write as many introductions as there were peoples in the surrounding settlements. Perhaps it is fortunate that I am a foreign import who, on my first journey here into the Siebenbürgen (a region inhabited from the 12th century predominately by 'Saxons'), thought it one of the most beautiful parts of Europe I had seen. In those Ceauşescu years it was unthinkable—and indeed impossible—to buy a house. It was hard enough to find a hotel, restaurant, petrol station or telephone. Tourists were really only encouraged into Moldavia, the part of Romania famous for its painted churches, which are Romanian Orthodox and were lightly supported by the Ceauşescu regime as monuments of the National Church. The Securitate were everywhere and, as a foreigner, one was followed. Everyone was suspicious of everyone, my bus driver of my translator. That is the way Communism ruled.

There have been huge changes since then. Communism has fallen (although there is some residue left). Romania has joined NATO and the EU. There has been mass emigration—most obviously, as relates to the subject of this guide, the Saxon exodus of the early 1990s. This has left entire communities to cope with a cultural change which would tax the most sophisticated. There has been restitution for some of the church communities and for the Hungarians and Romanians. There has been foreign investment as well as welcome interest from charities from outside

Romania, not only on humanitarian grounds but also in the fields of conservation and job creation, from bodies who realise how fragile is the beauty yet how important for all of us. I have listed some of them at the back of the guide (*p. 225*).

I have begun this guide in Odorheiu Secuiesc (Székelyudvarhely), the cultural centre of the Szekler communities. It is about an hour from the ancient Saxon citadel and town of Sighișoara—but could be a hundred miles away, so different is it culturally. Hungarian is the favoured language and much of the visual surroundings would sit comfortably in Hungary. Short journeys east will bring the traveller to the volcanic plateau which is the source of the Greater Târnava river.

Travelling west along the valley we explore the important town of Sighișoara, in the heart of the ancestral Saxon lands. It is not only beautiful, ancient and more or less complete, but it has a railway, hotels, restaurants and a buzz. From here I have suggested visits to villages and towns down the main valley road as far as Blaj, where the Târnava Mare converges with the Târnava Mică. There are journeys off this route: some are circular but most, I am afraid, are up and down to villages which are dead ends. I have tried to find places, usually private families, who, with due warning, can provide picnics or other meals and bed and breakfast. Hotels, plentiful in Sighișoara, Biertan and, increasingly in Mediaș, can be found in the listings (*pp. 11–15*) but also on the internet. Tourism is very important to this valley, an area which has so much to offer and which is, at times, concealed from the tourist. The concealment is not deliberate; I suspect it is largely because the Romanians themselves underestimate what they have.

The following little guide is only an outline of the area and its history. Others have written about the subject with greater competence but I have interlaced, in the descriptions of the churches, towns and castles, something of the general story of how they came about. I hope by the end of the journey from the source of the Târnava Mare to its meeting with the Târnava Mică at Blaj that any traveller will feel they have caught a glimpse of the many layers of this fascinating fragment of Europe.

Lucy Abel Smith

Acknowledgements

So many people have offered suggestions and given their time for interviews. Many have agreed to meet me and discuss everything from Transylvanian rugs, the niceties of the election or Coronation of historic rulers, to picnics. Like travelling in Transylvania, you never know what is going to happen next and those you meet or seek out can come from all over Central Europe. So much depends on who you encounter along the way and that is a matter of luck and timing. I have been very lucky and all those mentioned below have ensured that the journey has not been dull. Thanks and acknowledgements go to:

David Abel Smith, Rosie Abel Smith, Robert Abel Smith, Eliza Abel Smith, John Akeroyd, Jeremy Amos, Anna Balasca, István Barkóczi, Giovanna Bassetti, William Blacker, Alin Benghiac, Edward Bennett, Gladys Bethlen, Paul Billinghurst, Frances Cairncross, Adi Calaj, Ion Calinescu, Laura Chirilă, Letitia Nistor Cosnean, Annie Crutchley, Levente Csiszér, Levente Domokos, Jessica Douglas-Home, Miriam Eliad, Hermann Fabini, Caroline Fernolend, Roy Foster, Dieter Fröhlich, Anna Gergely, Juliana Grose, Anthony Hazeldine, Jan Hülsemann, Gheorghe Hundorfean, Caroline Juler, Hans König, Roy Lancaster, Klára Lázok, Henriette Lemnitz, Temple Melville, Dr Dóra Mérai, Mihai Mircea, Janet Page, Nat Page, Paul Philippi, Olga Pujmanová Stretti, Cristian Radu, Tony Redman, Anda Reuben, Eugen Roba, Andrea Rost, Christian Rummel, Clara Sarasan, Ioan Sarasan, Raul Sarasan, Hans Schaas, Jonas Schäfer, Ulrike Schäfer, Tony Scotland, Elisa Segrave, Ioana Serban, Sorin Serban, Fr. Gerhard Servatius, Noémi Simó, József Sisa, Mónika Soós, Tony Timmerman, Gerrit Timmerman, Gabriel Tudor, Beatrice Ungar, Wilhelm Untch, Laura Vesa, Paul Weldon.

My thanks also go to Attingham Summer School, which has given me the chance to make so many friends in Central Europe, and to Special Tours, my old company, who sent me to Romania in the first place.

GETTING TO THE VALLEY

Arrival in the Greater Târnava Valley can come in many forms. It takes about three days of intense driving to reach the valley from the UK. The quickest and most comfortable way is to fly to Sibiu or Târgu Mureș and hire a car. An attractive means of arrival is to take the sleeper train from Vienna or Budapest (it is the same line) and emerge in Mediaș or Sighișoara. Furthermore, this gives an understanding of the vastness of the old Austro-Hungarian world. Health and safety do not feature on Transylvanian train stations. One must leap with speed onto the adjacent tracks and hope for the best. Dinner is usually served on the train: always a goulash of sorts. The border stoppings are still long, passports are scrutinised and customs people still question. All this is in the middle of the night. But there is a real sense of travelling, now hard to find in other parts of Europe.

In the valley itself the most convenient way to get around is by private car. There is a railway line down the valley but it was being upgraded at the time of writing, with completion due in 2017. Rail travel in the valley is not advisable before this time.

A walking map of the area is available and can be bought in all Tourist Information centres and better bookshops. The MET also produce small brochures which include maps and suggested walks. These are available for Mălâncrav and Alma Vii and can be bought direct from the MET (*see p. 225*). There is a book of guesthouses in Romania, *Conace și Pensiuni din România* (Igloo Media, 2013).

For information on the churches visit www.transilvania-card.ro/fortified-churches. This is an resource on the main fortified churches in the area. There is a further site at www.fortified-churches.org.

The following site is more related to food and festivals in Transylvania: www.mytransylvania.ro.

WEATHER

The joy of this area is that is visitable all year round. The late spring brings with it the glory of the wildflower meadows (though the timing depends on how early or late spring arrives). It is probably safe to recommend early to mid-June. The summers are hot and the spring and autumn can be wet. Early November is a favourite: the colours of the beech forests are stunning and the sheep are in the lower pastures. The cattle still make their way home in the villages to be milked and the days can be warm with blue skies. There are also very few tourists in the honey traps. However, for those who wish to visit churches, note that Biertan is closed from November to Easter and that key-hunting for others becomes more difficult—though it can prove entertaining.

Winters are beautiful but the temperature can drop to minus 20°C.

SLEEPING AND EATING

Restaurants are still a rarity in many Transylvanian villages but you will usually find a bar or a 'Magazin Mixt' (general store) to produce the ingredients for a picnic. Lunches are possible in all villages where the MET has a guesthouse. Those covered in this book are Alma Vii, Biertan and Mălâncrav (*T: 0265 506 024, booking@experiencetransylvania.ro, www. experiencetransylvania.ro*).

Below is a short listing of places to stay or eat in the towns and villages covered by this guide. Note that in this listings here—and everywhere else in this guide—telephone numbers are given as if calling from within Romania. If you are calling internationally, add +40 (the country code) to the beginning of the number and drop the initial zero.

Alma Vii
The **Romanian School**, completely restored by the MET, can accommodate a total of 15 guests for B&B. (*T: 0724 000 350, booking@experiencetransylvania.ro*).

There are also two **MET guesthouses**, details of which can be found on the Experience Transylvania website (*www. experiencetransylvania.ro*). You can book online.

Axente Sever
Four **rooms in the church fortress** offer guest accommodation. Bookings and enquires can be made by phone

or email (*T: 0735 569 996; muzeulcetate@yahoo.com*). See the website (*www.axentesever.com*) for further information, details of bike hire, etc.

Bazna

For the B&B here, contact Mr Albert Binder (he is also the curator of the church) at house no. 21 (*T: 0269 850 101*). He can offer accommodation in two houses. There is a house called **Caminul Sasilor** which has three rooms, kitchen and living room. This house is managed by his son. There is more accommodation in the **parish house**, which has five rooms (sleeps a maximum of 20) with two shared showers and three WCs along with a large garden. To book, call Mr Binder as above. Mr Binder can also just supply lunch if this is requested in advance.

There is also the spa hotel, **Complex Balnear Expo**, a large modern building (*T: 0269 831 512, 0269 850 347, 0269 850 347, rezervari@bazna.ro, www.bazna.ro*).

Biertan

During the first Transylvanian Book Festival in 2013, we used the following accommodation and received nothing other than glowing compliments:

Accommodation in **renovated Saxon houses** close to the fortified church (*T: 0742 024 065, www. biertan.ro*); the MET guesthouse on the corner of the market-place (*www.experiencetransylvania.ro*); B&B at the **Casa Dornröschen** (*Str. George Coşbuc 25, T: 0269 244 165*).

The old school under the church walls is now the **Unglerus Restaurant**.

Copşa Mare

The Copşa Mare guesthouses, in the heart of the village, offer a very high standard of restoration of the ancient Saxon village house. Their interiors have great style and comfort, showing off the ceramics, textiles and furniture of the local communities with an Italian twist. There is also a restaurant using local food and recipes. Call to book (*T: 0746 064 200 or 0728 371 762, www.copsamare.ro*).

Criş

Picnics and horse-and-cart hire are available. Accommodation is also planned (*keresdguesthouses@gmail. com*).

Cristuru Secuiesc

A recommended place to eat is the **Bonfini** (named after the court chronicler of King Matthias Corvinus). *Piața Libertății/ Szabadság tér 51. T: 0726 244 499.*

Cund

The **Valea Verde** restaurant lies at the end of one of the most beautiful valleys in a region were there is tough competition for beautiful valleys (*T: 0265 714 399, www.discover-transilvania. com*). Valea Verde also offers accommodation; either comfortable apartments in their own building, or restored Saxon-style farmhouses in the nearby village (*booking details as above*).

Mălâncrav

The Apafi manor house can be rented from the MET (*www. experiencetransylvania.ro*).

Mediaș

A simple hotel in the main square is **Hotel Traube** (*T: 0269 844 898, hoteltraube.ro*). Also central is the new, small **Hotel Select**, which has a restaurant (*Str. Petofi Sandor 3; T: 0269 834 874, hotel.select@ yahoo.com*).

In the outskirts to the north is **Hanul Greweln** *pensione* and restaurant (*Str. Greweln 1; T: 0269 846 567, hanulgreweln.ro*). On the eastern outskirts is the **BinderBubi**, where the food is good. There is a pool, spa and the start of a Skansen (*Str. Plopului 30; T: 0269 843 089, binderbubimedias.ro*).

Moșna

Willy and Lavinia Schuster's organic farm, **Bio-Moșna**, offers visits and meals (breakfast, lunch, brunch, dinner or cheese tasting). You need to make an appointment, depending on the size of your group, at least one day before (*Str. Cetății 543; T: 0269 862 206 (landline), 0741 391 444 (Lavinia mobile) or 0752 108 184 (Willy mobile), willyschuster@yahoo. com*). There is also a comfortable *pensione*, **Casa Mantsch**, just two houses away, also managed by the Schusters, in a beautiful Saxon house with three double rooms (*Str. Cetății 540*).

The **Priest House** has three self-catering apartments and can accommodate up to a total of 20 guests. Contact Marianne Rempel (*T: 0744 624 776*).

The **Logean Vasile** guesthouse

at no. 69 sleeps four for B&B (*T:
0760 699 829 or 0269 862 150*).

Another guesthouse, **Diacu Ioan**
at no. 273, also sleeps four for
B&B (*T: 0760 699 828 or 0269 862
176*).

Nemşa

The **Borza Cornelia** guesthouse
at no. 58 sleeps six for B&B (*T:
0269 257 03*). **Pensiunea Liana**
can accommodate up to 25 guests
and also has its own restaurant.
Contact Elena Sarlea (*T: 0269 257
817*).

Odorheiu Secuiesc

For somewhere to eat, try **Pethő**,
on the southern edge of town
(*Rákóczi Ferenc u. 21; T: 266 218
161*).

Richiş

The **Priest House**, run by
Gerrit and Tony Timmerman,
will organise lunch or dinner
on request. They also offer
accommodation in the form
of camping in a walled garden
or guest rooms in the restored
Priest House itself (*T: 0269 258
475, www.lacurtearichis.ro*). B&B
accommodation is available in
Casa Noah (*T: 0742 980 250, www.*

slowlyplanet.org/casa-noah). The
MET has a beautiful, newly restored
house with a library, to sleep nine.

Saschiz

Anca and Charlie Dalmasso offer
rooms at **Casa de pe Deal** (*T:
0740 286 874, www.casadepedeal.
com*).

Hanul Cetăţii is an inn with
accommodation (*T: 0758 040 606,
www.hanulcetatii.ro*).

Other options are the **Cartref**
guesthouse (*T: 0745 981 139,
www.pensiunea-cartref.ro*) and
the **Pensiunea Violeta** (*T: 0265
711 837 or 0749 572 099, www.
pensiunea-violeta.ro*).

Sighişoara

In the citadel:
Casa cu Cerb (*Str. Şcolii 1; T: 0265
774 625, www.casacucerb.ro*). It is
very pleasant to eat outside in the
square. I am told that the tripe
soup is the best.
Fronius Residence, my current
favourite (*Str. Şcolii 13; T: 0265
779 173, www.fronius-residence.ro*).
Hotel Sighişoara (*Str. Şcolii 4–6;
T: 0265 777 788 or 0265 771 000,
www.sighisoarahotels.ro*). There is a
restaurant but it is inside only.
Casa Wagner (*Piaţa Cetăţii 7; T:*

0265 506 014, www.casa-wagner.com/en/home-sighisoara). It has become rather group-orientated of late but is still a lovely place to have a drink outside.

Casa Vlad Dracul, although for obvious reasons touristy, produces good, substantial meals (*Str. Cositorarilor 5; T: 0265 771 596*).

In the lower town:

Hotel Claudiu (*Str. Ilarie Chendi 28; T: 0265 779 882, www.hotelclaudiu.ro*).

BinderBubi (*Str. Nicolae Balcescu 8; T: 0372 088 888, www.binderbubisighisoara.ro*). The architecture looks as if it has come out of a kit but the hotel is good, as is the restaurant.

Gasthaus Alte Post (*Piaţa Hermann Oberth; T: 0365 430 270. www.gasthaus-altepost.ro*). Also good for meals.

Transylvanian food is, nowadays, very international, but traditionally has been a mix of Hungarian and Romanian. Expect delicious soups (*ciorbă, supă* and borsch); stuffed cabbage, schnitzel, salads and wonderful cakes. Romanian wine (homebrew excepted) can be a revelation (the Romanians have possibly been producing wine longer than the French) and the Târnava area is a large producer: its wine is the most likely to be found on menus in the region. There is also the schnapps, usually homemade, but none the worse for being so. Often offered as an aperitif, it is wonderfully warming after a long day's exploring, or even to start your day. If driving, it is worth remembering that there is zero tolerance for alcohol.

RECOMMENDED GUIDES AND AGENCIES

Ramona Cazacu: my_romania@yahoo.com;
Liberty International: geanina.diaconescu@liberty-international.ro, T: 0727 735 733;
Mike Morton: mike.morton@travelcounsellors.com, T: +44 1900 824329;
Reality & Beyond: lucy@realityandbeyond.co.uk, T: +44 1285 750358;
Andrea Rost: andrea.rost@gmx.net;
Laura Vesa: office@discoveromania.ro.

HISTORICAL OVERVIEW

Transylvania, lying partially protected by the Carpathians, is at the crossroads of Central and Eastern Europe and at various times in her history has combined the roles of buffer state and natural trade route, alternately facilitating links and protecting against conflict between East and West. She was also an early and exemplary haven of religious tolerance. For all these reasons, the region presents an intricate story.

Transylvania today makes up the entirety of western Romania. Once a political entity in its own right, it is now considered as an aggregate of 16 counties, with Cluj (Klausenburg/Kolozsvár) and Sibiu (Hermannstadt/Nagyszeben) the cultural centres. The population today is 75 percent Romanian, 20 percent Hungarian 3.4 percent Roma and under 1 percent German/Saxon. The numbers of Hungarians and Saxons have at different times been much greater. How this diversity came about, and why it shifted so dramatically, requires some explaining.

Dacians and Magyars: early settlers

Described from the perspective of the arriving Magyars, Transylvania was *Terra ultra silvam*, the Land beyond the Forest. The migrants arrived in the Carpathian Basin, led by their chieftains, in the late 9th century. Here they found peoples from the great migration period of the 5th and 6th centuries such as the Avars and Slavs. It is thought that there were also Vlachs (pastoralists still found all over the Balkans, who give their name to Wallachia) and a Hungarian-speaking people, the Székelys or Szeklers. But here, already, problems begin and the facts are contested. While one body of thought contends that the Székelys pre-dated the Magyars (some even claim descent from Attila the Hun), another believes that they arrived with Árpád and his Magyar tribal chiefs. And much Romanian scholarship has been devoted to demonstrating that the Vlachs were no mere pastoralists but proud descendants of those indigenous Dacians whom Trajan conquered in the early 2nd century, securing the wealth of Transylvania's gold mines for his imperial capital. Trajan is said to have sent a hundred thousand Dacian men in chains as slaves to Rome. In return he posted two of his legions permanently in Dacia. The joint descendants of those legionaries and the hundred thousand Dacian women left husbandless are the forebears of the Romanians of today, a theory which Romanian historians believe gives them prior claim to the territory and which they use to explain their language, which is an amalgam of Slavic and Latin.

What is known for certain on the Magyar side is that Prince Árpád's men founded a dynasty that gradually consolidated its power through old Roman Pannonia and the Carpathian Basin. Árpád's direct descendant, Géza (d. 997), sought to bring an end to the diffuse nomadic lifestyle of the Magyar tribes and condense power around a single leader. To do this, he founded a ruling house modelled on the Christian dynasties of Europe. Though in spirit always true to his pagan roots, Géza was baptised in 972 according to the Roman, not the Byzantine, rite, thus laying the foundation of Hungary's loyalty to the Pope and the Western Church. Géza failed, however, to still the squabbling among his tribesmen. It was left to his son, Stephen, to do this. Stephen defeated his elder kinsman and rival for power, Koppány, married Gisela of Bavaria, sister of the Holy Roman Emperor Henry II, and was crowned king of a united Hungary in 1000, with a crown which persistent legend claims to have been sent from Rome with papal blessing. Three years later, in 1003, he defeated another kinsman and rival, his uncle Gyula, plenipotentiary in Transylvania, thus bringing Western Christianity to the region. He founded the diocese of Transylvania, with Gyulafehérvár—the fortress of his defeated uncle—as its seat. Gyulafehérvár, in Romanian Alba Iulia, lies just beyond the confluence of the Târnava and Mureş rivers. However Latin the Romanian name may sound, it derives not from any member of the Julian clan in Rome but from the Hungarian *fehér* (white; in Romanian *alb*) and Gyula, the vanquished Magyar chief. With his defeat and that of Koppány, King Stephen broke the bonds of the traditional tribal system and reforged his realm into an early modern state. The borders of his Transylvanian territories survived almost without change until 1920.

Székelys and Saxons: the era of the House of Árpád

Under the continuous threat of invasion from the East, the early Hungarian kings had to think of innovative ways to protect their borders. The Hungarian-speaking Székelys (*for more on them, see p. 48*) were given the role of frontier guards in return for status, rights and exemptions. King Ladislaus I posted them to the Târnava Valley in the late 1070s.

Dauntless Székely soldiers and loyal Hungarian courtiers were one thing, but a land needed to be made productive and a people needed to be fed. King Géza II (1141–62) hit on the idea of immigration. He sent the Székelys further east, right to the fringes of the realm, and then, instead of giving their vacated lands to his Hungarian nobility, he invited settlers from northern Europe to farm them and to boost the economy with their skill as artisans and traders. These peoples, the *hospites teutonici*, became known as the Transylvanian Saxons (although they came from the Upper-Rhine and the Netherlands and not from today's Saxony around Dresden).

It was an important initiative. Each settler was given his own land as well as land to farm in common for each community. The communities were given royal guarantees that they could freely elect their own judges and follow their traditional customs. They were also permitted to elect their own priests and paid tithes to the local church rather than to the bishop (and hence to Rome). At a time when the papacy was flexing its muscles and feudalism was the norm, the concessions made to the Saxons were extraordinary.

The first written evidence of the rights of the Saxons is found in the famous *Andreanum* of 1224, drawn up by King Andrew II of the House of Árpád. It constitutes the legal basis for a community owing liabilities such as military service and tax (*terragium*) paid to the king, but also enjoying substantial privileges. At a stroke it both consolidated the power of the king and weakened that of the Hungarian aristocracy in the Saxon region. The historic name for the area stretching between the Greater Târnava and the Olt rivers is *Fundus Regius*, the Königsboden or 'King's Ground'.

In 1241, the Golden Horde of the Mongol Tatars, led by Batu Khan, senior grandson of the great Ghenghis Khan, invaded westwards and with swift efficiency wiped out most of the infrastructure of Transylvania and its population—in spite of the Székely defences. It says something for the organisational abilities of the House of Árpád that by the 1270s a huge rebuilding programme had completely reshaped the country. It is at this time that things begin to be written down. Many references to villages and towns, and also to trading activity, have come down to us from this period. Most of the villages and towns mentioned in this guide book were first documented in the late 13th century.

The House of Árpád became extinct in the male line in 1301. Its successor houses of Anjou, Luxembourg, Habsburg and Jagiello all claimed the throne through marriage.

The 'Three Nations'

By the 13th century in Transylvania, there were three recognised political and ethnic groups who made up the governing body: the Hungarians, the Székelys and the Saxons. The Hungarians dominated the northwest and provided the king's viceroy (the voivode). The voivode was head of the Transylvanian parliament, the Diet, which had no permanent seat but which held sessions once or twice a year in different appointed cities of the region (most frequently in Cluj, Turda, Târgu Mureș and Alba Iulia). The Székelys had their heartland to the east, organised in seats (*szék*) and led by a Székely count. The Saxon lands were also organised into legally autonomous seats which enjoyed special privileges and freedoms and the right to hold markets. The Saxons were forever vigilant of these freedoms and rebelled more than once at perceived attempts to curtail them. In 1324, a Saxon revolt was put down by the Hungarian king Charles I (Róbert Károly) and the Königsboden was definitively reorganised into the *septem sedes*, the seven autonomous districts or 'Siebenbürgen', which is the Saxon name for Transylvania. In 1437 the federation of the three peoples of Transylvania was officially codified as the *Unio Trium Nationum*. It remained a union of independent parts. The Hungarians and the Székelys, though they shared a common language, more than once found themselves in opposition (for example during the struggle between Michael the Brave and András Báthory; see p. 23). The Saxons always insisted on being a law unto themselves. The confederacy of their seven seats was once again recognised by King Matthias Corvinus in 1485 in the *Universitas Saxonum*, which acknowledged the independence of the administrative districts. There was also, at this time, a Wallachian nobility in Transylvania. Their interests coincided with those of the Hungarian ruling class and thus the Vlach peasants had no natural spokesman. As their numbers grew and they remained voiceless, they became, so to speak, the elephant in the room. But their time would come.

Despite the Hungarian monarchs' acquiescence in their people's wish to run their own affairs, the 14th and 15th centuries were turbulent times in Transylvania, mainly because of external raids by the Turks. The first fortifications had come at the time of the Mongol raids, but it was during the Ottoman incursions that defences of the kind so famous today began to go up. The finest and most elaborate were built by the Saxons: most of the Saxon churches in the Târnava Valley are protected by great rings of walls behind which the populace could retreat in case of onslaught. Great rooms for storage were built into these walls and the upper storeys of the churches and towers have missile emplacements and holes through which to pour boiling oil. From the mid-16th century, after the Reformation, *Ein fester Burg ist unser Gott*, Martin Luther's well-known paraphrase of Psalm 46 (God is our refuge and our strength), became one of the most popular mottoes to paint or carve over a defended Saxon entranceway. These extraordinary fastnesses remain one of the glories of Central Europe.

The Turks were soundly defeated at Belgrade by John Hunyadi in 1456, and during the peace that followed, Hungary flourished and developed into a European power. Until the discovery of America, Transylvanian mines provided much of the gold to the European market. A real beneficiary of these riches was Matthias Corvinus, a Transylvanian himself, son of the hero John Hunyadi, who became King of Hungary in 1458. His court was said to be second only to that of Lorenzo de' Medici in attracting artists and scholars. A humanist as well as a soldier, Matthias invited Italian philosophers and artists to his country. Renaissance ideas gradually trickled through to the towns and village churches in Transylvania. It was a prosperous age, but short-lived.

Habsburgs versus Ottomans and the Transylvanian Principality

Matthias was succeeded by Vladislav II of Bohemia, who died in 1516, leaving the throne to his ten-year-old son. That young king, Louis II, was to face the might of the army of Sultan Suleiman the Magnificent at Mohács in southern Hungary in 1526. The Hungarians were soundly defeated and King Louis drowned while trying to flee the battlefield. The mighty Hungarian kingdom fell apart.

King Louis' wife, Maria of Habsburg, sister of the Holy Roman Emperor Charles V, escaped north, taking with her the treasury of King Matthias, including the contents of the famous Corviniana library. Rival claimants for the Hungarian throne emerged in the form of Maria's other brother, Ferdinand of Habsburg, who had been promised the crown by Vladislav, and John Zapolya, who had been voivode of Transylvania and who was the choice of the Hungarian nobility. Struggles and skirmishes were ended by a treaty of 1538 promising the throne to Ferdinand on Zapolya's death. Zapolya died in 1540 but in the meantime his wife, Isabella, had given birth to a son, John Sigismund. Just weeks before he died, Zapolya retracted his treaty with Ferdinand. Sultan Suleiman, rather than see the land fall to the Habsburgs, threw his support behind Zapolya's baby son, installing the dowager queen Isabella as regent.

In 1541, Suleiman conquered Buda. Hungary was divided into three. To the north and west and under Ferdinand's control was Royal Hungary, with its capital at Preßburg (Pozsony, modern Bratislava). The territory in the centre, on either side of the Danube, went to swell the growing Ottoman Empire. To the east was Transylvania. Supported by geography— the mountains and the sheer distance from Vienna—the region tenaciously refused to yield sovereignty to Ferdinand but remained governed by the regent Isabella from her court at Gyulafehérvár (Alba Iulia). The Ottoman threat was kept at bay with hefty amounts of tribute. Queen Isabella oversaw the development of Transylvania as a kind of buffer state between two aggressive and intransigent powers, an intermediary known for its humanist culture.

John Sigismund began his reign on the death of his mother in 1559. In 1566 he went to Zemun (now part of Belgrade) to pay homage to the sultan and also, as his father had done, to pay a financial tribute. Two years later he issued his famous edict proclaiming freedom of worship (*see box*).

Freedom of worship in Transylvania

The Reformation had a major impact on Transylvania, under the leadership of the Saxon humanist, cartographer, publisher, jurist and theologian Johannes Honterus (1498–1549), who worked hard to disseminate Lutheranism amongst the Saxons of his homeland. The Hungarians looked instead to the teaching of Calvin. In the 1560s there were numbers of Hungarians who became Unitarian, a denomination who do not accept the Dogma of the Trinity. John Sigismund himself was born a Catholic, became a Lutheran in 1562, then a Calvinist and then, under the influence of his court preacher Ferenc Dávid, a Unitarian. The simplicity of Dávid's message, 'God is one', doing away with the thorny problem of the Holy Ghost, attracted many followers besides the prince. In 1568 John Sigismund proclaimed the Edict of Torda, granting freedom of worship to the four *religiones receptae*, the faiths of Transylvania's three nations: Catholicism, Lutheranism, Calvinism and Unitarianism. The Vlachs were categorised as a *natio admissa*, in other words a people who had been allowed to settle, and their faith, together with Judaism and Islam, was categorised as a *religio tolerata*. John Sigismund has gone down in history as the only Unitarian monarch. His edict was the first decree of toleration of its kind in Europe. Described by his contemporaries as a great Renaissance prince, his achievements were partly forced upon him by geography, partly born of self-interest, but his impact is still seen today in the multi-faith communities that are found in the Târnava Mare Valley.

In 1570 John Sigismund formally renounced his claim to the title of King of Hungary and was named instead Prince of Transylvania. This marked the beginning of new system whereby—not unlike the Italian city states of the period—the Transylvanian Diet elected its own rulers. From 1570 until 1690 the Principality of Transylvania existed as a semi-autonomous state, sometimes under Ottoman, at other times under Habsburg suzerainty, and almost always ruled by members of Hungarian noble families. One notable exception came in 1600, when the Prince of Wallachia, Michael the Brave (Mihai Viteazul), managed to add Moldavia and Transylvania to his holdings and for a few brief months united the three under his sole leadership. He took Transylvania after defeating Prince András Báthory, with the help of a band of disgruntled Székelys who felt that Báthory was eroding their historic privileges. After Prince Michael's death (by assassination) in 1601, Transylvania was taken by Rudolf I of Habsburg, who attempted to impose Catholicism upon the principality. Liberty was restored by István Bocskai, who led a successful rebellion against Rudolf and became Prince of Transylvania in 1605. The Ottoman sultan sent him a magnificent crown which he tactfully refused to wear: suzerainty was one thing; vassalage would be quite another. Bocskai ushered in the decades of Transylvania's 'Golden Age', an era when an unmistakable identity developed politically, economically and culturally. Transylvania, which until the 17th century had enjoyed only pockets of peace, being constantly under threat of sieges and incursions from the sundry claimants to power, at last began to settle down and enjoy a period when it could cultivate the finer things in life.

Transylvanian independence under threat

Under the princeships of Gábor Bethlen (1613–29) and György Rákóczi I (1630–48), a period of sustained peace arrived. The art of the goldsmith in Transylvania is notable at this time (*see p. 156*). Later, science blossomed, aided by international contacts, and printing presses were encouraged, leading to the spread of knowledge and ideas.

In 1683 the Turks were halted at the gates of Vienna by the combined Catholic forces of Leopold I of Austria, Charles of Lorraine and Jan Sobieski of Poland. Three years after that, the Habsburg armies expelled the Ottomans from Buda. Traditional schoolboy European history has seen these as unequivocally great victories. But for Transylvania, the result

Detail of the gown of Catherine of Brandenburg, wife of Prince Gábor Bethlen, sent to Budapest by the Bethlen family to safeguard it from looting after the First World War and now preserved in the Hungarian National Museum.

was more ambiguous. Over the centuries of her existence, Transylvania had built up a single great ruling obsession: autonomy. Long years of exemptions from taxation or military duties had taught her peoples to expect generous rights and a sizeable say in their own affairs. Freedom of religion and freedom of trade were their watchwords and the climate of shifting allegiances in which they lived had taught them to side with whichever exterior power would be most likely to grant these. The medieval Hungarian kings had been complaisant. So had the Ottoman sultans. But the Habsburg archdukes had no inclination whatever to follow suit and Transylvania knew it. Thus it was, ironically, that the victories over the Ottomans that were being cheered to the rafters in Austria and Hungary spelled Transylvania's undoing.

In 1690, the Prince of Transylvania, Mihály Apafi, died. His 14-year-old son, also Mihály, claimed the title. But history was never to grant it to him. Instead the Ottoman sultan threw his support behind the Porte's old ally Imre Thököly, who stormed into Transylvania with troops at his heel (the printing press in the castle at Criș had to be moved out of his way to safety) in an attempt to take possession. The Apafi faction appealed to the emperor Leopold to confirm the younger Mihály in authority. Leopold's response came in the form of the famous *Diploma Leopoldinum*, a document enshrining Transylvania's status and freedoms in 17 points. Its main provisions were as follows:

- The freedom of worship granted in 1568 to the Catholic, Lutheran, Calvinist and Unitarian congregations stands;
- The municipal rights of the Saxons remain in place;
- The apparatus of public administration and lawgiving remains unchanged;
- Only native Hungarians, Székleys and Saxons may be appointed to high office, regardless of religious denomination. The emperor may, however, make recommendations;
- One quarter of the members of the Privy Council and of the judiciary must be Roman Catholics;
- The Diet is to be convened annually;
- The governor shall reside in the province and he, along with Privy Council members and High Court judges, shall be paid by the Crown;
- The Crown shall receive revenue from salt tax, metal tax, tithes on trade from the Saxons and on land rents from the Hungarians, and taxes and excise duties shall not be increased;
- The free Székelys are to defend the realm at their own expense in return for which they shall be exempt from tax;
- Freedom of trade is guaranteed;
- Landowners shall rent their tithes from the Treasury;
- The province is required to maintain a body of troops for its own defence. These shall be under the command of an Austrian general who will, however, not meddle in day to day governance and shall only approach the Diet in time of war;
- The Saxons and other taxpayers shall no longer be obliged to provide free hospitality to travellers. Landowers and the provincial and town councils shall be responsible for inns and post houses.

By the standards of the day these were generous terms. But there is no mention of a prince. Transylvania is characterised as a province of Austria, independent of Hungary but nevertheless a governorate of the Habsburg Empire. Some historians have seen this as a calamity for Transylvania. Others, notably John Paget in his *Hungary and Transylvania* of 1839, have been approving. It is true, Paget concedes, that the princes of Transylvania were elected. But votes were most often obtained by force, bribery or other underhand means. The princes then presided over a Diet which although held up as a beacon of popular power is in truth made up of members 'in part elected, in part nominated, and in part, I suspect even hereditary.' The Habsburgs, in his view, had given Transylvania a better and more equitable system.

But equity might not quite have been Leopold's top priority. What concerned him most was winning the obedience of a docile people and asserting a Catholic hegemony. The *Leopoldinum* was issued in late 1690. The following winter a detachment of imperial soldiers was billeted on Mediaș and the villages of Biertan, Moșna, Șeica Mică and Valea Viilor. Leopold next moved to garner support though a rapprochement with the Orthodox Church and sent Jesuits to Transylvania to carry out the plan. In 1698–1700 the Uniate Church was signed into being. This was a hybrid denomination which retained the Orthodox liturgy but acknowledged the supreme authority of the pope rather than the patriarch. Many Orthodox clergymen refused to endorse it; some out of zeal for their faith, others because they were suspicious of Jesuitical Habsburg envoys bearing gifts. From its seat at Făgăraș and later Blaj, however, the Uniate Church grew to become a key focus of Romanian identity-building (*see p. 200*).

The Rákóczi wars and the 'Age of Absolutism'

Leopold's measures could not make Transylvania content, however. The old adage than men would prefer to be badly ruled by themselves than governed well by someone else is certainly true of the proud Transylvanians. But their very plurality was beginning to count against them. For centuries Transylvania had been a federation of independently autonomous peoples. As a united province it was discontented—and each class of person had a different motive for discontent, making it difficult for any leader to unite the disaffected groups into a coherent body. The man who came closest was Ferenc Rákóczi, stepson of Imre Thököly. Rákóczi's aim was to return to the semi-autonomous feudal Transylvania of old, but to achieve this he needed the support not only of the Hungarians, but of the Székleys, the

Saxons and the Vlachs as well—and, if it could be secured, of the Ottoman sultan. His 'Proclamation to the Peoples of the World' vowed to free 'our homeland' from the Austrian yoke. The difficulty was that in the eyes of many, the solution he offered could only be an alternative yoke, no matter that he was promising freedom of religion and liberation from serfdom. Importantly, too, he was a Catholic. The Porte would have preferred to recall Thököly from exile, and though keen as ever for power, Thököly was too old and gouty by this time to be of much use. In Transylvania, factions developed around the two potential leaders, causing chaos and disunity. Miklós Bethlen, who loathed Habsburg domination but equally dreaded the leadership of Rákóczi, dreamed of making Transylvania a significant player on the world stage as a neutral buffer between two mutually antagonistic powers—the way it has always been. The Porte, as well as Protestant England and Holland, would have been delighted with this. But when Bethlen outlined his vision in an essay entitled 'An Olive Branch borne by Noah's Dove' (*Olajágat viselő Noé galambja*), it was interpreted as sedition in an increasingly jumpy Vienna and Bethlen was imprisoned. Gradually the different groups in Transylvania coalesced behind Rákóczi. In the summer of 1704, at the Diet of Alba Iulia, he was elected Prince of Transylvania in a last brave bid to bring back the past.

Rákóczi's was a well-nigh impossible task. His army was ill-equipped, ill-trained, ill-disciplined and uncohesive. He did his best to unite his forces, placing Wallachians as second-in-command of some of his detachments. But his successes were mixed. Even when he won an engagement, his troops left destruction in their wake. There are reports of devastation in the village of Hosman, for example, where out of 400 households only 15 were left intact after the *kuruc* army, as it was called, had passed through. Citizens who retreated behind their walls to avoid the hurly burly found themselves falling prey to disease and plague. Rákóczi appealed to foreign powers, informing France, Sweden, England, Holland and Poland of his election as Prince. Louis XIV was encouraging and promised support, but this never materialised in any tangible form. Meanwhile János Radvánszky, Rákóczi's Protestant adviser, was forced to admit that the situation was abominable and that 'the enemy treats the Saxon people and the lower orders of our society with greater kindness than do our own men, and this is gradually winning them over.'

In the end, Rákóczi was one of history's colourful failures. Clumsy manoeuvres and a bloody battle lost in 1705 cost him support. His own side began to turn against him. A last ditch effort to proffer a solution and a cause to fight for, namely harking back to the Middle Ages and uniting Transylvania and Hungary under a single crown, could never appeal to non-Hungarian Transylvanians. The fighting dragged on until 1711 but it was increasingly hopeless, and eventually Transylvania was induced to swear allegiance once again to Austria.

Rákóczi ended his days in exile beside the Sea of Marmara, quietly doing carpentry and tending his vegetables. The Habsburgs tightened their grip on Transylvania and the 'Age of Absolutism' dawned. Now came the last push of the Counter-Reformation. In 1722, for example, a Roman Catholic elementary school was set up in Saxon Mediaș. Some members of the Transylvanian Protestant nobility, seeing no other way of enjoying a distinguished career, switched denomination for the sake of expediency.

Habsburg rule in the later 18th century, under Maria Theresa and her sons Joseph II and Leopold II, was, however, enlightened despotism and it brought with it some benefits. In 1766, Maria Theresa abolished witch trials. In 1783 Joseph II banned the ringing of church bells to prevent thunderstorms. In 1791 he made it illegal to extort confessions by torture. Other measures were aimed at creating a less fragmented society. The *Concivilitas* decree of 1781, for example, allowed Hungarians and Vlachs to establish themselves within the city walls, alongside Saxons. Calvinist and Uniate churches began to spring up in the town centres. The towns of the Siebenbürgen started to become more ethnically mixed. Modern attitudes will applaud this. But applied to the standards of the times, it was a case of dividing to rule.

And in the countryside, things were far from well. For hundreds of years, in order to cultivate the land using agricultural techniques that had barely changed since the Saxons were first summoned by King Géza, large numbers of immigrant Vlachs had been settling in the region. These downtrodden masses, with a high birthrate and low expectations,

1785 print of the execution of Horea and Cloşca,
showing preparations for breaking on the wheel.

condemned to serfdom, were slowly but surely beginning to outnumber
the other ethnic groups. Anti-feudal peasant revolts had been a sporadic
feature of rural life in Transylvania for some time but the mass uprising of
1784 was on a different scale. In response to a call from Joseph II for more
soldiers to guard the borders, large numbers of Wallachian serfs presented
themselves for duty. A soldier's life, in their view, could only be better
than their current slavery. When local authorities, feeling that they had
not been consulted, placed obstructions in the way of recruitment, the
simmering tensions came to the boil. Led by three men, Horea, Cloşca
and Crişan, a mob numbering many thousands seized what weapons
they could lay their hands on and rampaged across the land, attacking
Hungarian and Saxon landed targets. The aims of the three leaders were
extremely radical. Theirs was not only a revolt for better treatment but a
wholesale anti-feudal revolution which proposed to dismantle the nobility
and usher in an egalitarian society where each man would live by the
sweat of his own brow. When the emperor Joseph learned what was going
on, he called for order to be restored. The ringleaders were captured.
Horea and Cloşca were broken on the wheel outside Alba Iulia. Crişan
committed suicide in prison. To this day Romanians blame the Hungarians

for the deaths. Hungarians are careful to say that the army carried out the atrocity on imperial orders from Vienna. Whatever the case, the incident left Wallachian serfs in a state of suppressed revolt and Hungarian Transylvanians wary and resentful. Further conflict could only ensue.

Revolution and its aftermath: 1848 to the Dual Monarchy

The 19th century would prove another turbulent one for Transylvania. In 1826 a Uniate church was built in Mediaş inside the town walls. A Romanian-language school was established there in the same year. These facts are significant. The Transylvanian Vlachs, who until now had been tied serfs without land, education, law or a voice, were asserting themselves.

The fever of nationalism affected not only the Vlachs but the Hungarians too, and by 'the year of revolution' of 1848, the whole of Transylvania was caught up in a civil war. Hungarians were fighting for emancipation from the Habsburgs and fully intended, when crowned by victory, to unite Transylvania to Hungary. Already they were advancing plans to make Hungarian the official language of the region. The historian C.A. Macartney laconically notes that 'The Roumanians could be relatively indifferent to the language of an administration in which they did not participate and an education which they did not receive.' But their indifference was shrinking as the idea of a unity of the 'Romanian' people arose. The brief union of the three 'Romanian' states by Michael the Brave in 1600 began to take on an iconic significance. Romanian historians have seen it as the recreation of Dacia, that long-lost province of the Roman Empire. Prince Michael's achievement, according to Bodea and Cândea in their *Transylvania in the History of the Romanians*, 'enhanced... the consciousness of the Romanians of the three principalities regarding their existence as one people with a common language, common religion, common customs and common ideals.' Commentators in the Renaissance Europe of Prince Michael's day had rejoiced at the idea of the conquests of Rome being made good once again. Now, in the fervid climate of 1848–9, the Transylvanian Vlachs became vocal in claiming rights for themselves. They asserted the right of precedence ('we were here first') and the right of numerical superiority ('we are the most numerous ethnic group'). No longer were they content to be classed as the fourth nation. They were *the* nation, oppressed and marginalised, their birthright stolen from them. By the time of the 1848–9 revolutions, nationalist obsessions had utterly obscured the old Transylvanian ideal of a community of peoples. The 'freedom' that Hungarians were fighting for meant union with Hungary, an alliance that Vlach and Saxon strenuously opposed. At Blaj the *Cartea de aur*, or 'Golden Charter', spelled it out loudly and clearly: 'The people do not wish to recognise the union of Transylvania with Hungary. Instead it requests a Transylvanian parliament made up of Vlach, Magyar and Saxon representatives *in proportion to the population of each*.' [my italics]

The Hungarian bid for independence was crushed by Austria with the help of Russia. After a disastrous defeat at a battle just outside Sighișoara, Hungary laid down her arms in August 1849. The revolution had failed, but it had one great consequence: the final abolition of serfdom.

A mere decade after successfully exerting her authority, Austria suddenly began to look vulnerable. In 1859 she was defeated by Italy and France at the Battle of Solferino. To survive, it seemed that she would have to adopt a more constitutional form of rule. In 1862 the principalities of Moldavia and Wallachia were formally united in a single state called Romania, nominally under Ottoman suzerainty and ruled by a *domnitor*, Alexandru Ioan Cuza, counselled by a Moldavian-born hero of 1848, Mihail Kogălniceanu. Then, encouraged by Austria's weakness, at a diet in Sibiu in 1863–4, the Romanians claimed equal national rights in Transylvania and made Romanian the official language there. In 1866 Romania threw off the Ottomans and established herself as a kingdom, with Carol I of Hohenzollern-Sigmaringen on the throne.

But the Romanian claims on Transylvania were not destined to succeed just yet. Once again, Hungary stepped forward, securing her cherished goal of more rights within the Habsburg Empire with the establishment in 1867 of the Dual Monarchy of Austria-Hungary, with Franz Joseph as Emperor in Vienna and King in Budapest. Hungary had its own parliament and its own jurisdiction. Transylvania was attached to the Hungarian lands and immediately a programme of widespread Magyarisation ensued. Hungary entirely (and unwisely) disregarded the point of view of the Slavs

(Croatians, Serbs and Slovaks) in its domains; the Transylvanians too were expected to content themselves with the one-size-fits-all Magyar vest. The Blaj Pronouncement of 1868, demanding that Transylvania be returned to its old status of administratively and politically independent region, fell on deaf ears. Public Hungarian-language schools began to be set up, even in towns like Mediaş, where Hungarians had always been in a minority. Hungarian policy, dictated by the lessons of its history, held that the only way to survive was to be aggressively one-sided. To quote the words of Dezső Bánffy, written in 1903: 'The Hungarian state will have no secure future unless it adopt policies of the most extreme chauvinism.' A situation of intense passive confrontation grew up. Hungarian families chose for their children names like Csaba, which cannot be translated or Latinised. Romanians resisted Magyarisation by naming their sons Romulus and Trajan and their daughters Cornelia. It began to be difficult to see how an accommodation could be reached.

The First World War and Greater Romania

In 1914, Archduke Franz Ferdinand of Austria was assassinated at Sarajevo. The Hungarian prime minister sent a memorandum to Franz Joseph opposing Austria's ultimatum to Serbia; but Hungary now paid the price of its dual monarchy and was dragged into the war. Transylvania came with it and the consequences can be seen on every church memorial. On memorials in the Saxon villages, the house numbers are included to distinguish between so many fallen who have the same name.

Romania remained neutral for the first two years of the conflict. Her oil reserves and her grain were far too valuable for neutrality, however, and in 1916 Lord Kitchener sent an envoy to Bucharest to persuade Romania to join the Entente. A secret treaty was signed securing Romania's military support in return for Transylvania, the Banat and most of Bukovina. After initial unopposed advances, the Romanian military campaign quickly turned disastrous. The Central Powers overran two-thirds of the country, forcing the government to retreat to the Moldavian city of Iaşi. The October Revolution of 1917 and Russia's consequent withdrawal from the War left Romania alone and surrounded and with little option but to surrender and sue for peace. By the time hostilities finally ground to a conclusion in 1918, Austria-Hungary had been vanquished and Romania found herself on the winning side.

The victorious powers duly convened in Paris to allocate the spoils of a dismembered empire. Hungary could only now bitterly regret that she had not been more conciliatory towards her minorities. In 1918, vast numbers of Transylvanian Vlachs voted in Alba Iulia to join the Kingdom of Romania. In 1919, the Saxon community followed suit in a similar plebiscite in Sighișoara. At the negotiating table in Paris, Hungary had no chance. She was not only on the losing side. Her government had collapsed and a Communist Republic of Councils had seized power. She also had articulate enemies. The patrician diplomat Harold Nicolson, considered that the Hungarians 'had destroyed much and created nothing...For centuries [they] had oppressed their subject nationalities. The hour of liberation and retribution was at hand.' Another malign presence in Paris was the Central Europe expert R.W. Seton-Watson, whose anti-Magyar views were so strong as to be almost pathological and who certainly influenced opinion at the peace talks, contributing to a general perception that Hungary had for decades been wilfully suppressing the voices of her minorities.

Meanwhile, while the mandarins were deliberating, Romania had seized the initiative and sent troops westwards into Hungary, where they instituted a programme of wholesale looting and terrorisation. By the summer of 1919 they had occupied Budapest. Knowing that the allied victors would order them to fall back, their policy seems to have been to grab the maximum possible, on the grounds that they could only be ordered back so far. The Paris Conference awarded Romania the following territorial gains: Bukovina from Austria-Hungary (1919 Treaty of Saint-Germain); Bessarabia from Russia (1920 Treaty of Paris); and the Banat and Transylvania from Austria-Hungary (1920 Treaty of Trianon). The total area of land ceded by Hungary to Romania after World War One was greater than the truncated stump of a country that was left behind.

The Kingdom of Romania, on the other hand, suddenly engorged by several hundred thousand square kilometres of new territory, became known as *România Mare*, Greater Romania, and she entered upon her new existence with gusto, looking forward to a brave new future allied to rapid economic growth. Measures reeking of tit-for-tat spite were passed, such as the edict whereby anyone employed by the state had to speak Romanian. Sweeping land reforms were carried out, with an egalitarian aim no doubt, but the results were catastrophic for the Hungarians and Saxons. Hungarian noble families found themselves struggling to run their estates on the land that was left them. The Saxons lost the precious revenue that they had traditionally received from forestry. Both groups felt resentful and threatened, and as more and more Romanians moved into the country, rural overpopulation and technological underdevelopment took their toll. Despite the vast wealth taken from its vanquished neighbours (timber, salt, metals, railways, shipping networks, oil and gas), Romania tottered and the Great Depression of 1929 hit the country hard. The 1930s were an unstable decade, with 25 changes of government.

The rise to power of Hitler in Germany and the apparent success his financial policies caused many Transylvanian Saxons to favour him and many were sympathetic towards the Nazi recruiting drives in their towns and villages. Romania slid into Fascism and in 1940 joined the war on the Axis side. Hungary too had reasons for supporting Hitler: the Second Vienna Award of 1940, which gave her back a sizeable chunk of Transylvania. Most of the Târnava Mare Valley was not affected, but the Székely lands around the river's source, and the town of Odorheiu, were part of the agreement. Like the territorial promises made to Romania in 1916, this had the same aim: military support in the new world war. One can have nothing stronger than an opinion about Nazi Germany's ultimate design for Hungary. Whatever it was, she was fatally beguiled by the Vienna Award. In May of 1941, she also allied herself with Germany. Hungary and Romania, briefly, were on the same side.

The Second World War and its aftermath

In 1942 the Fascist regime of Ion Antonescu instigated the Holocaust in Romania, adopting the Nazi policies of genocide against Jews and Roma (the day the transportations to concentration camps began, 9th October, is now Romania's Holocaust Remembrance Day).

As the Russians advanced west, the young King Michael of Romania led a successful coup against Antonescu and in August 1944 Romania changed sides, joining forces with the Allies. This shifting of allegiance came at a price: forced labour. At the demand of the Russians, by January 1945 about 70,000 Transylvanian Saxons, men and women from the ages of 17 to 45, had been taken to Soviet camps in the Ukraine and the Urals. About 15 percent perished.

At the end of the war, with Germany and Hungary defeated, the Vienna Award was nullified and the whole of Transylvania became Romanian once again. Antonescu was convicted of war crimes and executed in 1946. In 1947 King Michael was deposed and Romania became a republic under Soviet control. On their return home from the labour camps in 1949, the Saxons of Transylvania found their homes and lands taken over by the Communist government. In the 1960s and '70s, under the hated Ceaușescu, many Jews and Saxons emigrated to Israel and Germany. 'Head money' was charged for each in hard currency, which in the case of the Saxons the West German government generally paid.

After the Romanian Revolution in 1989 and the execution of Ceaușescu and his wife, the Transylvanian Saxons were offered a new 'home' in united Germany. Many felt that the offer was too good to turn down. In and around 1990, the Saxons left Transylvania, the land they had helped create and which had been their home for 850 years. Villages which had once had majority German populations suddenly began registering single-digit figures. Romanians and Roma took their places.

The Hungarians, too, had suffered under the Communists, particularly the landowning class. Many were imprisoned or sent as slave labour to the Danube Canal. Estates fared poorly as ramshackle state farms. Manor houses were left to crumble. Restitution has taken a long time and has not always been generous. In some places where Hungarian was spoken before the war, you will scarcely hear it now. In others, notably the Székely lands, it is thriving.

So much evidence of the events and developments of this short history can be found in the Târnava Mare Valley.

Annabel Barber and Lucy Abel Smith

CHRONOLOGY

101–2 and 105–6 Trajan conquers Dacia in a series of battles that will later be depicted on his Column in Rome and which will come to constitute Romania's foundation story

972–97 Prince Géza. First Christians

1000 Pope Sylvester is said to have sent a crown to King Stephen I of Hungary, granting him the title of apostolic king. Hungary becomes a Christian kingdom within the Western orbit

1070s King Ladislaus I sends the Székelys to the Târnava Valley

1095–1116 King Kálmán. Development of churches and villages, monks from abroad supervising churches

1141–62 King Géza II calls in the Saxon *hospites*, not only to protect but also to strengthen the crown's economic power with farming and craft skills

1172–96 Reign of Béla III. Continuation of King Géza's policy of duties and liberties. There are now three political entities in Transylvania: the Hungarians under a voivode, the Szeklers under a count and the Saxons.

1224 Andrew II issues the *Andreanum*, a renewal of the liberties given to the Saxons by his grandfather Géza. They are given a political identity under the king's authority with scope for self administration

1241–2 Transylvania and Hungary devastated by Tatar raids

1235–70 Reign of Béla IV. Foreign architects arrive in Hungary to rebuild churches after the Tatars have passed through. Development of Buda

1301 The Árpád dynasty dies out at the death of Andrew III. Much fighting follows and through Andrew's wife, Charles Robert of Anjou takes the crown as Charles I. Sultan Osman I (d. 1324) founds the Ottoman state. The Byzantine army is routed

1308–42 The reign of Charles Robert ushers in a period of wealth and a great flowering of the arts in Hungary

1362 Sultan Orhan I captures

Edirne

1369 The Byzantine emperor John V Palaeologus seeks help from the pope

1384 Jadwiga, daughter of Louis I, is offered in marriage to Jagiello of Lithuania. Jagiello's sons make the House of Jagiello dominant in Central Europe

1387–1437 Sigismund of Luxembourg. Beginning of the Hussite dissention

1389 The Ottoman army under Murad I defeats the Serbs at the battle of Kosovo Polje

1391 Serbia becomes an Ottoman vassal

1394 Ottoman occupation of Thessalonica

1396 Battle of Nicopolis. The Ottomans rout the Crusader armies

1402 Battle of Ankara: Timur (Tamerlane) routs the Ottomans and the Anatolian emirates regain independence

1411 Sigismund is proclaimed Holy Roman Emperor

1422 First Ottoman attack on Constantinople

1437 Transylvania officially becomes a federation of three peoples, Saxon, Székely and Hungarian

1439 The Turks plunder Alba Iulia

1444 Hungarians and Wallachians are defeated by Murad II at the Battle of Varna

1446–53 The Transylvanian John Hunyadi is appointed Governor of Hungary

1448 Second battle of Kosovo Polje: Hungarians and Wallachians routed

1453 Sultan Mehmet II, known as the Conqueror, enters Constantinople. The cannon he uses to breach the walls has been made by a Hungarian

1456 John Hunyadi defeats the Turks at Belgrade

1458–90 Matthias Corvinus, son of John Hunyadi, is King of Hungary. Takes Bohemia in 1468. Marries Beatrice of Aragon in 1476, who brings Italian craftsmen to Hungary, including intarsia masters

1463 Bosnia and Herzegovina annexed by the Ottomans

1471–1516 Reign of Vladislav II Jagiello, son of Casimir IV of Poland. The throne of Hungary is offered to Bohemia.

1492 Granada falls to the Spanish. Spanish Jews are given sanctuary in the Ottoman Empire

1505 The Transylvanian Diet meets at Rákos and decides not to invite a foreign king or to recognise succession through the female line

1506 Tamás Bakócz commissions the first centrally-planned Renaissance building north of the Alps as his mausoleum in Esztergom Cathedral in Hungary

1512–20 Sultan Selim I conquers Egypt and assumes title of caliph. Ottomans are established as a naval power. The capital of their empire moves from Edirne to Istanbul

1514 Peasant uprising under György Dózsa, a Székely, who is defeated and killed

1516–17 Ottomans annexe Syria and Egypt from the Mamluks

1520 Accession of Suleiman the Magnificent to the Ottoman throne. Under him the Empire embarks on a period of territorial growth and cultural splendour. He rapidly conquers Belgrade and Rhodes

1521 Marriage of Maria of Austria, granddaughter of Maximilian I to Louis II of Hungary

1525 The stone carvers of Cluj receive their first charter of incorporation as a guild. From the 1530s Cluj becomes the centre of Transylvanian Renaissance art

1526 Battle of Mohács. Suleiman's army defeats Hungary and King Louis II is killed. Ferdinand of Habsburg claims the throne of Bohemia and Hungary but his claim is disputed by John Zapolya, who has the support of the Ottomans

1529 The first Ottoman siege of Vienna ends in failure

1530 Charles V is crowned Holy Roman Emperor

1541 Buda is taken by Suleiman the Magnificent

1541–51 Queen Isabella, daughter of Sigismund of Poland and Bona Sforza and widow of John Zapolya, starts to rebuild the palace at Alba Iulia in a Renaissance style with influences from Buda and Wawel Castle in Krakow

1543 Johannes Honterus and the beginnings of the Reformation in Transylvania. The Protestant movement attracts the lesser nobility and those opposed to the Habsburgs and papal power. The Ottomans occupy Esztergom

1547 The Ottomans take the Yemen and Basra. They are blocked from the Persian Gulf by the Portuguese

1551 Ferdinand of Habsburg occupies Transylvania

1552 The Ottomans capture Timișoara and most of Transylvania. The Diet votes to restore autonomy under the Ottomans

1555 Charles V abdicates. Ferdinand is elected Holy Roman Emperor

1568 Edict of Torda allows freedom of worship

1571 John Sigismund, son of Zapolya, is created the first Prince of Transylvania. He renounces the title of King of Hungary. The naval forces of Sultan Selim II ('The Sot'), son of Suleiman, are defeated at the Battle of Lepanto

1576 István Báthory succeeds to the titles of King of Poland and Prince of Transylvania

1583 Rudolf II moves his court to Prague to avoid the Ottoman threat to Vienna

1599 András Báthory, Prince of Transylvania, loses the support of the Székelys and is defeated by Michael the Brave of Wallachia

1600 Michael the Brave becomes ruler of Moldavia, Wallachia and Transylvania

1605 István Bocskai, the only

ruler acceptable to all factions, Protestants, Catholics and pro-Ottoman groups, becomes Prince of Transylvania

1608–13 Gábor Báthory is Prince of Transylvania and subdues Moldavia and Wallachia

1613–29 Gábor Bethlen is Prince of Transylvania, a formidable intellectual and statesman and patron of artists and artisans

1618 Beginning of the Thirty Years' War

1620 Battle of the White Mountain. Defeat of the Protestant cause in Bohemia. The outcome marks the beginning of the Counter-Reformation in the Habsburg lands

1629 Catherine of Brandenburg, widow of Gábor Bethlen, succeeds her husband as ruler of Transylvania, the only woman ever to do so. She is forced to abdicate by the Diet and converts to Catholicism

1630–48 György Rákóczi I is Prince of Transylvania. A period of stability and cultural prominence

1648 Treaty of Westphalia brings the Thirty Years' War to an end. Transylvania has not been affected

1648–54 György Rákóczi II brings

war to Transylvania with his ambition to conquer Poland. Allies himself with Sweden and the princes of Moldavia and Wallachia. The Porte calls upon the Transylvanian Diet to depose him

1661 Mihály Apafi I is elected Prince of Transylvania

1683 The Ottomans are repelled from the gates of Vienna

1686 Ottomans expelled from Buda

1689 With Ottoman power on the wane, Mihály Apafi I comes to an agreement with the Habsburgs to remain as Prince of Transylvania. He is the last of the independent princes

1690 Mihály Apafi II elected to succeed his father but is called to Vienna. Revolt against the Habsburgs led by Imre Thököly. The emperor Leopold I issues the *Diploma Leopoldinum*, asserting control over Transylvania but giving it a certain amount of autonomy

1691–1704 Miklós Bethlen is appointed Chancellor of Transylvania. However, his proposals for Transylvania's political future bring him into disfavour with Vienna and he is imprisoned

1699 Treaty of Karlowitz concludes the Austro-Ottoman war and signals the beginning of Turkish withdrawal from Europe

1703–11 Ferenc Rákóczi II. War of Hungarian independence, with repercussions felt in Transylvania. Rákóczi is elected the last Prince of Transylvania in 1704

1713 Death of Mihály Apafi II in Vienna

1714–18 Renewed war between Austria and the Ottomans

1719 Treaty of Passarowitz concludes hostilities between Austria and the Turks. The Turks lose the Banat and much of Serbia

1724 The Ottomans and Russians partition northwest Iran

1735 Russia declares war on the Ottomans and takes the Crimean capital

1739 Treaty of Belgrade concludes another Austro-Ottoman war. The Ottomans regain northern Bosnia as well as parts of Serbia and the Banat

1740–80 Reign of Maria Theresa. Catholicism reasserts itself in Transylvania. Reforms throughout the Empire

1755–65 Gábor Bethlen is Chancellor of Transylvania

1757–74 Reign of Sultan Mustafa III. War against Russia; Russia invades the Crimea in 1771

1774–87 Samuel Brukenthal is governor of Transylvania, in charge of the Siebenbürgische Hofkomission. Born in Nocrich, he is a great collector. His former palace in Sibiu is now an important museum

1780–90 Reign of Joseph II. Further reforms in Hungary and Transylvania, suppression of many religious orders and redistribution of their lands. The revolt of Horea, Cloșca and Crișan is brutally put down. German is declared the language of State

1782–91 The Transylvanian Chancellery is merged with the Hungarian under the chancellorships of György Bánffy and Sámuel Teleki

1783 Russia annexes the Crimean Khanate

1790–92 Reign of Leopold II. In 1791 he concludes peace with Turkey, bringing to an end the hostilities begun under his brother Joseph II

1793 The Ottomans are neutral in the European war against France. Execution of Louis XVI and Marie-Antoinette, sister of Joseph II and Leopold II

1798 Napoleon Bonaparte invades Egypt

1807 Serb forces occupy Belgrade

1815 Final defeat of Napoleon at Waterloo

1821 Beginning of the Greek independence movement

1846 Closure of Istanbul slave market

1848 Rise of Hungarian and Romanian independence movements. Transylvanian Vlachs demand representation and rights at the Assembly of Blaj

1848–9 Hungarian war of independence. The rebels are crushed by Austria with Russian help. Abolition of serfdom. The Transylvanian Chancellery is dissolved

1850 First official census in Transylvania. Romanian 59.5 percent; Hungarian 26 percent; Saxon 9.3 percent; Roma 3.8 percent

1853–6 Crimean War

1860 Institution of Chancellor of Transylvania reinstated

1862 Union of Moldavia and Wallachia to form the new state of Romania, under Ottoman suzerainty

1866 Romania establishes herself

as a kingdom under Carol I

1867 Dual Monarchy of Austria-Hungary formed at the expense of the Slavs. Transylvanian Parliament formally annulled and the Chancellery dissolved. Transylvania is joined to Hungary

1897 Czar Nicholas II and Emperor Franz Joseph agree on the partition of the Ottoman Balkans

1908 Young Turk revolution. The Ottomans lose Bulgaria, Bosnia Herzegovina and Crete

1912–13 First and Second Balkan War

1914 Archduke Franz Ferdinand murdered at Sarajevo. He had been sympathetic to greater self-rule for minorities within the Austro-Hungarian Empire. Outbreak of the First World War. Turkey and Germany are allies of Austria-Hungary. Romania is initially neutral

1915–16 Ottoman victory at Gallipoli

1916 Romania enters the war on the side of the Entente

1917 Russian Revolution. Russia withdraws from the war

1918 Defeat of the Central Powers and end of the First World War. Transylvanian Vlachs vote in Alba Iulia to join the Kingdom of Romania

1919 Saxon Transylvanians also vote to join Greater Romania

1920 Treaty of Trianon concluded between the victorious powers and Hungary. Hungary is shorn of two-thirds of her territory, including Transylvania and Slovakia. The Ottoman Empire is dismantled by the Treaty of Sèvres, although this proves unenforceable. Rise of Turkish nationalism. Charles IV of Hungary attempts to regain his throne, fails, and is escorted away down the Danube on a British gunboat

1922 Coronation of King Ferdinand of Romania and Queen Marie in Alba Iulia, the ancient Transylvanian capital. In Ankara, Turkey forms a new government under Atatürk, a veteran of Gallipoli. The Ottoman sultanate is officially abolished. Mehmet VI leaves Istanbul on a British warship. His brother Abdulmecit succeeds him as Caliph only. Population exchanges between Greece and Turkey

1923 Land reforms in Transylvania deprive Hungarian landowners of their estates and Saxons of their woodland. Founding of the Turkish Republic as a secular state with Ankara as its capital

1924 Abolition of the Ottoman Caliphate

1929 Great Depression. Transylvania badly affected

1933 Hitler comes to power in Germany. Many Transylvanian Saxons sympathise with his policies

1939 Outbreak of the Second World War

1940 Under the terms of the Second Vienna Award, Fascist Germany reallocates portions of Transylvania to Hungary. This strengthens Hungary's solidarity with Germany. Romania also joins the war on the Axis side

1942 Romanian Jews are deported to concentration camps

1944 Romania changes sides and joins the Allies

1945 Victory for the Allies. Transylvanian Saxons are deported to Soviet labour camps

1947 King Michael of Romania is deposed. The country becomes a republic under the Communist leadership of Gheorghe Gheorghiu-Dej

1965 Death of Gheorghiu-Dej. His successor is Nicolae Ceaușescu

1987 Warnings that Saxon villages are under threat from 'systemisation' leads to an international outcry

1989 Execution by firing squad of Ceaușescu and his wife. First free elections

1990–1 An invitation from the newly reunited Germany caused a mass emigration of Transylvanian Saxons

1992 Siege of Sarajevo

1993 Romania joins the Council of Europe. Slow moves towards restitution of property taken under the Communists. First visit of Jessica Douglas-Home and the MET to Viscri

1995 End of the Yugoslav war

1996–9 Kosovo war

1999 Historic visit of Pope John Paul II to the largely Orthodox Romania. Poland, Hungary and the Czech Republic join NATO

2000 The Whole Village Project set up by the MET to encourage responsible tourism to Transylvania

2004 Romania joins NATO

2007 Romania and Bulgaria join the EU

2014 Election of Klaus Iohannis, a Transylvanian Saxon, as President of Romania.

THE LAND OF THE SZÉKELYS
AND SOURCE OF THE GREATER TÂRNAVA

The western end of the Greater Târnava Valley is traditionally the home of the Hungarian military caste, the Székelys or Szeklers. The date of their arrival is disputed. According to some, they were here before the 9th-century migrations of Árpád and his chieftains. Others say they came at about the same time as the Saxons, in other words in the 12th century. They were posted to the far borders of the realm to protect the Kingdom of Hungary against invaders, receiving important freedoms and tax concessions from the king in return. They suffered badly in the Tatar invasion of 1241 and most of their settlements were destroyed. However, they reconsolidated and rebuilt, and have remained here ever since, a remarkable example of continuance and commitment in the region. All the road signs are in Romanian and Hungarian. Everyday speech is Hungarian.

In contrast to the other end of the valley, around Blaj, small manor houses replace grand country houses in the villages. The village houses are not linked together as the Saxons' are, but are set apart at intervals within small gardens defended by huge oak-carved gates like pieces of stage scenery—and reminiscent of Ireland, where huge gates belie the small bungalow behind them. The churches are different too, small and whitewashed, nothing like the Saxon fortresses, although in the Szekler lands there are also examples of fortified churches. The churches nurture the faiths of Catholic, Uniate, Unitarian and Calvinist congregations.

ODORHEIU SECUIESC

Odorheiu Secuiesc (Székelyudvarhely) is an interesting town, the largest in the Székely region and for many years the point of assembly for the Székely communities. Indeed, if Blaj at the other end of the valley was regarded as a 'little Rome', Odorheiu had a reputation as the Székely Athens because of its rich cultural life and its educational establishments. It was damaged by the Habsburgs at the end of the 17th century and again in 1848–9. It was given to Hungary as part of the Vienna Award in 1940, an arrangement which lasted until 1944. The Germans recognised Hungary's bitterness at losing Transylvania in 1920 and returned parts of the region to them to encourage them to join the Axis forces. The move caused a resentment amongst the non-Hungarian population that has lasted until the present.

The outskirts of Odorheiu today are unforgiving, but it is a great thing to have the majority population staying in their country and not emigrating. The Hungarian-speaking community here accounts for over 90 percent of the population. The industries are timber, iron ore (there are mining ventures everywhere), textiles (there is a Coats thread mill) and agriculture. The town boasts a Philharmonic Orchestra, founded in 2008; the Tomcsa Sándor Theatre; a folk dance studio, which also teaches contemporary dance; and many choral societies. There are local craft fairs too: most famous is the ceramics fair at **Corund (Korond)** in August, where you can find the characteristic rustic-patterned pottery. Corund is famous for its ceramics and some of the potters have open studios where it is possible to throw your own pot. Beyond it is the village of **Praid (Parajd)**, where there is a massive salt mine: geologists claim that there is enough salt in the area to last Europe for a hundred years. The surrounding landscape is interesting with good picnic places.

Odorheiu occupies an ancient site. Above the river to the southwest is an outcrop on which a castle once stood and where finds have revealed habitation going back to the Neolithic. The earliest building vestiges in the town centre are also the remains of old defences: the **site of the Roman castrum**, later a Dominican monastery and after that a contentious castle. The Székelys traditionally refused to have castles in their towns, seeing them as symbols of oppression: high walls from behind which an overlord could dominate the people. When István Báthori, voivode of Transylvania, began converting the Dominican monastery into a fortress, they complained bitterly to the king. Báthori was removed from his post and the castle was left unfinished. But when the Székelys rose up against a later voivode, John Sigismund, son of Zapolya, in 1562, they were ruthlessly put down and

46 | Travels in Transylvania

ordered to complete the castle so that the town could be fortified against its own inhabitants. Today it is rather a dull ruin. The last family to own it were the Kornis in the 1830s. Much of the building was destroyed when the Neoclassical National Academy was built in the 19th century. It is now the Agricultural School.

The **Haáz Rezső Museum** at Str. Kossuth Lajos 29 (*open March–Sept Tues–Fri 9–6, Sat–Sun 10–8; T: 0366 100 900*) is made up of two buildings on either side of the road, both worth visiting. The museum and library were assembled by the ethnographer and art teacher Rezső Haáz (1883–1958) and the collection was opened to the public in 1913. The library embraces the donations of Prince Mihály Apafi and chancellor Gábor Bethlen. There is also an interesting collection which belonged to the Calvinist College (*see below*) from 1797 and which is typical of the Enlightenment. It contains antiquities, coins and minerals, natural history, armorials and flags. Everything a child should know about.

At the top end of Str. Kossuth Lajos is the **main square**, Piaţa Primăriei (Városháza tér), which merges with Márton Áron Square. The 'square' takes the form of a broad street-cum-market-place. Around it stand grand buildings of late Neoclassicism and the Belle Époque. First Charles VI and then Maria Theresa attempted to keep the sputtering flame of the Counter-Reformation alight in Transylvania. Therefore, of prominence at one end of this long market-place is the Franciscan church and the adjoining Convent of the Poor Clares, begun in 1730. The altar is of 1780 and the whole was finished in 1928. At the other end of the square, further up the hill, is the Reformed (Calvinist) church, originally of 1633 but rebuilt in the 1780s. It is a charming building. Diagonally opposite, in extravagant French Renaissance Revival style, is the Town Hall of 1895.

Most thrilling from the architectural point of view are two seats of learning: the **Tamási Áron Gimnázium**, a Hungarian Catholic high school built in the Secession (Art Nouveau) style in 1910. It might be mistaken for a smart early 20th-century spa hotel, though at its core was the Jesuit College founded in 1593. Next to it is the **Catholic church** of 1788–93, and behind, a rather beautiful cemetery with a map to help you find the most important incumbents, which include the satirist Sándor Tomcsa (1879–1963), after whom the town theatre is named. The previous church on this site was used together by both Protestants and Catholics after the Reformation. The original building was damaged by the Turks in 1661. The architects of the current building were Pál Schmidt and Antal Türk. The sculpture is by Simon Hoffmeyer, whose work in Dumbrăveni is so remarkable (*see p. 98*).

The **Calvinist College** (Backamadarasi Kis Gergely Református Kollégium), opposite the west end of the Calvinist church, is more restrained but still influenced by Hungarian Art Nouveau (1910–12). This school was started by János Bethlen in 1670. Below it, on Márton Áron Square, stands the fine, if pugnacious, war memorial known as the '**Iron Székely**'. The Székelys, according to their own national mythology, took their role as border guards seriously and went gallantly to meet the enemy. They did not retreat behind defensive walls like the Saxons. Perhaps there is a touch of bravado here and disdain for the neighbouring Saxon who, after all, had been called to farm not to fight. The Székelys certainly were—and are—tenacious. If necessary, they hid out in the many natural caves that appear in the hills flanking the valleys, among them those of the Vârghiş Gorge east of Mereşti (Homoródalmás), where a vast and intricate cave system stretches for over seven kilometres.

There are also Unitarian and Greek Catholic churches in the town, as well as Orthodox, and two more slightly out-of-the-way museums that are worth seeking out. One is a **collection of Székely gateways** placed in a curve like a ski slalom down a hill on the outskirts of town to the north. This is part of the Szejke Spa and at the centre lies the tomb of Balázs Orbán (1829–90), the Székely writer and politician who travelled the length and breadth of his homeland with notebook and camera, documenting Székely culture and traditions. The Székely gateway takes the characteristic form of a single-roofed unit comprising a wider gateway, high enough for a laden cart to pass through, and a narrower postern alongside. The whole is usually made of hard-weathering Turkey oak, without nails, and is richly carved and sometimes painted. Nearby is the **museum of baths and mineral water** (Museul Apei Minerale/Fürdő és Ásványvíz Múzeum). At the foot of Mál hill to the north, on the road to Bisericani (Székelyszentlélek), is the **Székely Calvary**, constructed in memory of the Transylvanian Diocese and donated by the Ugron family. Fourteen reliefs by Walter Zavacki depict the traditional Stations of the Cross, linking the sufferings of Christ to disasters in Székely history.

A weekly market is held on Tuesday, close to the central bus station. Farmers from the surrounding villages come here to sell their produce. Once a month (on the last weekend of the month) a slow food market is held in the main town square.

The Székely People

There are two distinct groups of Hungarian speakers in Transylvania. Those in the west, next to the border with Hungary, are ethnically Hungarian. In the east you find the Székelys or Szeklers. It has been suggested that these Hungarian-speaking peoples were found by the advancing Magyars when they first arrived in Transylvania (some Székelys claim descent from Attila the Hun). Alternatively they may have been a militaristic clan advancing with the Hungarian settlers in the 9th century. Most now live as a homogeneous group in the eastern part of Transylvania, in the districts of Harghita, Covasna and the eastern part of Mureș county. They number around 700,000, roughly half of the Hungarian speakers in Romania, and are fiercely proud of their traditions.

The Szeklers were first documented in 1116 as an individual social class. Later they formed part of the elected Diet of the *Unio Trium Nationum* (with the Hungarians and Saxons). The Székely people were largely self-governing and were granted freedoms from taxes and given land in return for defending the borders of the Hungarian kingdom. They retained their freedoms until the 15th century, paying occasional tribute, such as when the queen gave birth to a boy, when horses or oxen were sent as tax. When later rulers threatened to curtail their freedoms, the Székelys responded with uprisings which were ruthlessly put down. Those who had taken part were condemned

Typical Székely gateway with its double arch.

to serfdom. Thus after the 16th century it was possible to find free Székleys and serfs in the same village.

At the Reformation many Szeklers became Unitarians or Calvinists and remain so today. The majority, however (about 60 percent), retain their Catholic faith.

The Székleys' history as border guards has made them resilient. The fact that in the last months of the First World War a separate Székely division held out against the Romanian royal troops not only illustrates their distaste for the future Treaty of Trianon, but also their fighting spirit. Szekler culture defines these people and separates them from other Hungarian speakers. As Mónika Soós, a Szekler from Odorheiu Secuiesc, puts it: 'For me to be a Szekler is not a uniform, but a support. It gives me strength and dignity. I don't feel at home when I go to Hungary and I avoid going to Bucharest. I feel in between somewhere and I feel good there, but it was a hard work to get there— and a long story.'

THE SOURCE OF THE GREATER TÂRNAVA

Heading east from Odorheiu on road 13A will take you to two famous spas spoken of in the 17th century and visited by Austrians, Saxons and English: Băile Selters (Székelyszeltersz) and Băile Chirui (Kirulyfürdő). However, to find the source of the Târnava, turn off left to Zetea (Zetelaka) and then on to Sub Cetate (Zeteváralja), where a dam was finally completed in the 1980s to prevent further flooding by the Târnava Mare. Here, rising to the volcanic plateau, the landscape becomes alpine and you are likely to see, being ridden astride down the streets, some of the splendid Székely horses, stocky and cob-like for extracting timber from the forest. The whole area is huge, about 30km square, and dotted with small homesteads. The area has become fashionable and in spite of a harsh climate there is much new-build. Some traditional wooden gates and a few ancient houses and barns remain to give a flavour but, in the main, the buildings are modern bungalows. After Sub Cetate there are a few mills and then you come into bear country. Here, at about Vărşag (Székelyvarság), the Târnava is a rushing stream and then, like the sources of many rivers—certainly the Thames though perhaps not the Nile—it becomes something of a disappointment. The journey, however, is worth it.

WESTWARDS TO CRISTURU

From Odorheiu the main valley road (the 137) leads to the smaller Székely town of Cristuru Secuiesc (Székleykeresztúr). The road (and river) run alongside the little private railway line between Odorheiu and Sighişoara, inaugurated in 1886. On the furthest outskirts of Odorheiu, on the left of the road, is the **Chapel of the Heart of Christ**, an unusual, walled, four-lobed structure, like some Byzantine baptistery. Many legends surround the origin of this strange little building. Perhaps the most likely is that it was built and donated by someone who was cured in one of the numerous baths/spas that dot the entire region. Now a museum (*open May–Oct Tues–Fri 10–5, Sat–Sun 10–2, closed Mon*), it is in the care of the Haáz Rezső Museum (*see above*).

View of the Chapel of the Heart of Christ (Jézus Szíve kápolna)
on the outskirts of Odorheiu Secuiesc.

Further on at **Feliceni (Felsőboldogfalva)**, the little church is Calvinist
(*T: 0266 245 277*). The fat, tub-like pulpit faces the entrance with seating
on three sides. No escape. Under the whitewash have been discovered
traces of frescoes of great charm. Note especially, on the chancel arch,
the Magi kneeling before the Virgin and Child. One of the Wise Men has
placed his crown on the ground in respect and the Virgin is encouraging
Christ to bless him: unusual iconography. There is also a St Veronica with
her veil, and on the panelled ceilings and balconies, lovely naïve paintings
in warm colours.

Beyond Feliceni, off the road to the right, are three small villages which
did not come under the sway of the Reformation and retained their
Catholic faith. They are Dobeni, Beta and Tăietura.

Dârjiu

If you have decided to explore this area in the leisurely manner which it deserves, make a detour south to Dârjiu (Székelyderzs), a UNESCO site which boasts further fine frescoes in its beautiful church (*open Mon–Sat 9.30–11 & 1–7. For the guide, T: 0764 160 619. I made the mistake of visiting on a Sunday, when the churches where bursting with worshippers in their black Sunday best; visitors at such times are frowned upon*). Much restoration work has been done on the church, which is fortified in the Saxon manner with high walls with a bacon tower and storage space for grain. Inside, on the north wall of the nave, is one of the best preserved **frescoes of the story of St Ladislaus**, a popular fresco subject in churches in the Hungarian lands. The story goes that at the Battle of Kerlés in 1068, fought by Ladislaus against infidel invaders (traditionally Cumans, but possibly Pechenegs), an enemy soldier was seen galloping from the field with a beautiful Hungarian girl as his captive. Although wounded himself, Prince Ladislaus valiantly rides to her rescue, calling to her to take hold of the Cuman's girdle and jump to the ground. She throws herself from the horse, dragging her captor down with her. A fight ensues between Ladislaus and the Cuman and the girl finally helps Ladislaus by cutting a tendon in the Cuman's leg. The Cuman is beheaded and the girl nurses the exhausted prince, resting his head on her lap. Ladislaus became king of Hungary in 1077 and was canonised in 1192, during the reign of Béla III. Béla had been brought up at the Byzantine court and was at one time betrothed to the emperor Manuel I Comnenus' daughter. Manuel's mother was King Ladislaus' daughter, a woman of great virtue, who married John II Comnenus and became the Empress Irene. Her tomb in Constantinople attracted a cult following which might have given Béla the idea to promote other Árpád kings as saints. The cult of Ladislaus as the ideal warrior king, which grew up a century and more after his death, is associated too with ideas of chivalry and the legitimacy of rule through virtue and wisdom.

Here at Dârjiu the story is told in a lively manner and was painted over an earlier series. The cycle begins with Prince Ladislaus seeing the girl being carried off by a Cuman. The fight between prince and Cuman looks as if it will have a dubious outcome as the Cuman puffs up his cheeks with effort.

Detail from the Székelyderzs frescoes: after cutting off the Cuman's head, St Ladislaus reclines in the arms of the Hungarian maiden. She is shown searching for lice in his hair, a motif used by medieval artists to suggest romantic intimacy and closeness.

The girl is called to help and chops off the Cuman's head. The last scene shows Ladislaus relaxing in her arms while she hunts his hair for nits.

On the south wall are further frescoes of bishops and a fine group of cavalry: one knight is looking straight at us and his banner has the name of the artist, 'István son of Stefan', and the date of the cycle, 1419.

Walk around the outside of the church and you will find, at eye level, many examples of **Székely runic script**, known as *Székely rovásírás*. After the establishment of the Christian Hungarian kingdom, the old writing was partly forced out of use and the Latin alphabet was adopted. However, among some professions (e.g. shepherds, who used a 'rovás-stick' to officially track the number of animals) and in Transylvania, the script remained in use by the Székely Magyars. It is different from the Germanic runic alphabet, with traces of Turkish and Greek. Today there is a revival of interest in this ancient form.

Excursion to the Homorod Valley

It is possible here to visit more Szekler churches off the beaten track. To the southeast of **Sânpaul (Homoródszentpál)** are some small lakes where the Romans extracted their salt. They are not particularly saline and freshwater fish can survive in them. The wells, however, are said to be full of salt and the locals cure their hams there. This is a protected area for migrating birds. On the hillsides in the surrounding countryside are groups of Scots pine planted in 1896 to celebrate the first thousand years of the Hungarians in the Carpathian Basin.

At **Crăciunel (Karácsonyfalva)** the church was listed in the papal archives in 1313. It became Unitarian in 1568 (*the key is at no. 49, the home of the priest*). The frescoes were discovered in 2005 and then restored. There is a fine 13th-century *Nativity* and a 15th-century *Adoration of the Magi* featuring St Helen and also, in the top right-hand corner, the cloth of Veronica, which she lent him to mop his brow on the way to Calvary and which was miraculously imprinted with his visage. The scenes of St Ladislaus are not of the quality of Dârjiu but are amusing to see all the same. The date is 1496. This village lies right on the old Roman border, a region where St Ladislaus was often invoked for defence against Eastern invaders. There is a fine coffered ceiling here of 1752. The sounding board of the pulpit and the altar are of 1798. The 19th-century organ is in the form of a triumphal arch. Just down from the church is a memorial to Empress Elisabeth, Sisi. She was much loved by the Hungarians as she learned their language and was a great supporter of their causes.

Mugeni, Lutița, Porumbenii Mari and Betești

Back on the main road, **Mugeni (Bögöz)** has a 13th-century Calvinist church (*T: 0266 245 427 for the key*), charming and whitewashed with the usual circular low wall. There is another fresco over the entry door. The interior has more decoration illustrating the life of St Ladislaus and more runic script. The frescoes are of the 14th and 15th centuries. Transylvania, incidentally, was the source of many of the mineral paint colours found in the frescoes, both here and in other parts of Central Europe. They imported their tin (white), however, from Cornwall.

Continue your journey along the river valley to **Lutița (Agyagfalva)**, which was the site of a national assembly of the Székely people in 1506. To mark this, and the Hungarian revolution against the Habsburgs in

Memorial to the Jews of Porumbenii Mari who died in the Holocaust.
The Hungarian inscription below the list of names reads:
'May their souls have eternal life'.

1848, there is a very Soviet-style memorial. Amongst the figures are the Hungarian kings of the Árpád dynasty.

The church at **Porumbenii Mari (Nagygalambfalva)** is Calvinist (*T: 0266 244 505 for the key*). There is a covered fresco over the entrance doorway. The door itself was given by one Clara Borsai in 1789. The lovely light decoration here is a signature of the interiors and furnishings of so many of the churches of the Székelys. The frescoes in the nave contain a fine late Gothic *Coronation of the Virgin*. As in many Szekler churches, just before the altar hangs a crown of straw or wheat ears, renewed each August as a harvest thanksgiving. In the little graveyard there is a memorial to members of the Jewish community who died in the Holocaust. Every village and town here had a Jewish population, but what is unusual is that the Holocaust victims from Porumbenii are recorded on a monument outside the inner walls of the Calvinist church. The Jews here were the commercial heart of the district, dealing in timber. Only one man survived the war and he returned from Israel and set up the monument.

There is a Greek Catholic church on the way out of the village. The countryside here is full of bear, lynx, wolf and boar.

At **Beteşti (Betfalva)**, in the local cemetery, you will see that, unlike in the Saxon villages, everyone from each denomination is buried in the same plot of land. There is an area here famous for its stone quarries, yielding material used in many of the Saxon settlements, although this district is best known for its wood carvings. There are basket-makers along this road too and, just before Cristuru, a specialist steel factory. The open countryside hereabouts is famous (among locals only) for truffles.

CRISTURU SECUIESC

Cristuru Secuiesc (Székelykeresztúr), in common with Odorheiu, has a Hungarian population of over 90 percent. The town was given the rights to trade as a market by Sigismund of Luxembourg (1419–37), King of Hungary and later Holy Roman Emperor. At first sight it may seem that there is little to hold you here. But don't be hasty. Head for the large grammar school (Berde Mózes Gimnázium or Liceul Teologic Berde Mózes), founded in 1793. The original, much smaller, school building is near the whitewashed **Unitarian church**. The church (*T: 0266 242 127 for the key*) is well kept due to a pairing with one in the USA. The pulpit is central to the general ground plan, which is quite different from any church layout further west and vaguely reminiscent of a Scottish kirk, where the pulpit and preaching are at the heart of the matter. Here the pulpit is opposite the church entrance on the wall and the pews face it on three sides. Although, in common with the Saxon congregations, the men, women and children are separately seated, each family has its own pew. The interior is delightfully painted. There is a large Unitarian college next door.

The **Catholic church** (*T: 0266 242 171 for the key if shut*) has retained its medieval site. There had been plans to build a cathedral here in the 12th century but the Tatar invasion put a stop to them. There are the foundations, at the west door, of a westwork. The chancel retains its Gothic vaulting and the nave its longitudinal plan.

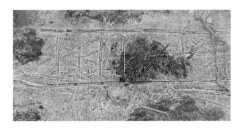

The ancient Székely runic script known as *rovásírás*.
Examples of it can be found at the churches of Dârjiu and Mugeni,
and in the István Molnár museum in Cristuru.

There are two town houses of note, one in the **main square** belonging
first to the Macskasys and then to the Hallers. It is now the hospital.
The Hallers appear in Mălâncrav and elsewhere and were governors
of Transylvania under the Habsburgs. The other notable building is a
charming manor house by the Târnava which belonged to the Gyárfás
family. It looks recently restored and is now a home for disabled children.
In it there is a **Petőfi memorial room**, curated by the Molnár István
Museum. The poet Petőfi spent his last night in this town before the Battle
of Sighişoara around Albeşti (*see below*), leaving the note: 'My only sorrow
would be to die among the pillows of a soft bed.'

The István Molnár Museum

*Piaţa Libertăţii/Szabadság tér 45. Open May–Sept 7.30–5, Oct–April 7.30–
3.30. The display of mills etc. is not open in winter. T: 0266 242 580.*

This small museum, started in 1946 by Dr István Molnár, is a must. In a
past life the building was the town's social club and cultural centre, until
reorganised in the 1960s. Such clubs (misleadingly known as 'casinos')
were a feature of Hungarian towns after the establishment of the Dual
Monarchy, functioning as places where the townsfolk could meet and
mingle, their purpose being to bring culture, the arts and ideas—and
concomitant gentrification and social mobility—to the provinces. When
the club ceased to exist, the house and land were given over to the

ethnographical and archeological collection begun in the Unitarian High School.

The first cases display finds from the Târnava Valley from the Neolithic period, also including the Iron Age and some fine Roman silver. Some of the Roman soldiers here were bought from Spain to build the Salt Road which skirts the area of this guide to the east.

Interesting too, in the next case, are the results of a dig on the site of a Saxon house near the museum. From it came a Saxon pike head, a Szekler stirrup and a Turkish bell. There are arrow heads with the owners' stamps on them, to ensure no poaching. There is also a bell for a foal with a stamp from Nuremburg c. 1580, a date when many workers came to Sibiu.

Due to the excellent clay found in the area, the potteries became third in importance after those in Budapest and Visegrád. The examples of stove tiles are fine and varied. One features old Székely runic script (*rovásírás*) and another a scene from the life of St Ladislaus (*see p. 52*). The first lead glazed tile is of 1573. Levente Domokos has reconstructed a stove from such examples in the museum.

There is also the studio of the local photographer, which is revealing about society up until the war. There is a rather strange exhibit of some funeral clothes as shrouds. More exotic is a Szekler costume of 1896, which the owner wore to represent his district in the Budapest parliament.

Outside, in the ethnographical section, is a series of ingenious mills of the kind used on the Târnava near its source. Some are for salt, others for extracting beech nut oil, cider vinegar for medicinal use, or for crushing oak and birch for use in tanning and the wool industry. The mill wheels all differ depending on the speed of water needed to turn them.

There are two Szekler houses in the garden. One, of 1834, has smoke vents at the end of its shingle (pine) roof. It was brought here lock, stock and barrel in the 1950s. The other house is interesting too. Note the cows' bladder hide for window covering and some fine horsehair sieves of a type made in the town for years. Tail hair only was used and that of stallions was preferred.

A display of stuffed animals illustrates the rich wildlife of the surrounding hills. Here are lynx, bear, wildcats, otters, wolf and badger (which the

Szeklers ate; they also used the oil and skin). The woods all around are renowned for their truffles.

ALBEȘTI AND BOIU ȚOPA

West of Cristuru Secuiesc, the village of **Albeşti (Weißkirch/Fehéregyháza)** lies close to the site of the last battle for Hungarian independence of 1849, when the Hungarian national army took its stand against imperial forces, both Austrian and Russian. This is where the charismatic revolutionary and poet Sándor Petőfi (1823–49), whose *Nemzeti dal* ('National Song') was inspirational for the Hungarian independence movement, was killed. There is poor signage to the little museum near the site of the battle (*turning to the left of the main street, just before the Casa Moda warehouse*). There is a further monument to Petőfi on the roadside. It is worth making the trek to the museum (although all the labels are in Hungarian). Emperor Franz Joseph called upon the Russian Czar for assistance and it was the Russians who won this last fight for the Habsburgs. Petőfi joined the army of General Bem as a major. His body has never been found and, as is the nature of things in this part of the world, rumours circulated that he had been killed by the Russians or just simply disappeared. It does seem most likely, however, that he did indeed die so far from home (although Transylvania was seen by Hungarians as their Motherland).

On the right of the main street is a sign to the villages of **Boiu (Bún)** and **Țopa (Alsóbún)**. On the banks of the river nearby are the remains of a fortified country house of the Bethlens. Today this is a ruin, the last fine façade having collapsed about five years ago. In its heyday it was important, built with ashlar and with spolia from a neighbouring Roman encampment (the practice of archaeological recycling is common in Transylvanian country-house construction). Boiu Țopa was begun by Farkas Bethlen, who died in 1618. He was a general of the Transylvanian army under Gábor Bethlen, his kinsman. His grandson, Miklós Bethlen, 18th-century amateur architect and statesman (*see p. 80*), made the Grand Tour through Holland, England, Italy and France. He planted an arboretum here, of which just a single oak survives. Much damage was done when, in the course of regulating the River Târnava in 1973–5, two towers were demolished. The Communists used the remaining buildings for offices and stores until the whole complex was abandoned in 1977.

SASCHIZ

The village of Saschiz (Keisd/Szászkézd), southeast of Albeşti, is not strictly in the Târnava Valley but I have included it because its church tower is so splendid and here too you will find an example of a peasants' citadel guarding the main road. The village is a UNESCO World Heritage site. The main road south from here will take you on to many other delights such as Viscri, which has become the template of conservation practices and is the birthplace of the MET's Whole Village Project in partnership with the Horizon Trust (*see p. 226*). The road leads finally to Braşov.

Saschiz is one of the earliest settlements in the valley, as the Hungarian-speaking Székelys (*see p. 48*) arrived in the 11th or early 12th century before moving on to defend the eastern borders of the Kingdom of Hungary (now the eastern limit of Transylvania), where most of them still remain. The Saxons moved in to replace them at Saschiz and started to build a church.

The village is split in two by the main Braşov to Sighişoara road. This was always, probably, a trading route and may have been the reason for the *cetate*, the **peasants' fortress**, that was built on a vantage point above the village. It has enclosing walls in the form of an elongated polygon once strengthened by six towers. To the east is a further defensive wall. The site is 90m long and 54m wide. In 1999, work to consolidate the structures, including the chapel, was started. This allowed for some limited archaeological digs to take place. Perhaps the most interesting finds were two coins, one of the period of Ferdinand I of Habsburg (1526–64) and the other of 1625.

The **church**, which is not inside the fortress, is dedicated to St Stephen of Hungary and is very sturdy. Building anew on early foundations, it was started in 1493 and construction lasted until c. 1525. All is well defended and the exterior is supported by buttresses. Above these is the area of defence, a walkway with piercings through the walls for throwing missiles

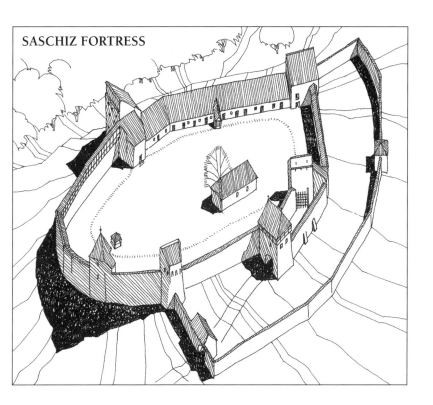

SASCHIZ FORTRESS

below. The church also has an impressive tower, modelled on the Clock Tower in Sighișoara. Restored in the 19th century, it stands separately from the church like a stout sentry.

The church interior has a single nave and chancel. The choir is one of the largest of its type in the valley, with slender brick ribs whose function is purely decorative. The sacristy has two upper floors forming a defensive tower in its own right. There was further investment in the 18th century providing for a pulpit, the altar of 1735 and the organ of 1778. The organ was extended twice in the 19th century, making the instrument one of the largest in the Târnava Valley.

On both sides of the main road there are charming streets of Saxon houses and there is a mill. The village pub can provide sandwich lunches. It is also possible to book lunch here in a private house (*see p. 14*).

Detail of the *Ship of the Church* fresco in Daia, showing the Crucifixion with Christ affixed to the ship's mainmast.

Saschiz is home to ADEPT (*see p. 226*), which has encouraged new plans for easier access to the *cetate* and for a revival of the famous Saschiz ceramics. There is an excellent information centre near the church, which also sells good local produce and guides to flora and fauna, etc. All this is actively encouraged by ADEPT, who work closely with the EU.

Excursion to Daia

From Dârjiu I recommend making a trip to Daia (Székelydálya), on a lovely untarred road. (NB: This area is very undeveloped as far as accommodation is concerned. Restaurants too are really only found in the two main towns. Beautiful picnic spots, however, abound.)

Daia has a tiny Calvinist church of 1505–35. It is worth finding the curator, Szabolcs Fülöp (*T: 0741 130 414*) for the key. The vault at the east end of the church was commissioned by Lenard Barlabasi; his crest is an ox head. The vault is decorated with vigorous lush foliage of the late Gothic/early Renaissance that would sit fine as a design on metalwork of the period. On the north wall is the unusual scene of the *Ship of the Church*. High on its mast is a depiction of the Crucifixion (*illustrated opposite*). The closest parallel may be the marvellous boat pulpits of Krakow.

SIGHIȘOARA

Only half an hour's drive separates Sighișoara from the Székely lands described in the preceding chapter, yet they are worlds apart in feel. Sighișoara is one of the great historic towns of the Saxons.

It was the Hungarian king Géza II (1141–62) who invited the first northern settlers. Here, on the site of the Roman garrison town of Stenarum, they built a wooden castle and settled around it on the hilltop. As with all these towns, though, we have no written evidence until after the destruction by the Tatars in 1241. There is a document of 1280 (a copy is in the Monastery Church) which mentions the town as 'Castrum Sex', that is, 'Camp of the Saxons'. It was a free royal town from 1367 and flourished as a centre of trade, agriculture and craftsmanship. After the Battle of Mohács, the townspeople (in common with many Saxons) sided with Ferdinand of Habsburg against Zapolya. Troubled times followed: Ottoman invasions, a Székely rebellion bloodily put down, struggles of Hungarians versus Habsburgs, and then a devastating fire in 1676 which claimed much of the citadel. Today's walls and bastions are from a mix of dates. Some of the foundations are early, with 15th- and 16th-century emplacements on top, and some are later, post-dating the fire.

To absorb the atmosphere of this remarkable place, I suggest that you take in both the citadel, now a UNESCO site, and the lower town below, which lies along the banks of the Târnava Mare. The citadel, at the height of the tourist season, has a tendency to veer towards Disney. Its beauty, plus associations with the Pied Piper of Hamelin and Vlad Țepeș (Dracula), have encouraged this. But it is only part of the picture of this beautiful, yet industrial and prosperous town. A few steps behind the Monastery Church stands the grand 19th-century Town Hall. This is a real Austro-Hungarian statement and brings home that there is so much more to Sighișoara than the tourist centre it has become. And now that the lower town is also being restored and offers hotels, the whole city appears less claustrophobic, and more layers of Transylvanian life and history are apparent.

THE CITADEL

I recommend visiting the citadel first. In the summer months it is advisable to park in the official parking at its foot and walk up. If staying in one of the many hotels in the citadel, they will send transport for the luggage. The short ascent through the double walls gives both a sense of the danger from the East and of the wealth of the city guilds who were responsible for this spectacular defence. The Sighișoara citadel is one of the few fortified towns still intact in Europe. As you climb, look out over the pre-war area near the hospital, with its charming villas of the '20s and '30s and which a friend, born and bred in Sighișoara, described as 'Belgravia'.

Huge strides have been made in restoring the fortifications. The MET (*see p. 225*) has repaired two of the existing towers using one, the Turnul Cojocarilor ('Tower of the Furriers'), as their central office. Attached to this is a shop making leather goods.

Piața Cetății
The old main square of the citadel is Piața Cetății. Sighișoara has wisely retained its cobbles, which give texture and sit well with the details and materials of the buildings. The centres of Brașov and Sibiu have all been re-paved to their detriment. The hoteliers in the citadel have also retained some of the original elements of the ancient buildings: as you look around this enchanting mix of architecture it is difficult to believe that most of the buildings are of the late 17th century and later. Have a drink in the **Hotel Sighișoara** to see the frescoes, and enjoy the carved stag's head rearing from a frescoed body on the **Casa cu Cerb**, which gives this hotel its name. The square also contains the putative **house of Vlad Dracul**, now a restaurant. Vlad Dracul was one of the warriors against the Turks and was the father of Vlad the Impaler, notorious as the inspiration for Bram Stoker's Dracula. The Canadian author never set foot in Transylvania and the Dracul house is much later than Vlad. Alas, in this case, fiction is stronger than fact and, as a result, shopping in the citadel is a dispiriting experience unless you want teeth or T-shirts. All the antique shops have gone. In the 1990s there was an ill-conceived scheme to build a Dracula

SIGHIȘOARA

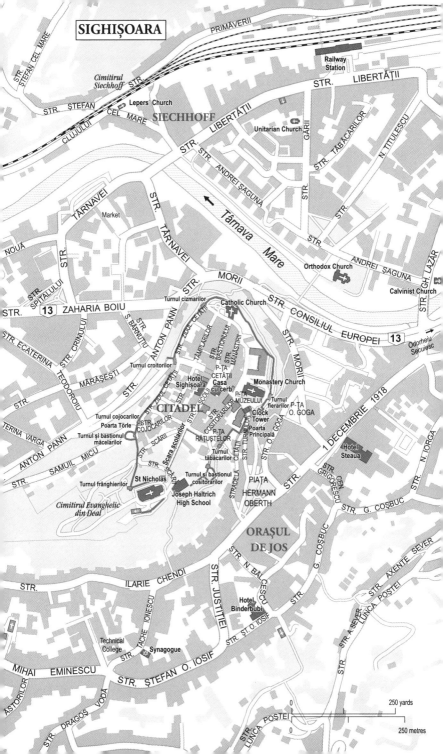

STR. ȘTEFAN CEL MARE

PRIMĂVERII

Railway Station

STR. LIBERTĂȚII

STR. ȘTEFAN

CLUJULUI

CEL MARE

Cimitirul Siechhoff

Lepers' Church

SIECHHOFF

LIBERTĂȚII

Unitarian Church

GĂRII

STR.

STR. TĂBĂCARILOR

N. TITULESCU

STR.

STR.

STR.

STR. ANDREI ȘAGUNA

Târnava Mare

NOUĂ

STR.

TĂRNAVEI

Market

STR. TĂRNAVEI

MORII

STR.

STR.

ANDREI ȘAGUNA

STR. GH. LAZĂR

Orthodox Church

Calvinist Church

STR. SPITALULUI

13 ZAHARIA BOIU

Turnul cizmarilor

Catholic Church

STR. CONSILIUL EUROPEI

13

Odorheiu Secuiesc

STR. ECATERINA TEODOROIU

STR. CRINULUI

S. BĂRNUȚIU

STR. ANTON PANN

STR. ZIDUL CETĂȚII

TÂMPLARILOR

STR. BASTIONULUI

STR. MĂNĂSTIRII

Turnul croitorilor

P-ȚA CETĂȚII

STR.

MĂRĂȘEȘTI

Hotel Sighișoara

Casa cu cerb

Monastery Church

STR. MORII

STR. O. GOGA

STR.

STR.

STR. ZIDUL CETĂȚII

SCOLII

Turnul fierarilor P-ȚA O. GOGA

TERINA VARGA

Turnul cojocarilor

CITADEL

STR. COSITORARILOR

STR. TURNULUI

Clock Tower

ANTON PANN

Poarta Törle

STR. COJOCARILOR

P-ȚA MUZEULUI

Poarta Principală

STR. SAMUIL MICU

Turnul și bastionul măcelarilor

SCĂRII

P-ȚA RĂȚUȘTELOR

1 DECEMBRIE 1918

STR.

STR.

STR.

Scara școlarilor

STR. SCĂRII

Turnul tăbăcarilor

STRADELA CETĂȚII

Hotel Steaua

STR. GEN. GRIGORESCU

STR. N. IORGA

Turnul frânghierilor

St Nicholas

Turnul și bastionul cositorarilor

PIAȚA HERMANN OBERTH

Cimitirul Evanghelic din Deal

Joseph Haltrich High School

STR. G. COȘBUC

STR. N. BĂLCESCU

ORAȘUL DE JOS

ILARIE CHENDI

STR. JUSTIȚIEI

Hotel Binderbubi

STR.

STR. G. COȘBUC

STR. AXENTE SEVER

STR.

TACHE IONESCU

STR. A. SEVER

STR. LUNCA POȘTEI

MIHAI EMINESCU

Technical College

Synagogue

STR. ȘTEFAN O. IOSIF

STR. ȘT. O. IOSIF

ȘTRII

STR. DRAGOȘ VODĂ

STR. LUNCA POȘTEI

250 yards

250 metres

0

0

park overlooking the city, amidst the ancient oak forest. At the last minute the project was halted—but not without many old tricks of intimidation on the part of those who had hoped to make their fortunes.

St Nicholas on the Hill

To reach the highest point of the citadel, start by ascending the Scară Școlarilor, the Saxon **Schülertreppe**, a covered stairway for scholars to reach their School on the Hill (Școala din Deal), which gives as its foundation date c. 1522 but is probably earlier. The present building is a neo-Gothic structure of 1901 and today is the Joseph Haltrich High School. Local resident Mr König remembers running up the stairs to school; but also when, in 1975, he was among the 100 candidates for confirmation and 5,000 Saxons still lived and worked in Sighișoara. Now there are only 500 and the Saxon Church still has responsibility for three churches and three cemeteries.

Facing the school is the **Church of St Nicholas on the Hill** (Biserica din Deal), the parish church before the Reformation (*it keeps to museum times and is closed on Mon; there is an excellent guide who will be delighted to take you around if you wish*). First built in the 13th century in this strongly defensive position, it was enlarged in the 15th. There is a series of fine but weathered statues between the window bays on the exterior of the choir. The interior seems all the more grand after walking up the dark, covered steps. It is a hall church, light and airy with fine vaulting completed in the early 16th century. In the 18th century the frescoes were painted over but some traces remain, including two scenes of *St George and the Dragon* and a fine *St Michael*. Under the west tower there is an inscription of 1488 declaring that: 'The maker of this work is Jacobus Kendlinger of Sankt Wolfgang'. Emese Sarkadi believes this to be the name of the fresco painter who executed the *trompe l'oeil* paintings, which she links to the workshop of the altarpiece in the Schottenstift in Vienna. Much of the decoration of this great parish church was due to the patronage of Michael Polner, '*purgermeister*' in the late 15th century. The majority of the frescoes visible today were uncovered in 1934. There may be more yet to come.

St Nicholas is also a depository for **altarpieces**, including three very fine

The Saxon covered staircase known as the *Schülertreppe*, which leads to the School on the Hill.

examples from the early 16th century. The Altar of St Martin (first south pier) is from the Monastery Church. It shows scenes from the life of the saint, including the famous scene of him giving his cloak to the beggar. It is the work of Johannes Stoss, the son of Viet Stoss from Nuremberg who also worked in Krakow. The younger Stoss had a workshop in Sighişoara for nearly 20 years and was heavily influenced by Dürer. Also in the south aisle is the altarpiece from Cund (*see p. 101*), showing scenes from the story of St Nicholas with outer panels of scenes of the Passion of Christ, a cycle whose iconography was still acceptable to the post-Reformation Lutheran communities. The high altar at the east end has a fine retable from Şaeş. In the predella are scenes of the *Prayer in the Garden*, *Crucifixion* and *Descent from the Cross*. The subject matter of the main panel, however, takes as its theme the Family of the Virgin (as does the predella of the Biertan altar), depicting the relatives of Christ on his mother's side. It has been suggested by Ciprian Firea that it was made up from the altarpiece originally in Copşa Mare.

A sculptor whose work is also found here is Elias Nicolai. His are the mid-17th-century **tomb slabs** of Georg Heltner and Stephan Man. Elias, a native of the Szepes area of upper Hungary (now the Spiš region of Slovakia), introduced the early Baroque to Transylvania. His work is seen also in Biertan. It was he who made the monument to Mihály Apafi I, now in Budapest, moved from its original position in Mălâncrav. His monuments to the elite of these wealthy towns give an insight into the strata of 17th-century Transylvanian society: the gowns as portrayed in this series of monuments seem to sum up the dignity, faith and status of the elders and leaders of the Saxon community. Clerical costume for the Saxons is largely unchanged. One monument, against the wall to the left of the main entrance, clearly once had a hinged wooden cover. In general these monuments were put against church walls for convenience, although originally set in the floor.

When you leave the church, I recommend descending into the town through the **Lutheran Cemetery** (Cimitirul Evanghelic; *open May–Oct 8–8, Nov–April 9–4*). It is not only beautiful, but a reflection of the community who once lived here. The cemetery chapel stands on the site of the old Goldsmiths' Tower in the walls.

The Monastery Church

The entire area of the Piața Museului was destroyed in the devastating fire of 1676. As for the Monastery Church, only the walls and the window tracery were left standing. The interior, therefore, is Baroque. The church was founded by the Dominicans, who had to leave at the Reformation. It is now the main Lutheran church in the town. Before entering, take a moment to look at the intarsia work of the doors, dated 1678 (there are actually two pairs of doors). Ceaușescu was rumoured to want them for Bucharest. To thwart him, the people of Sighișoara covered the intarsia work in black paint. The doors remained in place and have now been restored to their former beauty.

Inside, this hall church is surprisingly small, with simple quadripartite vaults and a lower chancel. There is a beautiful font. Painted panels flank the galleries, naïve in comparison to the other objects in the church. The resplendent organ of 1680 (dated in the scrolling woodwork on the organ case) boasts beautiful, faceted pipes framed by trumpeting angels and stringed instruments. Close to the organ loft is a fine Renaissance door to the upper gallery. Every Friday in summer there is a concert in the church.

The pulpit itself is undistinguished but the canopy is delicate Rococo. The pews around the edge of the nave are for members of the various guilds and bear their symbols. The mayor's pew, again with charming panel paintings, overlooks the chancel. At the east end is an enlivening altarpiece, also installed after the fire. Indeed, it has similar woodwork to the organ case, with *Christ Triumphant* at its apex.

The rest of the deep, rich colour of the interior is provided by the superb collection of Transylvanian rugs (*see p. 203*). Indeed, the first mention of carpets in this area comes in 1538 when John Zapolya, voivode of Transylvania, met the ambassador from the Porte, Mehmed Bek. Four rugs were brought here from Brașov for the occasion. The fire of 1676 destroyed most of them but there were enough locals who realised their value and did what they could to salvage the remainder. The rugs were catalogued for the first time in 1914, and in the same year 30 pieces were sent to Budapest on exhibition. There are 34 rugs in the church's collection, some with rare donor inscriptions.

The figure of Diana (Monday) in the Clock Tower.

The Clock Tower and walls

Nine defensive towers remain today out of the original fourteen that studded the city walls. Going clockwise from the Clock Tower in the east, they are the towers of the Tanners, Tinsmiths, Ropemakers, Butchers, Furriers, Tailors, Cobblers and Blacksmiths. Between the two last is the Catholic church, in the neo-Byzantine style. The Clock Tower itself (*closed Mon but otherwise open 9–4*) was begun in the 14th century, but again was damaged in the fire and restored in the 17th century. It is now roofed with coloured tiles. There are many steps inside but it is worth a visit for the magnificent clock at the top and its mechanism of 1677, replaced by an electric-driven Swiss movement fitted in 1906. There are two clock faces. The one that looks over the citadel features figures of Peace, Justice and the Rule of Law. Justice and Law are shown joined at the hip, respectively bearing a set of scales and a sword. There are also figures of Day and Night. Overlooking the gateway from the lower town is a revolving drum (electrified in 1963) with oak figures of the days of the week, personified by Roman deities bearing their planetary, zodiacal symbols on their heads and each associated with a metal in a happy mix of pagan theology and medieval alchemy. The figures are as follows: Diana (Monday); Mars (Tuesday); Mercury (Wednesday); Jupiter (Thursday); Venus (Friday), Saturn (Saturday) and the Sun (Sunday).

The other exhibit to be recommended is a room dedicated to the work of the Transylvanian Saxon pioneer of rocket science, Hermann Oberth (1894–1989). He was educated at the School on the Hill. His family left Romania in 1938. Together with his pupil Wernher von Braun, he was involved with the V2 rocket at the end of the Second World War. Von Braun went on to develop the rocket technology responsible for the first landing on the moon.

If staying in the heart of the citadel at high season, you have to contend with men in armour and ladies in distress. When the groups leave, though, it is lovely to have a drink in the square and walk around the defences counting the towers and imagining the wealth and pride of the guilds who built them. Even more, wonder at Sighișoara's survival at all.

THE LOWER TOWN

Access to the lower town is through the Clock Tower. Make your way down through the walls to the river and find a turn-of-the-20th-century commercial centre with churches, colleges, hotels and restaurants as well as the tiny synagogue.

The heart of the lower town is **Piaţa Hermann Oberth**. This was the main market-place and the site of gatherings, fairs and parades since the Middle Ages. The citadel rises above you. The main street is filled with a range of 19th-century architectural styles and it is here that it is easier to find an ATM and shops selling attractive tourist items. There are one or two notable buildings, such as the old **Hotel Steauă**, on Str. 1 Decembrie 1918, by the architect Fritz Balthes. It still retains a faded version of its splendid Art Deco façade, though alas nothing else of its past glory remains. In its heyday this was the Hotel Zum Goldenen Stern. It had a huge interior courtyard with orchestras playing and restaurants. It was the most fashionable place to be seen. The name of the street is a popular one in Romania. The date, 1st December, is Unification Day, a national holiday commemorating the annexing of Transylvania (along with Bukovina and Bessarabia) to Romania after the First World War.

Across the Târnava Mare, the vast **Orthodox church** makes a political statement outside the Saxon walls. It was planned as part of the Unification celebrations in 1918–19 but not built until 1934–7. It was badly damaged in floods in the 1970s, restored in 1991 but now only seems to open for services. This whole area suffered twice from flooding in the '70s, when the Târnava rose up to three metres. It was during this period that Nicolae Ceauşescu was attempting to 'systematise' towns and villages by bulldozing large sections of them, as he did in Bucharest. At this time, much of the old Mühlgasse (Strada Morii) was cleared and new buildings were put up. Many of Sighişoara's Saxons began to leave at this point. They found it easy to get work in Germany due to the excellence of their training at the technical colleges in their native town.

Not far from the Orthodox church is the neo-Gothic **Calvinist church** of 1888, built to plans by the Hungarian architect Ignác Alpár.

Fritz Balthes

In the Saxon area of Transylvania, the architect and engineer Fritz Balthes was perhaps the most outstanding practitioner of what has come to be known as Transylvanian Jugendstil. Balthes was born in Sighișoara in 1882. After studying architecture and engineering in Germany, he worked for the architect Otto March in Berlin, where he came closely in touch with Bavarian Jugendstil and the Munich Secession. In 1909 he conducted the restoration works on the fortified church of Cisnădie (Heltau) near Sibiu. Soon after that, he opened his own office in Sighișoara, drafting plans for a number of buildings. Works by his hand in the area covered by this guide include the Hotel Steauă in Sighișoara (1910) and the Stephan Ludwig Roth High School in Mediaș (1909–12).

The Saxon community way of life, organised around village neighbourhoods, is reflected in Balthes' approach. The ordered structure of Saxon village houses and the need for the right architectural context lies at the root of his projects. 'A building must have its homeland,' he wrote, 'which means it must stand in the right place and be in harmony with its neighbours.' Balthes' style successfully merges geometric shapes with organic forms and avoids excessive decoration. 'Architecture,' he said, 'is reality rearranged. Some might say, architecture is order.'

Individual houses were one thing, but the true test of architectural ability, Balthes believed, was town planning. In the decades when the garden city was the keynote of so much urban design, it would have been interesting to see how Balthes would have developed his ideas. He was killed in Serbia in 1914, at the outbreak of World War I.

It is an astonishing fact that Balthes' buildings are not protected. Many have fallen into disrepair or have been wrecked by later additions. An association dedicated to their conservation is now being formed. For further information, contact James de Candole at james.decandole@outlook.com.

On Str. Garii there is a **Unitarian church**, built in 1936 and used by a Hungarian congregation.

On this side of the river there is also the **Lepers' church** of the 15th century, described as the *Leprosorium* in the 16th century, with an outside pulpit. The Saxons gave it to the Greek Catholics.

Back on the south side of the river, diagonally opposite the Technical College on Str. Ionescu, is the small **synagogue**, built in the early years of the 20th century. The key is held in the neighbouring house and the building has been newly restored.

Continuing westwards from Sighișoara down the valley, the road passes the **Romanian cemetery** on the left, spreading up the hill to the edge of the oak woods; and close by is the **Jewish cemetery**, nearer the road. There are several second-hand furniture shops with imported goods from Germany. These also sell modern copies of Saxon/Hungarian furniture. The days are gone of finding original painted wooden furniture from the homes of Saxons or Hungarians.

There are so many guides to this beautiful and important town. I would recommend especially *Sighișoara, Transylvania* by Eronim Alexandru Crișan, which is not only well produced but has a programme of the numerous cultural events that happen if you are here at the right time of year.

DANEȘ, CRIȘ & IACOBENI

West of Sighișoara is **Daneș (Dunesdorf/Dános)**, which has a small, picturesque Saxon church. There is great village pride here, with beautiful beds of flowers and cherry trees. On the left-hand side of the road is the Hotel Dracul. Early on, when there were no hotels in Sighișoara, this was one of the few possible places to stay. It was also the unlikely home of an ostrich farm. Now there are riding stables where you can rent a hireling. By horse is one of the best ways of seeing the countryside, either on its back or in a cart. There are endless ancient tracks made by the Saxons' wagons over hundreds of years. The deciduous forests are magnificent at any time of the year and there are no fences. Many of the roads are still unmade. It is a good idea to take a guide with you and a flower book. The biggest danger are the shepherds' dogs. Take a stick too.

CRIȘ

The road to Criș (Kreisch/Keresd) is best reached via Daneș. It is the seat one of the great Hungarian Transylvanian families, the Bethlen of Bethlen, who founded both the village and its castle. Criș is first documented in 1305 as a fortress, built in stone (although there may have been an earlier wooden castle on a site further up the valley). Only once, since its founding, has it been out of the family's ownership and that was under the Communists. It has, in the last few years, been restituted to the Bethlen family. Along with Beclean further north (home to another branch of the Bethlen family), it is among the most important transitional late medieval and Renaissance castles in Transylvania.

Perhaps here it is worth recalling a little of the background to Renaissance ideas in this part of the world, as the only other example in the valley of Italianate architecture of this date is the Apafi Castle in Dumbrăveni (*see p. 99*). The Renaissance came late to Transylvania, from Italy via Hungary, in the reign of King Matthias Corvinus (1458–90). He was tutored by

Stucco 'defender' decorating the Bethlen castle at Criș.

the humanist János Vitéz, later Archbishop of Esztergom, and then by the archbishop's nephew, the humanist poet Janus Pannonius. During Matthias' stable reign, the forms and ideas of the Italian quattrocento arrived in Hungary and Italian artists and philosophers were attracted to his court in Buda. Matthias' great library, the Bibliotheca Corviniana, was famous throughout Europe, surpassed only by that of the Vatican. Renaissance influences increased when Matthias married Beatrice of Aragon, daughter of the King of Naples, in 1476, an alliance which led to contacts with the Italian states of Naples, Urbino and Ferrara. Beatrice brought with her Italian artists and humanists. Matthias also collected works by many of the great masters of the quattrocento and introduced to his kingdom not only architects and philosophers but also craftsmen and cabinet makers skilled in intarsia work, hence the polychromatic inlaid wooden panels which are found in several of the churches in the Târnava Valley.

The Battle of Mohács in 1526 and the subsequent fall of Buda to the Turks in 1541 resulted in the division of the Kingdom of Hungary. Power was split between Ottomans and Habsurgs in the north and west of the realm, while in the east the semi-autonomous Principality of Transylvania came into being. Under Queen Isabella (1519–59), acting as regent for her infant son John Sigismund, the court at Alba Iulia became the Renaissance model for the aristocracy. Queen Isabella was the daughter of the King of Poland and the formidable Bona Sforza (who had previously been considered as a bride for Lorenzo the Magnificent) and she looked to Buda and Wawel Castle in Krakow as prototypes for her court style. Italian architects finally came to work in Transylvania, though only the wealthy could afford one. For example, Prince István Báthory (d. 1586), believed by some scholars to have been educated in the humanist tradition in Padua, continued to build fortifications in the Renaissance form at Oradea in the 1570s and '80s and worked on his castle at Făgăraș, which is not far distant from Criș.

There was an important guild of stone carvers at Cluj which ensured a continuous source of Renaissance forms. Their Charter of Incorporation was first in place in 1525, and the guild in turn attracted Italian craftsmen throughout the 16th century.

The fact that the Saxons were also adopting Italianate techniques and forms in their Gothic church interiors, while at the same time fortifying these otherwise Gothic structures, is a mirror of the times. Of course there were many countries in the north of Europe which took on the forms of the Renaissance only in small details, not least of which was Tudor England. Yet not so far distant, in Prague, Ferdinand of Tyrol was building a summer house for his queen with ideas taken from Brunelleschi. This was a totally new form of building, Italianate in form and Renaissance in idea. But Prague is further west than Vienna. It called for no defence against the Turks.

At Criș, then, the early fortress and donjon, already built by the 15th century, were added to by György Bethlen and his wife from 1559. They built a two-storey wing with traditional Lombard twin windows on top of the medieval donjon. This included the chapel. Throughout there is a mix of late medieval and Renaissance details. Péter Farbaky describes Criș as 'a fine example of a traditional, irregular, free-planned Transylvanian castle', although the Bethlens were not innovative patrons. The defensive tower was given another two storeys, creating more of a viewing platform over the garden than a form of defence.

The Bethlen Family

The Bethlen family are one of the great dynasties of the region, having provided, over the centuries, a pool of enlightened leaders and members of the intelligentsia of Transylvania. With the Reformation they had embraced Protestantism (Unitarianism and later Calvinism) and they flourished during the relatively stable years of the 17th century. There are two main branches. From the Iktár branch came Prince Gábor Bethlen (1580–1629), who became one of the most successful rulers of Transylvania. The other branch are the Bethlens of Bethlen, and it is they whom we encounter in this book.

János Bethlen (1613–68), the 'Transylvanian Tacitus', was born at Ţopa (*see p. 59*). He served as county lieutenant, wrote a contemporary history of Transylvania, and was nominated chancellor under Prince Mihály Apafi I. He founded the Calvinist College at Odorheiu Secuiesc. His son Miklós (1642–1716) was fascinated by architecture and travelled extensively, visiting England, Holland, France and Italy in preparation for his position at court. His great legacy is the Renaissance manor house of Sânmiclăuș (*see p. 191*). His political career foundered as a result of his efforts to position Transylvania as a neutral buffer state between the Ottoman and Austrian empires. Such ideas were inimical to Vienna and the Habsburg military commander Rabutin condemned him to prison for life, first in Sibiu and then in the Austrian capital. In prison he wrote his memoirs.

On the Criș side of the family was another writer and scholar, Farkas Bethlen (1639–79), who embarked on a great history of Transylvania for which his brother Elek set up a printing press at Criș (it was moved to Sighișoara in 1690, out of the way of the troops of Imre Thököly, who was attempting to claim the principality with Ottoman support). Kata Bethlen, the niece of Farkas and Elek, married Thököly's rival for the princeship, Mihály Apafi II (*see p. 100*). Another Kata Bethlen (1700–59), the staunchly Calvinist daughter of Miklós's half-brother

'B K', the initials of Kata Bethlen on her painted wedding chest (1695),
flanking the coat of arms of the Bethlen of Bethlen family. The paintwork
is very worn, but its curling serpent emblem can still be made out.

Sámuel, was forced into an unhappy arranged marriage with a
Catholic relative but proved a remarkable diarist. Her published work
is redolent of the Enlightenment and her letters and autobiography
have led her to being compared to Mme de Sévigné (although rather
more pious and Protestant).

A later Bethlen, Gergely (1810–67), was commander of the Hungarian
cavalry during the 1848–9 revolution against the Habsburgs. When
that failed, he escaped Italy where he put himself at the service of
Garibaldi. Count István Bethlen (1874–1946) was Prime Minister
of Hungary between the wars. A fierce opponent of the Hungarian
alliance with Nazi Germany, he was nevertheless taken prisoner by
the Soviets in 1945. He perished in a Russian gaol the following year.

The defensive character of the tower is emphasised by the amusing Székely 'defenders' in stucco, portrayed hand on hip, which were introduced when the building works were continued by György's son Mihály in 1598. They say much about the change in attitude to security in the 16th and early 17th centuries. The colonnade of fat, vaguely Ionic columns also looks more to Italy and to decoration than defence. It has been recently suggested that the colonnade was built under Miklós Bethlen in the 1670s (though it may be earlier, from the time of Mihály). The angular bastions were added by Prince Alexius (Elek) Bethlen from 1675–91. Of note is the English landscaped garden with some good specimen trees. These give a real sense that Criş was once a home.

With the coming of Communism, the house—and indeed the family—received poor treatment. Count Bethlen was imprisoned and the house was nationalised in 1948. Much that was of value was stolen. The precious library, put together by Kata Bethlen (1700–59), was burnt in the castle courtyard. For a time the house was a Pioneers' camp and an agricultural college. Restoration began in 1974 but stopped in 1977. Since then, the roof has been replaced, although the tiles are not in keeping and there is cement everywhere. The 'cementfest' comes from pre-restitution restorations by the Romanian state, when there were efforts to turn the house into a hotel. Even the stairs have gone, to be replaced by a ramp. Since then the family has founded the Pro Castellum Bethlen Association to try and save this important building. A saviour recently appeared in the form of the remarkable 'St Francis Foundation of Deva', started by a Franciscan monk, Csaba Böjte. He has a good reputation for transforming important buildings to new use most sympathetically (as well as for running a remarkable charity). The castle has been leased to the foundation for 50 years. Under their care there are already huge improvements. At present, it keeps museum times (*open 10–5, closed Mon*). There is a custodian who is happy to take visitors around. There are also helpful labels about the history.

Nikolaus Bethlen, grandson of the last occupant, is buying properties in the village which he plans to restore and use for tourism, to reinvigorate Criş and create economic activity for the local population, as well as to preserve family and Transylvanian heritage.

IACOBENI AND BEYOND

After Criș, instead of returning back to the main road, I recommend continuing to **Iacobeni (Jakobsdorf/Jakabfalva)**. I have never managed to get into the church but Fabini describes it as follows: 'a hall church built in the 14th century on earlier foundations. The net vault was replaced in the 19th century and the galleries are "rural Baroque".'

Continue through **Netuș (Neithausen/Netus)**, which also has a charming, small, fortified church with woodwork of 1770 by Johann Folbarth.

From Netuș it is only a short distance to **Brădeni (Henndorf/Hégen)**. Here the church interior has the usual simple charm (*for the key, ring ahead or visit Mrs Bálint at house no. 210; T: 0722 335 884*). The church is first documented in 1350 and is dedicated to St Andrew. In common with many of these churches, its fortifying walls came later, in the latter part of the 15th century. We know that they were put to the test in 1658, when the Ottomans overran the village and the people took refuge in the fastness around their church. The reason for visiting Brădeni are the storage chests in one of the towers. There are over 80 of these; why and how they arrived there, and in such numbers, remains a mystery. Research was carried out on them when the church roof was restored and a few were taken to Sighișoara, where they remain, in the Church on the Hill. Grain chests are not unusual in the Saxon communities, but to be found in such a quantity makes the journey and the climb up the tower worthwhile. Perhaps they were made *in situ*? They sum up the resilient and defensive character of the Saxons. The Priest House here is unusual (there is another similar in Pelișor). English 19th-century pattern books may have been consulted for its design.

From Brădeni continue to **Apold (Trappold/Apold)**, where they have received funding to uncover their frescoes; and **Șaeș (Schaas/Segesd)**, where the church is a charming early 18th-century building with a little Baroque bell-tower. The important pre-Reformation altarpiece from the earlier church on this site is in Sighișoara, again in the Church on the Hill.

MĂLÂNCRAV

To reach Mălâncrav (Almakerék/Malmkrog) from the main valley road, you must pass through **Laslea (Großlasseln/Szászszentlászló)**. The turning is between Sighișoara and Șaroș. Laslea shares a priest with Mălâncrav. It is not really worth a special stop unless you are buying some food in the shop, but if you feel like exploring, the key to the 19th-century church can be obtained from Johannes Halmen (*T: 0740 172 015; please call a few days before you plan your visit as, although he keeps the key in the Priest House, he is usually only there two or three times a week*). Alternatively, ask in the blue-painted shop on the corner. Beside the church is the hospital with a matching façade. It was possibly built in the 1840s (perhaps by the Hallers, who bought Mălâncrav from the Bethlens?). The earlier church was of the 13th century and now only the west tower survives. It is a curiosity.

For Mălâncrav, take the road to the left by Laslea's corner shop. Your journey is along another beautiful valley and will take about 20mins from the turn-off. En route you will pass hop fields. This was a very successful crop during Saxon days. Even today some farmers are succeeding in selling to Germany. It is labour-intensive.

The road to Mălâncrav is now tarred, but there is still a great sense of arrival at this beautiful Saxon village. Mălâncrav, as with Dumbrăveni and many other villages in the Târnava Valley, was the property of the Hungarian Apafi family (*see p. 100*), from among whose number came one of the most successful of the elected Princes of Transylvania. There are tales of secret tunnels from Mălâncrav manor to Dumbrăveni—which must be questionable but it is an attractive thought.

Today there is a higher proportion of Saxons in Mălâncrav than in most villages in the Siebenbürgen, which may be due to two factors. The first is that the priest lives in the village, in the Priest's House near the church. He is from Germany but, at the time of the Saxon exodus, was on secondment to the priest of Mălâncrav. The original priest failed to return from his holiday so Father Joachim Lorenz remained and, along with him,

Transylvanian Saxons in 1938.

his congregation. The second factor may be the long restoration process carried out in the village by the MET (*see p. 225*) and Horizon (*see p. 226*). This 'Whole Village Project' provided work for the villagers and restored many village houses.

The manor house

Although the village itself was inhabited by Saxons, Mālâncrav Manor, sitting near the church above the village and separated from it by a flower meadow, could hardly afford a more perfect example of a Hungarian aristocratic seat. The house itself has great charm, mixing Transylvanian Renaissance and northern European features. Its fine colonnaded façade recalls that of some of the great houses of the Hungarian aristocracy, including three covered in this book: Sânmiclăuș (Bethlen family; *see p. 191*); Dumbrăveni (Apafi family; *see p. 99*) and Criș (Bethlen family; *see p. 77*). The dumpy Transylvanian Ionic columns became a leitmotif of the

Transylvanian Renaissance and even appear again on the 20th-century Town Hall in Târgu Mureș.

There has been a house on this site since the 15th century, built by the Apafis. The present structure was up by the 17th century and rebuilt again in the 18th and 19th centuries. Inventories survive describing the alterations between 1679 and 1778. They make mention of frescoes in the north rooms. The manor was rebuilt in the 1830s by the then owner, Count Haller, and then after the First World War it was owned by Baron Pál Szentkereszty. This latter family built the Calvinist church in Valea Lungă. Deeds of the house record that in the 1920s the house was sold by its last private owner to the village's Lutheran community. The property was confiscated by the Communists in 1947. It was then used as an entertainment hall with a stage. A concrete kitchen was added in the 1950s. Little of the original interior detail remained but the external form—as it was in 1920—stayed more or less intact. The manor house was bought from the community by the MET in 2000. Both house and garden, inside and out, were reconstructed with British knowhow. The interiors were designed by David Mlinaric and the garden by Katherine Fitzgerald.

The manor has been transformed into a luxurious guesthouse, run by the MET, with lovely rooms and a library. Most of the contents have been made locally, including curtains and carpets woven by Maria Nistor (*house no. 302; T: 0269 448 606*) and Elena Neagu (*no. 162; T: 0269 448 769*). Please note, if you wish to visit either of these two craftswomen, telephone a day ahead to make an appointment (*to make reservations at the manor house, see the MET contact details on p. 13*).

The village

Downhill from the manor is the Saxon village, sitting snug in the valley, the houses filling two wide streets divided by a small stream. Ducks, geese, turkeys etc., abound. The settlement is ancient and used to belong to the Hungarian Becse-Gergely clan, from whom the Bethlen, Apafi and other great families, many of whom furnished Princes of Transylvania, were descended. After the Reformation, the Apafi family gave the church to their Lutheran subjects. When the Apafi family died out, their property went to the Bethlens, in 1775. By the mid-19th century, Mălâncrav belonged to Countess Susanna Haller, and in 1865 she built the present-day green-stuccoed Catholic church in the street below the Lutheran church. Perhaps, in the Transylvanian spirit of freedom of worship, the Roman Catholics and Lutherans shared St Mary's until the Roman Catholic church was built. The Hungarian Catholics no longer use the little church but, once a year, on the first Sunday in September, a service and a grand procession is held in honour of the Virgin. The church was also restored by the MET, whose logo consists of a distinctive blue plaque with a laurel wreath taken directly from the plasterwork relief of Mălâncrav's village symbol. It can be seen all around Mălâncrav.

A Romanian Orthodox church also exists on the outskirts of the village.

The fortified church

Now turn to the 14th-century fortified Lutheran church (*the key is to be found at house no. 307*). The church is dedicated to the Virgin and obviously played an important part in the life of the devout Apafis. Miklós Apafi, a member of Emperor Sigismund's court and curia, received a papal indulgence for the building of a chapel of the Blood of Christ here in the early 15th century. He also made generous bequests to other churches on his estates, including, presumably, Ighişu Nou (*see p. 162*). St Mary's became a rare place of pilgrimage in 17th-century Transylvania. A mausoleum was built in 1635 where György Apafi, Lord Lieutenant of the Târnava region, and his wife Borbála were buried. The monument was carved by the celebrated Elias Nicolai (*see overleaf*). In 1908/9 the remains of Prince Mihály Apafi I (d. 1690) and his wife Anna Bornemissza (d. 1688), together with that of Prince Mihály II (d. 1713) and his wife Kata Bethlen (d. 1724), were discovered in the sacristy here. Prince Mihály II was the last of the line and his property was subsequently transferred to the Bethlen and Haller families. The remains of the two princes and their wives were reinterred in Cluj. The monument to György Apafi is now in the Hungarian National Museum in Budapest. If you are in Budapest, it is well worth seeking out. Also on display in the museum is the golden cup of Anna Bornemissza, a ten-ducat coin of Mihály Apafi I and the marriage chest of Kata Bethlen.

Detail of the tomb-chest of György Apafi, signed by Elias Nicolai 'Cibinium manens', resident in Sibiu.

Elias Nicolai

Elias Nicolai (fl. 1635–60) is Transylvania's only well-known stone carver of the 17th century. Unusually, he signed some of his work and has become something of a cult figure for later scholars. His monuments, portraying priests, princes, leading townsfolk and their wives, conjure up the world of grandees, clerics and burghers in Transylvania and Wallachia. His work is to be seen in Biertan, Sighișoara, Mediaș and Sibiu. He was also commissioned to carve windows and doors in country houses for the Bethlens. His most elaborate monument is to Prince György Apafi (d. 1635), commissioned for the family vault in Mălâncrav, and now in the National Museum in Budapest.

It is believed that Elias came from the Spiš region in what is now Slovakia, once part of the Kingdom of Hungary. Spiš has a very fine late Gothic stone-carving tradition. Gábor Bethlen invited a number of skilled masters from Upper Hungary to work in Alba Iulia in the 1620s and Elias Nicolai is thought to have been part of this group. It is assumed that he settled down and made a career in Sibiu after 1629/30 due to his skill in figure carving. His name is linked to the later alabaster and limestone pulpit in the Calvinist Church in Cluj (c. 1646). It appears he subcontracted this work, a fact which throws an interesting light on his workshop practices, which are unclear, but he must have had a large studio. The first documented information about Elias is from 1636. The last written sources are from 1654, and scholars suspect that he died in the plague of 1661.

His style derives from Northern Renaissance pattern books, for example those of Vredeman de Vries (1527–1606), illustrating the love of strapwork. He carves in high relief and his subjects are shown half-length or, after 1638, full-length, resplendent in dress, accompanied by their coat of arms, religious motifs and symbols of *memento mori*. His style is stolid and conservative. Traces of polychrome paintwork have been found on the tombs recently restored in Biertan.

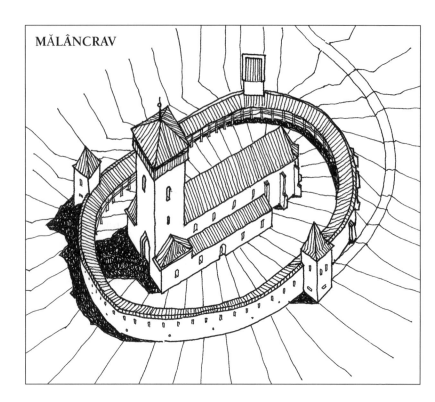

MĂLÂNCRAV

The interior of the church has a remarkable series of frescoes, both on the north wall and in the chancel. Those on the **north wall of the nave** are possibly from the 1370s. They constitute the most extensive ensemble of Gothic linear narrative painting in Transylvania and are in five registers comprising 53 separate scenes. It has been suggested that they may be influenced by painters from Slovakia, in particular the artist of the legend of St Dorothea in the Church of St James in Levoča, which is dated 1370–1400. Slovakia was then part of the Kingdom of Hungary. There were many connections between the two parts of the kingdom. Slovakia is rich in original altarpieces and carvings, which would throw light on those in Transylvania. Indeed, Elias Nicolai, the sculptor of the Apafi monument, came from the Spiš region of Slovakia.

The **frescoes in the choir** date from the late 14th or early 15th century and were completed during the life of Miklós Apafi (c. 1398–1451). They are of an extraordinary intensity of colour and design. In the ribbed vault above the altar are the Evangelists and scenes from the life of Christ and the Resurrection as well as the Fathers of the Church. In the Annunciation scene, God is seen behind Gabriel, throwing the infant Christ plus dove at the Virgin. Unlike those on the north wall, these remarkable frescoes were not painted over. The style has a strong narrative feel, with strange divisions of frilly seaweed, which possibly derive from Bohemia. The

Reclining effigy of György Apafi from the top of the tomb-chest by Elias Nicolai. The deceased is shown in full armour, with every detail carefully rendered: the leather straps and buckles, the damascened breast plate, the undercoat of mail. His face is turned towards the family coat of arms: a sword piercing a helmet from which sprouts a vine frond laden with fruit. Vine branches curl around the borders of the sepulchre, interspersed with emblems of *memento mori*. The tomb was commissioned by György's wife Borbála Petki (who is also buried inside it) and was completed by their son Prince Mihály I. It is now in the Hungarian National Museum in Budapest.

closest models cited are the c. 1370 frescoes found in the Chapter House of the Benedictine Monastery at Sázava, close to Prague. However, frescoes have just come to light under lime wash some 50km away at Ighişu Nou, south of Mediaş. They have similar love of human profile and gesticulation. The foreground uses the same barren rock convention of distant Byzantine art and *trompe l'oeil* architectural painting at dado level. At Ighişu Nou (*see p. 162*), according to Fabini, the church was on land owned by the Apafi which later became Crown Land. An exact date is not given. It would be interesting to know what part, if any, Apafi played in the commissioning of the frescoes in Ighişu Nou. Similarities with Mălâncrav are clear.

The **frescoes in the chancel** at Mălâncrav were suffering from damp. They have been monitored by the Horizon Trust and the MET, and, more

Mălâncrav altarpiece: work-day side

St Michael	Annunciation	Visitation	St George
	Circumcision of Christ	Presentation in the Temple	

Mălâncrav altarpiece: feast-day side (illustrated)

Nativity	St Catherine	Maestà	St Agnes	Assumption
Adoration of the Magi	St Barbara		St Margaret	Dormition of the Virgin

importantly, steps have been taken to stabilise the environment around the frescoes, including repairs to the building fabric and the provision of proper surface/ground drainage. Funds were also donated by the Prodan Romanian Cultural Foundation.

The Mălâncrav **high altarpiece** is outstanding, testimony to the patronage of the next generation of the Apafis. At the base of the central 'Maestà' of the feast-day side are the donors Mihály Apafi and his wife Klára. This was an earlier Mihály, not the later Prince. He came of age in 1450 and was dead by 1469, marking the latest date of the panels. At the feet of the Virgin, who appears almost archaic, with angel musicians behind her, Mihály is being introduced by his titular saint, the Archangel Michael. Both Michaels, donor and saint, are wearing rich brocade. Mihály's wife, Klára Macedoniai, is being introduced by her titular saint, St Clare of Assisi. The mendicant orders were much favoured by the Hungarian court. It is known that the Macedoniai family had strong links with the Franciscans. As Ciprian Firea has shown, it is unusual but not unique to have a portrayal of a female donor. There is a beautiful balance of pattern and colour and the incised gilded gessoed background glows.

Open, the panels depict the Madonna and Child and donors flanked by saints, again in alternating green and red. They are Sts Catherine, Barbara, Agnes and Margaret. Enclosing them are two scenes of the life of Christ (*Nativity* and *Adoration of the Magi*) and two from that of the Virgin (*Dormition* and *Assumption*). The panels from the work-day side are given in the diagram on the previous page. The painted backgrounds of St George and the Archangel Michael are finely detailed, showing fields and a small settlement. In place of the gilding of the other side of the altar, the landscape of these panels is acutely observed. The sky fades towards the horizon, the sky itself is dotted with gold stars. The altarpiece was restored in 1974.

The **rood** on top of the panels is complete, with the Crucifix flanked by the Virgin and St John the Evangelist. The figures themselves are earlier than the surrounding tracery and are an extraordinary survival by any standards. The **organ** is of 1925 and it was in 1913–25 that the nave paintings were discovered. There is a fine **aumbry**, similar to those at

Ighișu Nou, Bazna, Dupuș and Valea Viilor, dating from the beginning of the 16th century.

The village orchard

Next to the fortified church is the Priest House. The village also has a 200-hectare orchard which is famed for its organic apple juice. This is made from apples of ancient German and Romanian varieties, including Batul, Renet Bauman, Frumos de Boscop, Parmen Auriu and Gustav Durabil. There are pears too, often planted with quince rootstock for durability. There are several varieties of plum, including Tuleu Gras and Anna Spath. The juice can be bought near the Manor House, close to the apple processing plant. The MET bought the orchard from the state in February 2002 and is returning it to traditional management.

DUMBRĂVENI & CUND

Dumbrăveni (Elisabethstadt/Erzsébetváros), on the main road between Mediaș and Sighișoara, retains a somewhat down-at-heel feel and is often by-passed. However, the recent translation of its history into Romanian from a 19th-century Hungarian monograph may bring more people to this remarkable place: and one may well hope so, for it is a fascinating showcase in miniature of the last of the Transylvanian princes, the Apafis. The town owed its later trading success to the Armenians, who arrived from Moldavia in the middle years of the 17th century. It finally became an administrative seat of the Dual Monarchy. The Armenians were given special concessions by the Habsburgs (Charles VI, Maria Theresa and Joseph II). They paid no tax nor were they required to serve in the Habsburg army. They traded in leather, textiles, jewellery and cattle. For the latter, the method was to take calves at foot and fatten them on the route to Vienna, selling them there for a handsome profit. Ion Calinescu, the translator of the town's history, has pointed out that it was similar to trading in oil today. For all this, the Armenians had to ensure that, although they were allowed to retain the Armenian church rites, they recognised the papacy, as loyal Habsburg subjects.

It is difficult today to piece together the town's development. It has been gently disintegrating since the revolutions of 1848–9. In spite of the patronage from Vienna, the Armenian community was supportive of the Hungarian separatist movement. A few kilometres down the road in the garrison town of Mediaș, the Saxons chose the Habsburg side. So civil war was only too close to home and the countryside in chaos. In a battle just east of Sighișoara, at Albești in 1849, the Hungarians lost. After their defeat many Armenians left the country for Italy, France, the United States, and also Argentina, where they helped found the army. János Czetz, for example (1822–1904), was a Hungarian freedom fighter of Armenian origin who rose to become the first director of Argentina's national military academy.

Don't let the sparse, shabby station and railway line put you off crossing it, and the river, and making your way into the heart of the little town. The view from the road is not deceiving: the town was once grand, and once you are in it, you enter Austria-Hungary and the lands of the Dual Monarchy (1867–1918). Just before the revolution of 1848, the population of Dumbrăveni reached 3,000. Land was drained and the streets, some of which still retain their cobbles, were laid out in the grid pattern still extant and characteristic of this town. At one end of the central Strada Mihai Eminescu there is a huge confection of a building, the palatial Court House, installed by the Habsburg governors—and perhaps it would be more at home in Austria. At the other end of the street is a church with twin belfries (originally of equal height; one has now lost its steeple) which tower over the Saxon landscape for miles. This is the Armenian Catholic cathedral. Other grand buildings include a large neo-Baroque school and the important Agricultural College.

The Armenian Cathedral

Maria Theresa gave permission for the construction of this cathedral, dedicated to St Elisabeth of Hungary, as part of her efforts to spread the Counter-Reformation in Protestant Transylvania. Her two letters for its foundation are said to be in the surviving tower cupola. Dumbrăveni's Armenian community paid for it themselves—with intercessions, it was said, from St Elisabeth herself.

An earlier church of 1725 was flooded when the Târnava burst its banks in 1763. The present building, begun soon after this on a new site, is built in a cold and forbidding Neoclassical style. It has echoes of the Uniate Cathedral in Blaj, but it is later, from the 1760s, completed in 1777, with the interior finished by 1791. The architect, Franz Gindtner from Cluj, was inspired by the Martinelli workshop, which was responsible for a number of buildings in the Austrian crown lands. Internally it is light and elegant, although much in need of restoration. It takes the typical Counter-Reformation form of a three-bay nave with nothing to obstruct the view to the pulpit. The main altar, dedicated to St Elisabeth, is poorly painted by Albert Csávási from Vinţu de Jos (Alvinc), but the gilded wooden

Gold ten-ducat coin of Prince Mihály Apafi I.

statues of Sts Peter and Paul are fine, the work of Simon Hoffmeyer. The whole ensemble lights up, making the east end of the church look like a fairground. Hoffmeyer was also commissioned to make the statues for the Roman Catholic church in Odorheiu Secuiesc, which was consecrated in 1793. There is a good font, by the side of which is a charming, naïve portrait of Dr Karácsony, the priest who, under Maria Theresa, was responsible for the church. The painting of the side altarpieces is patchy; the best are near the west end, especially the *Crucifixion*, *Stoning of St Stephen* and *Presentation of the Virgin*. The side chapels are of different dates. The painted wooden sculptured figures of saints are generally of good quality. The organ case is an elegant, Neoclassical work but the organ itself needs restoring. The carpenter who worked on the church was Antal Überlacher and the stonemason, Jakab Marini.

Although this is still the cathedral of the Armenian Catholics, there are now only 24 practising members of the congregation remaining in Dumbrăveni. They hold three services a year according to the western Armenian rites. The rest of the year the services in the cathedral are Roman

Catholic. There is only one Armenian priest in the whole of Romania serving a surviving population of around a thousand. The main Armenian towns, along with Dumbrăveni, are Gherla (Armenopolis, north of Cluj-Napoca), Frumoasa and Gheorgheni. The Armenian priest Avedik Lukács (1847–1909) was the first to translate the Armenian rites into Romanian, in 1871. He also wrote a history of Dumbrăveni in Hungarian and it is this work that has now been translated into Romanian by Ion Calinescu, a member of the Armenian congregation (*and key holder if you would like to visit the church; T: 0745 257 524*). Mr Calinescu could not be more welcoming or knowledgeable. I recommend finding out about the feast days as the services are splendid and there are processions around the town.

The Apafi Castle

The Apafi Castle (*open 10–4, closed Mon*) is just south of the cathedral. Building was begun in 1552 by Gergely Apafi. In 1604 it was attacked by Saxon troops from Mediaş but not taken. In Ottoman times it was moated. Mihály Apafi I, Prince of Transylvania from 1661 (the last one under the Ottomans), welcomed many Armenians to Dumbrăveni in 1658 as they escaped persecution in Ottoman and Orthodox Moldavia. When the Apafi family died out, the Armenians took over the building. The entrance door is in the 17th-century part of the building. There is little to see inside except a show of suitcases, a reference to the peripatetic life of the Armenians. At least the historical importance of Mihály Apafi and the Armenians has been recognised and there are schemes to restore what is, potentially, a fine building (it has been estimated that two million euros will be needed).

By far the most interesting façade is found by walking around to the left: look up to see a lively stone lion on the side elevation. At the back and to the right is the early, fortified octagonal tower, possibly from the 16th century. There was another defensive [tower?] on the left. The adjacent wing and portal have a plaque over the door with the date 1552, the year that Gergely Apafi began construction. This might also refer to the once-open arcade ahead. This architectural form is a sign of Italianate influence and is found all over Central Europe at this date, being especially common in Renaissance Bohemia and Moravia. Here it is an important reminder that

Transylvania was a cauldron for ideas from both East and West. Similar Renaissance influences are found at the Bethlen Castle in Criș, from 1559 (*see p. 77*).

The Apafi Family

The Apafis were one of the great Hungarian ruling families of Transylvania. György Apafi of Mălâncrav (1588–1635) was Lord Lieutenant of Küküllő (Târnava) County. His magnificent tomb-chest is now in Budapest (*see p. 91*). György's son Mihály was elected Prince of Transylvania in 1661, the last prince under Ottoman suzerainty. According to some, he had little head for politics, preferring to leave matters of state in the hands of his able wife, Anna Bornemissza. He seems to have been a *bon viveur*: remembered for introducing tobacco to Transylvania and for enjoying his wine. Civic records from Mediaș for the year 1676 note that the copious quaffing of Apafi and his retinue cost the town 155 pieces of gold.

Mihály's son, also Mihály, is known as Prince Mihály II (1676–1713) because he was elected as such by the Diet, although he was never confirmed in the appointment. By the time of his father's death in 1690 the Ottomans had been repelled from Vienna and expelled from Buda, and the future of Transylvania was squabbled over by differing factions. Imre Thököly, with Ottoman support, attempted to restore Transylvania's independence under the Turkish aegis. Leopold of Austria, however, had other plans. Mihály II was summoned to Vienna, where he died in 1713. The Apafis died out with him.

Both Mihály I and Mihály II, together with their wives, were buried in Mălâncrav. Their remains were reinterred in the Calvinist Church in Cluj in 1909 and are marked by a stone designed by Károly Kós in 1942. It was Prince Mihály I who also gave the church at Mălâncrav to his Lutheran villagers. Here at Dumbrăveni he offered asylum to 200 Armenians in 1658. AB/LAS

Other sights of Dumbrăveni

Altogether there are three churches and a convent in Dumbrăveni. In its heyday, the congregations must have been huge in this flourishing trading town. In the **main square** was a convent of Armenian Catholic nuns. The building later became a school and is now a shop painted puce, but the Armenian Cyrillic is still above the entrance. The square is the old trading centre and market-place. It contains an obelisk to the Armenian community, an attractive monument put up by the Communists (not normally known for this sort of thing). There are plans to erect another monument to the Armenians who died under the Nazis and the Communists.

The pretty, white Baroque **Church of St Peter and St Paul**, one block south of the square, once belonged to the Armenians too, and before that to the Calvinists. It was taken back by the Catholics in 1727.

There is a third church, which the Armenians gave to the Saxon community. This is at the west end of Strada Eminescu next to the **Court House** and the gaol (within easy walking distance). The Court House was the most important court of law in the area. It stands out from a distance— symbolic of its function under Austria-Hungary. Today it is a hospital.

The **Agricultural College** was used under Communism to train managers for the state farms. It taught the all-important subjects of animal husbandry and viticulture, forestry and orchard-keeping. Back on the main road towards Sighișoara you will notice the cattle pound, today a mere metal enclosure painted red and white.

THE ROAD TO CUND

Leaving Dumbrăveni on the main road to Sighișoara, you will see on the left the outlines of **Hoghilag (Halvelagen/Holdvilág)**, where the church was dedicated to St Mary. Only the church tower survives from the former mid-14th-century building. On my last visit it had been turned into a dairy collection point. Better seen from afar.

Travelling in the other direction, it is recommended to eschew the main road and instead make your way to **Cund (Reußdorf/Kund)**. Not only does Cund offer comfortable B&Bs in the Saxon houses, but there is also an excellent restaurant. Even if you receive no answer by telephone or email (*given below*), I still recommend the drive, perhaps with your own picnic.

Heading north from Dumbrăveni there are no signs to Cund nor to the Valea Verde complex. For some reason signs are not allowed. Once out of Dumbrăveni, past some very poor Roma houses, if you remember to take a left fork in the road once you are past the fishing pools, all will be well. In a country of outstanding valleys, the route to Cund wins the prize for being most beautiful: broad and generous with views through woodland and vale to further beauty, sheepfolds and arable land. Here is the reason why those Saxons who were brave enough to leave northern Europe found a better life in Transylvania in the 12th and 13th centuries. Such beauty makes the exodus of the 1990s all the more difficult to explain.

This village is one of the most remote in the region, not as the crow flies, but because the road from Dumbrăveni is not only unmarked but also untarred for most of its length. Nearing the village, there is a former state orchard, then the small church and the straggle of houses. Cund retained its Saxon community until the last possible minute. In 1986, the date of the last census, it was 95 percent Saxon; by 1996 there were only four Saxons left, with two or three Hungarians and one Roma family. The church in its present form dates mainly from the 15th century and has a net vault over the choir. Major restoration is planned and it is hoped that its early 16th-century (pre-Reformation) altarpiece, currently in Sighișoara (*see p. 70*), will be able to return here.

The driving forces in Cund today are Jonas Schäfer and his wife Ulrike, who run a successful tourism business. They have restored several houses in the village, which they rent out. As well as providing local employment, they are contributing to the restoration of the church and organising transport to the nearest High School for the village children.

In 1990, Schäfer's father arrived from Germany with a charitable mission, when the full horror of the plight of Romanian orphans hit the Western press. He thought the area was wonderful. Jonas was less than enthusiastic but gradually the Schäfers decided to settle and develop Valea Verde by letting out houses in the village, both their own and those of others. They have been in the village since 2003 and married here in 2007.

The road to Cund.

Now there is an excellent restaurant, where Jonas himself started as a keen amateur chef. He has since trained up locals and all the ingredients are sourced locally (*T: 0265 714 399, info@cund.de, www.discover-transilvania.com/en*). 'Nowadays,' he says, 'it is local women who have never had a fine dining experience in their lives who are cooking their heart out with amazing food...We have a network of small farms. We have one farm that supplies our cheese and another breeding Angus beef calves. We have another place where we go to buy our mozzarella from organic buffalo and we have about two and a half hectares where we grow our organic vegetables.'

The 200 hectares of state orchard which lie adjacent to the village have been restituted to the original Saxon owners, who have sold it—or rather, just the trees—to others. The new buyers did not realise that they did not own the land but only the trees and fruit. There is something of an impasse. These sort of land issues are happening all the time in Transylvania.

ȘAROȘ, BIERTAN, COPȘA MARE & RICHIȘ

Three good fortified churches are Șaroș, Biertan and Richiș. Before the Reformation they attracted a rather high quality of clergy, who were prepared to commission religious works of art during their tenure, an indication of the valley's wine wealth and available artists and craftsmen. Șaroș, it seems, did not quite have the status of Richiș or Biertan, since priests wishing for promotion moved to either of those.

ȘAROȘ

Șaroș pe Târnave (Scharesch/Szászsáros) straddles the junction of the main road and has a fine church dedicated to St Helen. In comparison to such glories as Mediaș and Biertan, perhaps it takes time to recognise the dignified gathering of buildings around the church: Priest House, school and council offices. The church itself, standing up above the village street, is next to the school, which is typically Austro-Hungarian, similar to all the others in the area. This is best viewed from the other side of the road. There are shops and a bar here but the roadside houses have suffered from the insertion of plastic windows and an 'alpine' makeover. The key for the church can be obtained from Stan Vasile at no. 380, the house on the corner opposite the church (T: 0740 912 465).

The walls surround the church in an oval. There is a nice covered staircase, which leads through the walls, by the Priest House. The entry passage takes a turn to confuse enemies. The church portal is Baroque. There is fine flowing tracery in the lancet windows at the east end and in the courtyard are thoughtfully-placed benches—all peaceful, unlike the street.

Inside the church, there is a charming altarpiece, similar to that of Richiș; it must have been created by the same carver, Johannes Folbarth, in the late 1770s. Here in Șaroș, the Old Testament figures of Moses and Aaron frame the Crucifixion. The surrounding panels are of fruits of the Passion such as grapes and pomegranates. They are similar in style to those

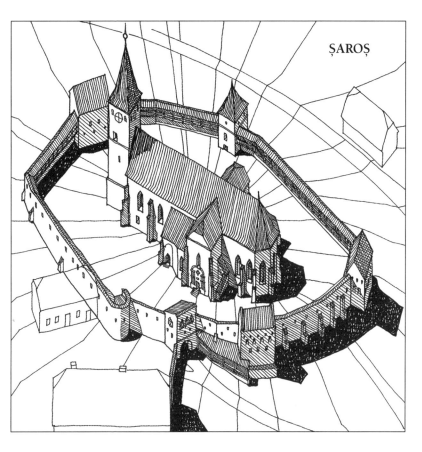

ŞAROŞ

in Richiş. The nave was restored in the 18th century although there is a gallery for dignitaries with a net vault on the south of the nave. The galleries, where the men sat, have been well restored. The organ has good organ pipes. Note the orchestra of painted putti in the organ loft. The west end is gutsy with Baroque mouldings. All the pews are in place and the seats at the east end are good. Take note of the typical Saxon banners, too. These are not banners of the guilds, just admonitory sentences: 'Be a Man and keep your values' and 'We want to stay what we are'. They are of typical Saxon gold-thread embroidery on black velvet of the 19th or early 20th century. This type of embroidery was a staple of Saxon textiles. They are fine and all rather taken for granted. Many are in need of restoration.

Deeper into the village, on the other side of the road from the church, there is another church, possibly Orthodox but it might be Uniate. There are several streets of largish houses, a circumstance which points to wine wealth. On the road between Șaroș and Biertan there is a field growing solar panels but surrounded by security lights, which must defeat the object. You are here at the head of what was once a famous wine valley, stretching south to Richiș. Alas, the crop is, for the moment, no more: the local winery has closed and the terraces are empty of their vines.

BIERTAN

The road to Biertan (Birthälm/Berethalom), coming from either direction, is flanked by hills. Those on the west side are terraced, the result of work carried out after 1950 by the Communist government to prevent erosion of the vineyards. However, this was ineffectual and a more likely reason was to give employment to the Communist youth. Many of the terraces are now unkept and grow saplings. Ahead of you, the fortified church of Biertan stands on a hill above the village. It is a wonderful sight.

There is a quiet dignity about this once-prosperous little town of about 2,000 inhabitants, which is a surprisingly complete statement of what we have come to expect from the Siebenbürgen. In the past its income was mainly from wine: at one time there were more taxpayers recorded here than in the major town of Mediaș. Now it is a World Heritage site and has become a tourist honey pot: but don't be reluctant to join the bees; the attractions are obvious. The Lutheran church here is one of the most beautiful in Transylvania and definitely has one of the most spectacular altarpieces. From 1572, forty years after the start of the Reformation and lasting until 1867, when the Dual Monarchy of Austria-Hungary came into being, Biertan was the seat of the Lutheran bishopric. It appears that the first bishop, Unglerus, was born here. He obviously decided that his birthplace was worthy. That is as good a reason as any. Now the bishopric is in Sibiu.

But this does not really explain the glory of this church, as its construction was completed and its magnificent altarpiece commissioned before the Reformation. The glory, in fact, came from the income from wine, which led to Biertan being on trade routes for artists and ideas. It also reflects a sophisticated community who were able to elect, even before the Reformation, their own priests and judges.

The beauty of the church comes from its site and the proportions of the citadel walls, with the towers visibly creating a sense of completeness. The church's high-pitched, red-tiled roofs spilling down towards irregular towers and outcrops of brick and timber buildings tie it all together, creating a visible link with the elegant Saxon houses at the foot of the citadel. From some angles the citadel looks as if it might have fallen from the moon, or at least from some fairy story. It is the second church on the site and dates from 1493 to 1522. It was built during the time when Renaissance ideas were arriving from further west and was completed four years before the Battle of Mohács, when the Kingdom of Hungary was still intact.

A walk around the walls

I would recommend a walk around the citadel walls at street level before visiting the church, as this will give a real impression of the grandeur of the place. Take the path between the walls to the left of the citadel entrance off the village square. The Priest's House will be on your left. At the end of this short path you return to the street. At no. 14 is an unusual two-storey house with a beautifully restored façade. During restoration, a note was found written by the previous Saxon owner, Sara Römischer. This tells a harrowing tale of what happened to her and her fellow Saxons as the Russians arrived at the end of the Second World War. She was taken from her children along with all those from her age group and sent as slave labour to the mines in the Ukraine. The text may be found at www.transylvaniadreaming.eu/?p=41.

You will now be at the foot of the cartway into the citadel. The door is rarely open but there are wonderful views up to the roofline and the buildings in the bastion (there are endless tales of secret tunnels between the citadel and the town). You will pass the old Saxon school, which is now the Unglerus restaurant.

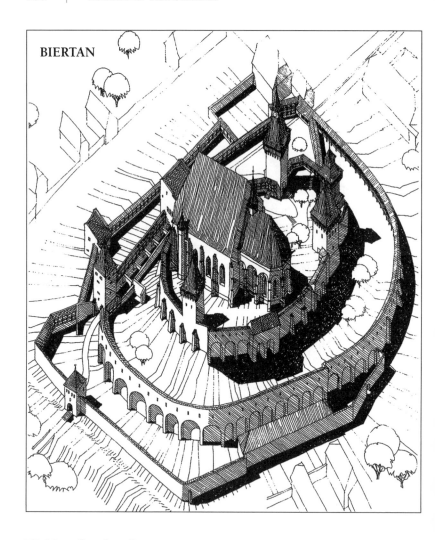

Visiting the church

NB: The church is closed from the beginning of Nov to the end of March.

The church is dedicated to the Virgin Mary. Take the beautiful covered **wooden stairway (2)**, newly restored, up to the ticket office (*open 10–1 & 2–6; the office contains an adequate bookshop*). From the stairway, if you take the first exit on the right you will find yourself looking down on the cart entrance, with sturdy flying buttresses. Continue to the entrance ahead,

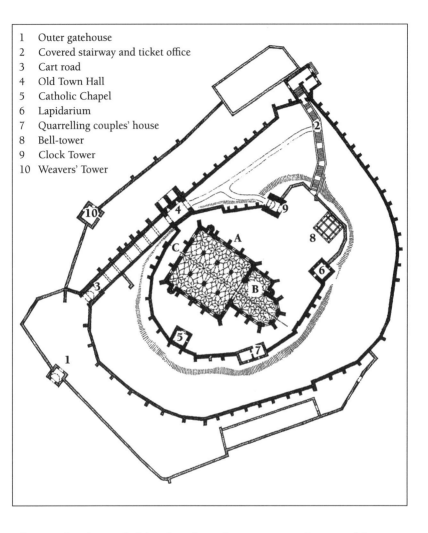

1 Outer gatehouse
2 Covered stairway and ticket office
3 Cart road
4 Old Town Hall
5 Catholic Chapel
6 Lapidarium
7 Quarrelling couples' house
8 Bell-tower
9 Clock Tower
10 Weavers' Tower

where under the roof of the church are fragmentary architectural frescoes. The **north entrance (A)** has a Baroque wooden door, surrounded by a jamb with carving by Ulrich from Brașov, who arrived in Biertan in 1523. The carving echoes that on the pulpit inside.

On entering, the grace and light of this hall church is a delight. The interior is both rich and airy, the net vault over the chancel having been repainted after damage by the severe earthquake in Bucharest of 1977.

This lovely style of vaulting finds echoes in Bohemia and Slovakia and in the revolutionary architecture of the Parler workshop in Prague. The vaulting in the nave is less intense. It was restored in the 17th century. Over the **chancel arch** is written in Latin, in thick Gothic script:

Anno Nat[ivit]atis Domini n[ost]ri 1522. Erecta est hec edis sacra ac instituta impendiis venerabilis do[min]i baccalaurii Joha[n]nis qui tum parochiani hic fungebatur munere quem tandem eiusdem nepos magister Lucas subsecutus eandem ex sua legatione testamentali finire per industriam Iacobi cementarii civis cibiniani curavit.

The church, in other words, was erected at the expense of the parish priest, the venerable Master Johannes, and completed in 1522 by his nephew Lucas, who employed for the purpose the stonemason Jacobus, a citizen of Sibiu. The coat of arms of Johannes, which features a chalice and the initials I.O., can be seen three times: painted on the high altarpiece; inscribed on the sacristy door; and on his tombstone in the Lapidarium.

The great **polyptych above the high altar** is the chief glory of the church. Eighteen painted panels frame a carved Crucifixion group of Christ with the Virgin, St John and Mary Magdalene. The centre panel at the top also shows the Crucifixion, with the Virgin Mary and St John in contemporary dress tending the base of the Cross as if it were the Tree of Life. Mary is pouring water from a pitcher and John is delving. Beyond them are crowded the Saved, saints and martyrs. To the left is the emperor Augustus' Vision of the Virgin according to the Golden Legend, and on the other side, the Vision of the Prophet Ezekiel. The central panels show scenes from the life of the Virgin in the top register and the life of Christ in the lower. These scenes were painted in the 1480s and repainted when the altarpiece was commissioned again in 1515 to fit in with the 16th-century work. They are heavily influenced by the master of the altarpiece of the Scots' College (Schottenstift) in Vienna, as is the contemporary retable in Mediaș. The abbot of the Scots' College came from Transylvania. Below these is a fine predella of the Holy Family, with Joachim and Anne (the parents of the Virgin), Mary and Joseph and the Christ Child as if already a sacrifice. All have an interesting dark background. All 25 figures are named, and the panels offer an unusually wide-ranging representation of

Biertan high altarpiece

		Vision of Augustus	Crucifixion	Vision of Ezekiel		
Joachim and Anne	Birth of the Virgin	Marriage of the Virgin	Crucifixion (sculpture group)	Annun- ciation	Visitation	Nativity
Circum- cision	Adoration of the Magi	Presentation in the Temple		Flight into Egypt	Christ in the Temple	Baptism of Christ
		Holy Family	Holy Family	Holy Family		

the Holy Kinship. The images are of not only of St Anne, but also her parents and her sister Esmeria and the offspring from her second and third marriages (to Cleopas and Salomas). The same subject matter is found in the altarpiece of Șaeș, now in the Church on the Hill in Sighișoara. It is, however, very rare. It is interesting that the Holy Family members are all named. Might this indicate the obscurity of the subject, which was perhaps chosen by the donor but needed interpretation for the congregation? The stylistic influence of the northern Renaissance is strong. The whole is a mix of beautifully-seen details yet still using the Gothic gilded and stamped gesso background. For costume historians, these panels are a treasure trove, especially since the altar is dated. There are coats of arms of donors to left and right of the predella. The one on the left bears the chalice emblem of Johannes, the priest commemorated above the chancel arch as having financed the initial stages of the church's construction.

The **choir stalls** were made in 1514 by Johannes Reychmuth and have panels of intarsia work. They are very fine. So too is the cresting of the stalls, which look Art Nouveau but are late Gothic and would be at home in Prague (the choir stalls in Richiș, 5km down the road, may have had this form and were probably made in the same workshop).

The other highlight of the east end is the **door to the sacristy (B)**. It was restored to be shown at the 1889 Paris Worlds' Fair. It is dated 1515 (above the coat of arms of Master Johannes) and is similar to the unrestored door in Richiș, which is one year later, and to fragments of intarsia in Aţel. This is an Italian technique, brought in by Italians working at the royal court in Buda. In the sacristy there is another intarsia panel, but of the early 20th century, illustrating the church before the roof was restored to its original late Gothic profile, in 1938–43, strangely, in the middle of the war.

The **font** is of the 17th century. The **pulpit** is splendid and was carved by the sculptor Ulrich from Brașov, whose workshop must also be responsible for the carved surrounds of the north entrance doorway. The pulpit panels portray the *Mater Dolorosa* with her breast pierced by a sword, the *Crucifixion* and the *Garden of Gethsemane*, the latter composition contained within an interesting woven fence. The medieval historian Ciprian Firea has suggested that the kneeling figure with a book in front of the *Mater*

Dolorosa is the donor of the work, Lucas, the nephew of Johannes, who was priest here from 1520–47. By the end of his tenure, Reformation ideas were already taking root in Transylvania. He was the last Catholic priest of this church. The fine wooden tester is of 1620s and is typical of the auricular style coming in from pattern books from the north of Europe.

The **organ** is neo-Gothic. There are good summer concerts in the church. The guild represented in the south pew is that of the Carpenters. There was a still a furniture workshop in the village, working in the Biedermeier style, in the late 19th century.

Biertan church also displays some **carpets** of importance, such as the beautiful fragment of a 16th–17th-century white-ground rug from Selendi in west Anatolia (*illustrated on p. 202*); an early 17th-century Lotto rug; and a single-niche Transylvanian rug, also of the 17th century. In all, Biertan has seven rugs. One includes an inscription '*In symbolum gratitudinis ofert... anno do 1708 ian*', a rare example of a donor inscription on a rug.

The churchyard and citadel

Outside, walking around the church, the double **west door (C)** is framed with delicate late Gothic stone tracery (1510–16). It is the same date as the door to the sacristy and was no doubt also created under Master Johannes. The same form is also found in Sighișoara, Sibiu and in much late Gothic/ early Renaissance stonework in the Kingdom of Hungary as far west as Bohemia. Here too, above the doors, are the coats of arms of King Vladislav Jagiello, also King of Bohemia (d. 1516) and the Voivode of Transylvania John Zapolya (d. 1540). These are in terracotta, a material obviously commonplace since the Middle Ages in bricks and stoves etc., but much favoured during the early Renaissance. It is also used on the Renaissance chapel of the cathedral in Alba Iulia.

The buildings attached to the inner wall are four towers including the usual **Bacon Tower**, where the bacon of each household was stored; the old Town Hall and the Clock Tower. Two of these towers deserve a visit. The first is the **Catholic Chapel (5)** set aside for the those who refused to adopt the ideas of the Reformation. This symbol of tolerance is also found in Mediaș (*see p. 148*). The frescoes are late Gothic, probably of the early

1500s. Above the entrance is the Virgin Mary and Christ offering a wreath to St ?Catherine. On the right is King Ladislaus. On the west wall is the *Last Judgement*, then to the south the *Annunciation* and the *Adoration*. To the east are the Archangel Michael and St George with the Veil of Veronica, thought to protect against sudden death. On the north wall is a *Pestbild*, a sacred image for protection against the plague, where God rains arrows upon Man protected by the Man of Sorrows and the Virgin of Mercy. At the time, between 1493 and 1495, an Ottoman invasion was followed by two years of famine and plague.

There is also the so-called **Lapidarium (6)**, set up at the beginning of the 20th century and containing the funerary monuments of priests and then bishops from the 1570s by carvers from Sighișoara and Sibiu. These have recently been restored. Fascinating remnants of their original colour have come to light in the cleaning. They had been badly affected by damp and salts but protection has now been installed. Dr Dóra Mérai believes that the earliest of these monuments were originally set into the pavement at the east end of the churches. In Brașov and Sibiu this was the case, therefore there can be a presumption that this was so elsewhere. In Sighișoara, there is evidence of a hinged top to one of these monuments. The effigies carved on them would have been examined from above (not knelt beside or processed around), in all their polychromatic, comforting normality. The deceased wear clothing illustrating their status, origin and wealth (indeed, priestly dress for the Lutheran pastor has barely changed today). Frequently the priests are shown with a chalice. The Biertan effigies were moved in the second half of the 19th century from the east end of the church and were set up against the walls in the Lapidarium in 1913. In Sighișoara too they were moved from their original positions. It is not always clear why these moves were made. Later monuments are of painted wood and are found in many of the churches, erected more like memorial plaques on the walls. From the 19th century, monuments were placed in the town cemeteries outside the church walls. Here in the Biertan Lapidarium, the following priests and bishops are to be found: Johannes (1520, patron of the church and altarpiece), Franz Salicaeus (d. 1567), Lucas Unglerus (d. 1600, who established the bishopric in Biertan),

Mathias Schiffbaumer (d. 1611), Zacharias Weyrauch (d. l621), Franz Graffius (d. 1627), Georg Theilesius (d. 1646), Christian Barth (d. 1658; he had the foresight to book Elias Nicolai to make his monument in 1649 before his death), Christian Haas (d. 1686). In front of the tower can be found the tombstones of the bishops D. Graeser (d. 1833) and G.P. Binder (d. 1867). The societies who funded this restoration are Siebenbürgisch-Sächsische Stiftung, World Monuments Fund and Deutsche Stiftung Umwelt. They donated one third of the costs each.

Another building within the inner walls (**7**) is more a curiosity. It is said that quarrelling couples were locked in here for a week with just one bed, one knife, one cup, one plate, etc. between them so that they had to learn to get on with each other. It appears that this form of marriage counselling was largely successful. I suspect the truth was that separation and divorce were out of the question anyway. The building is now a small museum.

Around the town

The countryside, seen from the walls, is wonderful and portrays a well-to-do market town of Saxons and Romanians. A quick walk around the streets will tell you most of what you need to know. The square at the foot of the church, travelling anti-clockwise, contains one of the most ancient houses in the town, the **Priest House**, to the left of the church entrance. There follows a fine row of Saxon houses and at the bottom of the square is one of the guesthouses owned by the MET, which can be rented (*see p. 12*). The **old school** of Biertan is under the walls of the church on the square and is now the Restaurant Unglerus, named after the first bishop, elected in 1572. The Saxons founded their schools very early in the life of the Siebenbürgen and are still very proud of the standard of education, which was always closely linked to the church. The German secondary schools are still considered the best in Transylvania. Traditionally the schools were paid for with the revenue from forestry. Following land reform in 1923, the Saxon community lost this vital resource and had to pay an extra tax for the schools, which caused much bitterness.

Just off the square, past small bars and a couple of general shops, is the Post Office (*open 9–11*) and the **Tourist Information Centre and Library** (*open 9–5; T: 0269 868 321*), not only providing information for tourists but also a service to the local community. Codruța Plăiaș is most helpful. The centre is funded by the Town Hall and Astra Library in Sibiu. There is an ATM here. If interested in contemporary art, ask for directions to the studio of Ion Constantinescu at Str. George Coșbuc 17. He makes fine woodcuts.

The **Town Hall** is at the church end of the square. The mayor is responsible for Richiș, Biertan, Șaroș and Copșa Mare. To the right of the Town Hall lies the road to Richiș, along which are some very imposing houses. The old retirement home has at last closed and the pensioners have moved to a good modern building just out of the village. It opened later than planned, as so many who might help here are in other parts of Europe doing the same work. On this street too, with a porch, was the homeopathic chemist, sadly now closed down (there had been one on this site since the 19th century). On the other side of the road is the **Saxon Cemetery**.

Return to the Tourist Information Centre and walk about 100 yards following the sign to Copșa Mare. Ahead, on the right, is the small **Uniate church** and the primary school and further along and to the right is the **Orthodox church**, which is grand and has some early tombstones near the entrance. This stands on a hill, in competition with the Saxon church, and it is from here that you get a good view of the Saxons' citadel. Straight on, the road leads to Richiș through a lovely valley (well marked for walking). Here too is the road to Copșa Mare, another recommended walk. On leaving the town are the smaller houses of the Roma community.

COPȘA MARE

The road from Biertan is well signed to the lovely small village of Copșa Mare (Großkopisch/Nagykapus) about 5km away. Alternatively, the walk is charming too, taking you past the small houses at the edge of Biertan with wide verges and wells, through fine beech forests which grow down to the edge of the unmade road. The gentle undulations produce different views until you are above the village, offering possibly the finest view of all of the church down to your right.

THE GREATER TÂRNAVA VALLEY | 117

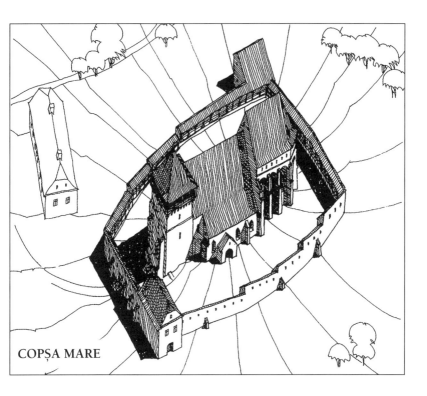

COPŞA MARE

Head for the church. The entry point is at the side of the shop. The key can be found from the caretaker, who lives within the walls. The church has an early sandstone base and the entrance is, unusually, under the fortified bell-tower. Its present form dates to the 16th century, although the foundations date from 14th. The church is a slight disappointment inside. But the bell of 1550 is worth climbing to. Its fine casting echoes early baptismal fonts such as the one in Mediaş. There are also the original workings of the organ with its huge cow-skin bellows. These wonderful instruments are found in many of the churches down the valley.

Copşa straggles and at the end of the main, wide street is the Orthodox church. The Town Hall, which is a most imposing building, seems almost out of place and is very much in the architectural style of the Dual Monarchy. It has recently been restored and conceals stabling behind. The hire of horses and carts can be organised here, with picnics to the surrounding hills. There is also truffle hunting at the right time of year.

The village has been much restored by an Italian family, who have fallen in love with the valley, making Copşa well placed for eating and sleeping. Guesthouses have been beautifully restored, with their interiors comfortably and stylishly Italian but using local furniture and ceramics (*see the listing on p. 12*).

An excursion

If you have a four-wheel-drive vehicle and would like to see over woods and hills to the Carpathians, there is no better place than Copşa Mare from which to wend your way up into the hills to find the local shepherds and their *stâne* (sheepfolds). You will pass hunting huts and gas pipes along the way, reminders of how rich this area is in gas (Mediaş is home to the head office of Romgaz, the main gas supplier in Romania). Turn right at the well at the end of Copşa village and at the second crossroads turn left. You will always think you have made a mistake. Go through a wood with a stream on the right and a forester's hut now on the right. Eventually you will find yourself in open country. The road turns to sandy hardcore and some sheep should start appearing. Continue until you reach a plateau. Ahead will be the Carpathians; alongside you are the Biertan shepherds with dogs, donkeys, pigs, guinea fowl and sheep. All ahead is Transylvania. The drive will take about 30mins.

These shepherds still practise transhumance, the annual moving of the animals from summer ground to winter pastures. Here they move them to the plains of Satu Mare, where the winters are milder. Special corridors for transhumance are needed for such vast flocks, and in most other European countries such practices have had to cease. Ask the shepherds about their traditional sheepskin coats, which are ankle length and ensure they can sleep outside, even in winter. Milking takes place at sunset.

You will now be on the back road to **Agnita (Agnetheln/Szentágota)**, where there is a good church and on the way there a memorial to those who took a stand against the Communist government after the war. They fought on, hoping in vain that the Americans would arrive. Many were killed or ended up in Sighet prison.

If you simply retrace your steps, look out for good flora and fauna on the way. The road is lined with gentle hills, many of them terraced. You pass gas installations and beehives and a tree nursery. The valley is quite wide at this point with strip farming and then, beyond, the pastures once held in common by the Saxons. Golden rod has become invasive but is loved by the bees. See Roy Lancaster's extensive plant lists, compiled after only a few days staying in Richiş and walking to Biertan (*p. 212*). See too, the notes by Wilhelm Untch on bees (*p. 207*).

RICHIŞ

Following the road South from Biertan, you will arrive in Richiş (Reichesdorf/Riomfalva). Although it is believed that this and many of the villages in this area were founded before the end of the 13th century, the period of the most specific recording came only after the disasters of the Mongol invasions of 1241. Thus it is that the first documented mention of Richiş is in 1283.

One of the largest villages in the valley, its lanes and houses lie along the bottom of the valley in the most satisfactory manner. The hills on the west side of the road to Biertan have grown vines since the Middle Ages. The soil on the hills is light and sandy; that of the valley floor is rich and dark. Under the Saxons, everywhere the plough could go grew crops and, on the hills where it could not, vines were cultivated. The grape was the source of wealth here and is a frequent motif for stucco decoration on house façades, not only throughout Richiş but in all the surrounding villages. The wealth is evident in the breadth of the house façades, many of which have a quiet, classical elegance. The houses nearest the church are large with spacious gardens. It is not surprising in such a church-centred society (the community always voted for their priests from the 13th century) that the most important houses are those near the church. Where there is no room for an orchard or vegetable garden, ground was allocated across the street.

There are few Saxons left in Richiş today. In the 1930s there were nearly 900. In the 1880s phylloxera struck the vines and 300 Saxons emigrated to the USA. However, the village is gradually seeing a revival. The shop, bar and camping site, and the restoration of the **Priest House** as a *pensione*, is due to the Timmermans, a Dutch couple who have been in Richiș since 1991. They have been the moving force behind the revival. There are two further general shops and another bar, also in the centre. The MET and Horizon have achieved thoughtful restoration at the heart of the village. ADEPT has advised on and supported the milk collection from the cattle in a countryside where now there are too many sheep. Much, too, is due to the work of those Saxons who chose to remain in the village after 1991, Mr and Mrs Schaas and Mr Wilhelm Untch. They have kept the church community going and their knowledge of the past is invaluable.

The church roof was restored in 2009–10 with a private donation from the UK. This came just in time to prevent the collapse of the whole structure. Next to the church is the charming 18th-century Town Hall of the Saxons, called the **Old School**. This has been restored by the MET and the Horizon Foundation. The ground floor is both the Tourist Information Centre and a community help desk, and holds a small museum of weaving (*T: 0269 258 585*). There is also a doctor's surgery here one day a week.

The MET and Horizon have also restored the spacious **Saxon Meeting Hall**, complete with stage, where the first Transylvanian Book Festival was held in 2013. The hall dates from 1910. It was here, on Sunday 14th January 1945, that all men and women between 18 and 46 were gathered to be marched to the railhead in Dumbrăveni to be taken as slave labour to the Ukraine and the Urals. There were 85 women and 36 men, of whom 14 people died.

On a happier note, in the early '60s, a travelling circus used to arrive in Richiș, presenting a dancing bear on the stage along with knife- and axe-throwers (their target, a lady in a swimsuit). Fire eaters and conjurers, complete with rabbits and hats, added to the fun. People came from miles around, mainly on foot or in carts. The circus was open to all, not only the Saxon community, but to Hungarians and Romanians too. There was theatre here, both professional and amateur. There were dances for children and adults, including the great Carnival Ball, which took place in February (masks were worn). At midnight children were removed and food was

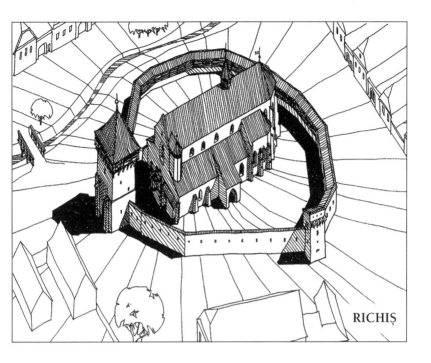

RICHIȘ

brought, ladies went home to change and the whole thing continued until six in the morning. There was one dance, unmasked, when the ladies could ask any man they chose to partner them. This happened in those brief years when those who had survived the gulags returned and before the full impact of Communism under Ceaușescu had made itself felt. There were many such festivals in the villages. I have been lucky enough to interview neighbours who took part in them. Wilhelm Untch is one of them. He can also remember people walking around the village singing the songs of Georg Meyndt, villager and composer who died in 1902 (*see p. 127*).

The church and churchyard

The church foundations were laid from 1350–1451. The fortified walls were built c. 1500 against the threat from Ottoman Turkey. In the early 1900s, due to greater prosperity and a growing population, the stone from the walls was reused for the school and hall.

The church is one of the least known but one of the most important in Saxon Transylvania. It is on trade routes and was open to international influences and wealth. It is earlier than Biertan's, and though it lacks the latter's architectural splendour, it retains a quiet dignity and spirituality. It may have been founded as a monastic church, possibly Cistercian. It is the Cistercians who are credited with teaching farming methods to the Saxons.

No excavations have been conducted but the monastery buildings may be under the present Priest House and Town Hall. The cellar of the Priest House has 15th-century arches and massive foundation stones (pinkish sandstone) from the Făgăraş Mountains. The bell-tower is mainly 19th century but its doorway is part of the late medieval fortifications. The church has three entrance doors. Those to north and south have deep portals. The **west door** has keeled orders with bases. The capitals are vigorously carved with seaweed foliage of a type found also in Sibiu and Mălâncrav. The tympanum is unusual in Transylvania in that it is figurative. It portrays the Crucifixion with the figures of St John, the two Marys and the Centurion (on a horse) who was converted at the foot of the Cross. Above the Crucified Christ are two angels. At some stage the heads of the figures have been knocked off. Perhaps damage from the Reformation.

Walking around the interior, note that the two side aisles and nave are lit by fine, slim lancet windows with delicate tracery. However, the most notable feature of the interior is the rich decoration. The simple quadripartite vaulting is in contrast to the energetic carving of the capitals. Throughout the church there are several examples of 'Green Men', pagan, amorphous faces within foliage. These are common in English churches but not so in Transylvania. There are also more heads of men and women decorating the springers beneath the vault. On the northwest pier capital, and only recently discovered, there is carved a tonsured monk.

The quadripartite **nave vaulting** includes carved bosses with the Godhead, the Agnus Dei, the Hand of God, the Pelican in her Piety and armorials, possibly of the church patrons. There is definitely a shield of the Stonemasons and other small shields with insignia. The medieval historian Ciprian Firea notes, on the west side of the chancel arch, an inscription marking the construction of the vault in 1451, at the time of the priest

Christian (1451–3): '*Anno dni mccccli completa est testudo hec tempore Cristanni decretorum doctoris.*' Christian went on to become a cathedral canon in Alba Iulia, the capital of Transylvania. This valley seems to have attracted priests of high calibre.

The **choir** was restored in the 17th century. The stalls at the east end are mainly 16th century but are much damaged. They were probably by the same workshop as those in Biertan. On a panel under the priest's chair there is an image of a knight on a horse with a lance, perhaps St George.

The **high altarpiece** is of the Crucified Christ flanked by Sts John the Baptist and Evangelist. It is signed and dated 1775 by Johannes Folbarth and is a fine piece of painted woodwork, albeit stylistically a century out of date. It is interesting that in the Protestant Siebenbürgen the old forms of the Catholic Church were retained, unlike in most of Reformation Europe. However, in the late 19th century, when a powerful group of local ladies requested that the frescoes in the chancel be whitewashed over, they also demanded that the legs of the Baptist be covered in painted and gessoed linen. Young girls and children sat at the front of the church and his bare legs were considered a distraction. The aumbry cupboard, for the bread and the wine for the Eucharist, is to the left of the altar, and is carved with the Pelican in her Piety (the bird is shown drawing blood from her own breast to feed her young, a symbol of Christ's sacrifice).

The **sacristy door** has good Renaissance intarsia work of 1516, similar to the door at Biertan, which was also executed in the atelier of Johannes Reychmuth from Sighișoara and has the same complex locking system. It has a coat of arms which is assumed to have been the emblem of Richiș (the Saxon name of the village may perhaps derive from *Reiher*, a heron). Ciprian Firea, however, suggests instead that this is the coat of arms of the priest Petrus Wol, who after studying in Rome and Padua (1505, Padua: *Petrus Pannonius plebanus de Șaroș de Transilvania*), moved up from Șaroș to Richiș and lived here as prebend from 1509–29. He commissioned the inlaid door and an altarpiece (1520–5) displaying his coat of arms, which was moved to Nemșa and is now in Mediaș. In 1529 he became *decanus generalis* and was the last Catholic priest in Sibiu before his death in the 1530s. These were the years when the Reformation came to Transylvania.

The sacristy door at Biertan was restored for the 1889 Paris World's Fair. This was an interesting choice: the aim perhaps to illustrate craft skills and nationalism. The Richiș door is not restored and shows the marks of the disruption of the Reformation, when it is recorded that the villagers forced out the monks here. In the sacristy are two fine tomb slabs.

The Transylvanian Saxon church community

The seating in the nave and aisles was hierarchic in all Lutheran churches, with the priest's wife, the schoolteacher, etc. in places of prominence. Everyone else, from child to pensioner, had their place assigned according to sex, marital status and age, until finally taken on the last journey up to the cemetery, behind the church, forever overlooking the village. Fine costumes were worn for Sunday services and festivals until the early 1990s. Many hours could be taken in preparation, especially with the elaborate headdresses. Every costume betrayed something of your status. Here, in Richiș, green dresses were worn by brunettes and blue by blondes. Richiș even had a special dress for married women who were yet to have children: their role in ensuring the future meant they were the most cherished. Each village retained individual forms of greeting and dress, something Ceaușescu was keen to eliminate. The exodus of the Saxons in the 1990s has almost succeeded in destroying this unique part of European culture. The Reichesdorf Saxons have gone to Germany. The reason for their leaving was mainly a sense of this being their 'only chance'. Many had relations in Germany already. The priests went and the congregation followed. Those who had agricultural skills were able to get work; others, who had clerical and managerial skills, would have found it hard. Still today they make an attempt to keep the spirit of the community alive. They return to their village in the summer and for reunions. But their customs have gone with them. They must have been one of the last true church communities in Europe.

Young married women who have not yet become mothers, assigned to particular
pews in church and dressed in their own costume and headdress.

The **War Memorials** in the north aisle are to the dead of the two World
Wars and the deportations. Transylvania entered the First World War as
part of Hungary. They were shocked to be invaded by Romanian troops
in 1916. During the Second World War, Romania came in in 1940 on the
Axis side. They withdrew from the conflict in 1944 when the young king
led a coup against Antonescu and the German allies. In January 1945, at
the insistence of the Soviet Union, 121 men and women were deported
from this village. That, on top of war losses, must have made working the
land difficult in such a farming community. These memorials tell much of
the tragic history of the Saxons in the 20th century. Without doubt, in spite
of threats from the Ottomans and the civil war in 1848–9, the last century
was the most traumatic period in the whole of the Saxons' 850 years in
Transylvania. The memorial is repeated outside in the village square.

The little holes in the stone jambs of the west doorway and behind the
altar at the east end are curious. They are said to have been made by
transgressors who had to sit in full view of all, twisting their fingers into
these holes. There may be a fault in the stone.

The community paid Daniel Prause in 1788 for the **organ**. Over the last three years a remarkable collaborative effort has been made possible by a generous donation from Anna David from Richiș, who was herself taken to the Ukraine as a young woman. Romanian and British organ builders and conservation workshops in Sibiu have ensured that the organ will be heard again. The church's two 'Transylvanian' rugs are to be seen in Mediaș church (*see p. 152*).

At the top of the **bell-tower** is a bell of 1708 with the inscription *Venite Laudate et Glorificate Deum*: O Come, sing and glorify God. The others were melted down in the First Wold War, after which new bells were donated. The largest has an inscription in German that translates as: 'Heroes' Bell. Dedicated in 1922, with Love and Faith, to the Memory of our Brothers killed in the 1914–1918 World War, by the Saxons of Reichesdorf living in America.'

In the churchyard is a **memorial to Georg Meyndt** (1852–1902), the local songwriter and composer. The memorial was moved from its original position in the Saxon graveyard by Herr Schaas, with the aim of preserving it. Meyndt lived in house no. 17, opposite the church. It is now a shop and retains its attractive neo-Baroque façade. Meyndt's music was still sung in the village within living memory.

Walks around the village

There were nine districts in Reichesdorf, with each district taking care of all those within it. All nine districts then worked for the common good of the church, maintaining it, along with the school. Each district (*Nachbarschaft*) was headed by a neighbourhood leader or 'father' (*Nachbarschaftsvater*), who helped neighbours and organised social events. Each neighbourhood father had a neighbourhood sign (*Nachbarschaftszeichen*) which was used to display notices: births and deaths, invitations to social events, notifications about when communal work was due to begin. This sign was carried from house to house by children. Once a year, everybody attended a so-called judgement day (*Richttag*), meeting around the age-old neighbourhood chest. Grievances were publicly aired and forgiveness had to be asked if necessary.

Georg Meyndt and the music of Transylvania

Transylvania is a treasure house of music where some of the most ancient tunes and dances in Europe survive, incorporating influences from the Steppes, the Balkans and from Western Europe. Folk tunes were already being collected in the 19th century and provide inspiration for the Hungarian composers Franz Liszt and Ferenc Erkel. In the last century two other Hungarian composers, Béla Bartók and Zoltán Kodály, as well as the Romanians Constantin Silvestri and George Enescu, also collected music from the Transylvanian villages and composed for traditional instruments.

Dancing in the villages took place in the so-called 'Dance Houses' (a community house like a barn) on Sunday evenings, and in full national costume. The tradition still lives on today at weddings and baptisms.

As emerges from the museum in Sighișoara, in the Saxon communities, everyone was a member of a choir or a brass band and joined some kind of musical association from an early age. Every Saxon village had, as a matter of custom, a dancing area where everyone met and danced.

Georg Meyndt was a Saxon Transylvanian, born in Biertan in 1852, who lived in Richiș for most of his life. Although a lawyer by profession, his real love and talent was for music, and he wrote poems, composed and collected songs in the traditional Saxon dialect. They were sung around the village on engagements and festivals, still within living memory. His music has been published in Germany and can be found on CD. There continues a rich vein of choral singing and church music to be found in many of the Saxon churches, hence the emphasis given to organs in many of the churches in the Târnava Mare Valley.

The church presbytery had two members from each neighbourhood who met once a month for the business of church, school and managing the landholdings that provided the money to operate them, as well as caring for the forests, the church hall, etc. The system ensured a close community and the physical endurance of the Saxon settlements. The houses really need to be restored every three years or so, a fact that has led to the current popularity of cement as the cheaper and unskilled option. So many of the old skills left with the Saxons. It is interesting that Andreas Nemenz chose to write all this down in an invaluable compilation of the history of Reichesdorf (*see Bibliography, p. 238*). He lived in the house which I spent ten years or so restoring.

Several walks can be taken around Richiș. Three short rambles are given below:

The centre of the village contains three shops and two pubs. The most attractive of the shops retains its old façade and the name of the original shopkeepers. There is also an attractive camping site here. In the village centre the stream splits, creating an island on which are (or rather were) some of the most charming houses. The MET has restored the green Neoclassical house opposite the church. It operates as a guesthouse and includes a large library, part of which is dedicated to the work Georg Meyndt (*see previous page*). His works will be performed in the music room, along with other concerts.

On the other side of the street is the Town Hall of the Saxons and then the Village Meeting Room. Outside of this, in the gardens, is another war memorial. There are fine buildings of the state farm (note the grapes portrayed in the plaster work). At no. 12, part of the old state farm, is the joinery workshop which has been revived and where they take on journeymen. The idea of the 'journey', serving as an apprenticeship for traditional craftsmen which lasts for three years and a day, is still continued in Germany and France. Traditional journeyman uniforms are still worn: look out for the big hats, waistcoats with pearly buttons and bell-bottomed trousers. They are now in demand for making traditional cart and carriage wheels. Christian Rummel, the head of the workshop, also organises carriage ides in a nobleman's journey carriage from 1884 (*christian.rummel1@gmx.de or T: 0269 258 401*).

Continue on, keeping to the wider street as far as the water trough,

Eric the journeyman making a cart.

where the horses, goats, sheep and cattle still come. This is also where the villagers scrub their carpets. Note house no. 30, which is one of the finest and largest in the village. It was here that the German commander lived in 1943–4, when a tank regiment was billeted in the village. They moved out as the war moved east. There is a fine hill, terraced again, on your right, where children waved to the Luftwaffe as they flew over. In the last few years the wine company that took over the vineyards in the village has withdrawn and the vines have been taken. Sheep are now trampling the hills and soon the terraces will be gone.

Heading around the east end of the church, cross the brook. Either continue straight on, up the most beautiful of the village streets, where the Saxon graveyard rises above the church and is worth a visit; or turn left along a grassy lane which is lined with wooden barns (a feature which may not survive much longer). Return to the village centre again and ahead you will see the school of 1904, a typical Austro-Hungarian building. There was a rise in population at the turn of the last century and the walls of the church were used for the school building. Cross the stream and two buildings facing you tell of the self-sufficiency of the Saxons: the attractive double-storeyed building is the dairy. The ground floor still retains its white tiles. Next to it was the butchers' shop. The road leads to Biertan past the Orthodox graveyard, the tiny Orthodox church and the small houses so typical of the edges of Saxon villages, where the gypsies lived who worked alongside the Saxons for hundreds of years.

The most attractive walk of all, perhaps, is to take the main road towards Biertan, turning right at the old Fire Station and before some more state farm buildings. There are attractive houses here, beyond which hay fields open up. To the left there is a cart track running parallel to the Biertan road; or you can continue into an attractive valley to the edge of the beech woods and the sad remains of the communal village hut. It was accidentally burnt by the charcoal burners who were working there.

THE ROAD TO SIBIU

This is not strictly in the Târnava Valley but **Pelișor (Magarey/Magaré)** sits in attractive countryside and on a route which is well worth taking if you need to make your way to or from Sibiu airport. The main road from Mediaș to Sibiu is busy, yet slow and nerve-racking. The route via Pelișor, Bârghis, Alțâna, Nocrich and so to Sibiu is lovely. Allow plenty of time though, as there are lots of sheep, cows and water buffalo to hold you up, as well as horses and carts.

On the western outskirts of Pelișor, to the south of the road near the Zlagna turning, is a nunnery. The land was given by an Orthodox family from the far south of the country, and there are plans—indeed, the foundations are already in place—to build a huge Orthodox church here within the seven hectares of land. The nuns are energetically collecting money to build their ideal, from pilgrims and visitors. This is definitely making a statement in the middle of ancient, Saxon Protestant lands. If you can, try and come here for a feast day such as All Saints, 1st November, when you will be given a special 'cake'. The small basilica on the site is charming with a well-painted iconostasis, with panels from the 1950s which have been re-used. The community is very welcoming and the tables groan with food. The nuns are vegetarian and they grow most of what they eat themselves, as well as farming hens, sheep and fish. You will also be served carp in all sorts of sizes. They have one priest and four nuns and lay brothers to help. People come from afar to this beautiful valley as a place of retreat.

Pelișor itself has a fortified church in a poor state of repair, with a neo-Gothic priest house that would sit happily in any English village. It may be that the designs were taken from an English 19th-century pattern book.

The route south to Sibiu will take you on to **Alțâna (or Alțina/Alzen /Alcina)**, owned for 300 years by a single noble family. The first mention of the village is in 1291, but nothing much remains of the buildings of those years. **Nocrich (Leschkirch/Újegyház)** is next, where in 1454 the Archbishop of Esztergom ordered any valuables to be sent to Sibiu. It is thought that the Saxon community had disappeared by then. The old church was demolished in 1807.

At **Hosman (Holzmengen/Holcmány)**, the magnificent fortified Saxon church stands proudly in the landscape just off the main road. It has an important doorway, well worth making the detour to see (*contact Diana Maria Mureșan in advance, T: 0742 153 005 or email jzholzmengen@ gmail.com*). It has splendid fortifications and fine interior, especially the Neoclassical font and galleries of 1803–4. To be recommended, too, is a visit to the old mill, which has been restored from a ruinous condition by the Hosman Durabil Association, and supported by the MET. The mill is in working order, as is the smithy. There are guided tours of the mill in English. The local kitchen will provide a meal made of locally-grown produce (*T: 0740 959 389, info@moara-veche.ro*).

From here you will start to see the peaks of the magnificent Carpathians ahead of you. You will soon start to descend to Sibiu.

AȚEL & DUPUȘ

There is a tarmac road leading to AȚel (Hetzeldorf/Ecel), again along a lovely valley—though farmed with machinery more than with horse and plough. There is a long village street with small, single houses linked by archways leading to the fortified church.

As for the fortified church itself, the defensive walls have been partially demolished and the church entrance, under the 15th-century tower (which holds two bells), is dated 1380. The key is held at no. 171 adjacent to the church, a home for retired Saxons (*NB: You might be asked for ID*). Opposite the church entrance is the large Priest House, with barrels of wine at the base of the walls. I was lucky enough to find the key holder, a tall man in his eighties and with a fine voice. Unbidden, from the chancel of the little church, he intoned, in a rich baritone, the Saxon baptismal service, over the font, and then gave me an apple.

The nave vault is dated 1499 and the interior, on a simple cruciform plan, was finished in 1516, just before the Reformation. The interior is fine with rich sculptured details, but it is quite difficult to take in the whole picture. Some of the stonework (for example the nave columns) may have been re-used. As some of the sculptural forms are of the quality found in Moșna (*see p. 166*), the architectural historian Fabini has suggested that Andreas Lapicida was also at work here. The choir was heightened for defence and there is a fine set of 19th-century sedilia on the south side. The altar (1792) is by Johann Folbarth, a master wood carver from Sighișoara. His carvings are frequently found in the surrounding churches. Some pieces are dated. The organ, by Samuel Maetz, dates from 1802. There is a panel of intarsia work, dated 1516, in the nave, the same date as that at Richiș. The vestry portal dates from 1499 and is also possibly by the hand of Andreas Lapicida. In the attic of the sacristy are fragments of the story of St Ladislaus seeing off the Cuman (*for the story, see p. 52*).

The village buildings at the west end of the church, where the defensive circuit has been demolished, are not an improvement.

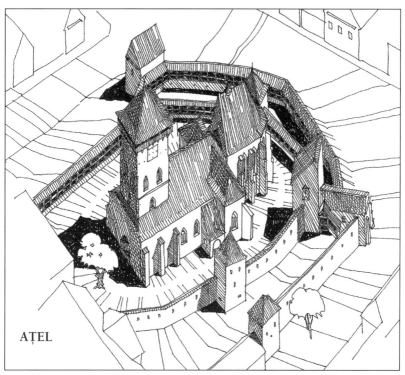

ATEL

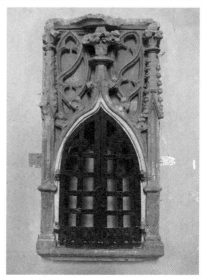

Aumbry cupboard in the church at Atel with richly carved and traceried surround, an example of the fine Gothic stonework to be found here.

Aţel: west doorway.

DUPUȘ

The route from Ațel to Dupuș (Tobsdorf/Táblás or Tóbiásfalva) is slow and poplar-lined, with other valleys opening up along the short distance. However, just to see the remarkable organ case it is worth the rather bumpy journey. The case is dated to 1731 but looks much earlier. It is in a vigorous, late Mannerist style filled with angels playing instruments. It is quite one of the best organ cases in the Târnava Valley.

The village is first documented in 1267, the same date that the Saxons took over Medias from the Székelys. It was a free, rather than a feudal, village (*see p. 159*). The church, dedicated to St Tobias, is a hall church built in the first quarter of the 16th century on the site of an older building. It has a free-standing belfry replacing the original tower, which collapsed in the late 18th century, and retains its defensive walls. The raised level for defence and refuge above the nave and choir of the church is well seen in the drawing reproduced below.

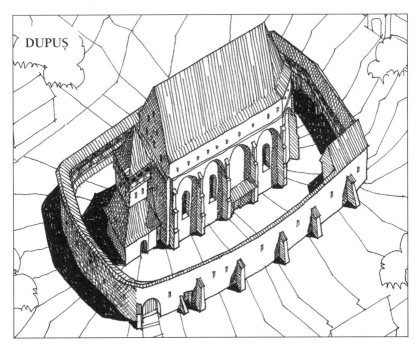

DUPUȘ

Florid early 18th-century organ case at Dupuş.

The church key is with Péter Szombati, who is not only the local school teacher but also organist, composer and biker (T: 0747 530 014). To reach the Priest House, where he lives, walk up the hill and you will find it behind the church. Szombati is, I would guess, the only person who can play the wonderful organ, as the keys are so stiff. It was last restored in 1908. The huge organ bellows still exist; if someone is playing the organ, then someone else has the work of pumping the air through the instrument by foot.

The date 1524 is inscribed behind the organ. The church's high altarpiece is now held, for safe-keeping, in Mediaş (see p. 151); its frame is in the same auricular, late Mannerist style as the organ. The pews, of 1537, are possibly the work of Johannes Reychmuth of Sighişoara.

BRATEIU

Brateiu (Pretai or Pretau/Baráthely) is an ancient Saxon settlement. The first recorded mention of it is in 1283. Nowadays there are Romanians, a few Saxons, Hungarians and gypsies living here. The last group are probably in the majority.

Old Saxon Brateiu

Brateiu has a fine **fortified church** dedicated to St Mary Magdalene (*the key is found at no. 30 on the right of the church before the chemist shop and Town Hall; T: 0787 694 821 or 0269 863 019*). The church was reconstructed in the 14th century and building work continued into the 15th. On the north wall of the chancel are remains of a frescoed *Adoration of the Magi*.

The gate tower holds a small **museum** (*closed for restoration at the time of writing*). When open it is worth climbing to the top to look out over the village, which has been laid out on either side of the main road with a very impressive long square functioning as a **market-place**: the perfect trading centre. An acute sense of priority—religion; education; civic administration—is reflected in the buildings. The church is at one end with the school at its base, and at the other end is the Town Hall.

There are the usual rows of Saxon village farms on either side of this lovely wide market-place. The Saxon **graveyard** at the entrance to the village, as you come from Sighişoara, is only one third filled, with the latest burials dated to the 1980s. Many of the monuments reflect the dignity of those who traded and farmed here.

Roma Brateiu

However Brateiu is two villages in one. At the Mediaş end of the village, the Roma community have turned their backs on the Saxon houses which they occupied when the Saxons left. Indeed, many of the original Roma arrived in the area about 1845, around the time of their emancipation in the middle years of the 19th century. The Roma were among the last groups in Transylvania to receive the right to work as free men and receive wages, as opposed to working as serfs. The present families arrived in Brateiu in 1968. At this time they were known as *corturari* (*cort* means tent in Romanian). They used to be nomads moving from winter to summer pastures.

Today, they have doubled the size of the village by building in their own style, unique in Europe as far as I know. Few of the houses are finished but they are large enough to hold several generations of one family. The materials are red brick with cement columns around doors and holding up tiered balconies. The window glass is convex to allow total privacy, i.e. you cannot see through it. The façades are then covered with aluminium. Some are highly decorated like a Hindu temple, with intricate star shapes: echoes of India, the Motherland, but occurring six centuries or so after their westward migration. Why and who first built in this now distinctive 20th-century gypsy style?

The Roma of Brateiu belong to the *căldărari* caste (*see p. 221*) and specialise as boiler-makers and coppersmiths. During the Communist period they were forbidden to produce stills for plum brandy; only tin-smithing and guttering were allowed. Today along the roadside at Brateiu, you will see stalls selling everything from a jug for your Turkish coffee to a large still for your fruit brandies. Bargaining is expected.

The women dress in wonderful clashing patterns and colours, elegant in their long pleated skirts, aprons, blouses, waistcoats and scarves. The men are bearded or have long moustaches. They wear white shirts and black trousers and black felt hats, a costume they say they adopted from the Saxons. Up until recent times the Roma population would simply have added further colour to the diversity of dress in any village. Now that the Romanians and Hungarians have given up their national costumes, however, the gypsy inhabitants of Brateiu stand for wonderful exotica.

There are many related families here from the villages of Dârlos, Buzd, Aţel, Richiş and Dupuş. Some of the most traditional gypsies from Brateiu have built their houses with just one floor, as women are not allowed on a higher one. A married woman is not allowed to step in front of her husband (or of her husband's horse), nor is she supposed to drive a car.

Suburban villa meets Hindu temple, with horse and
rubber-wheeled wagon. An example of the extraordinary juxtaposition
of styles and centuries to be met with in Transylvania.

There are several families in Brateiu who welcome visitors: contact Emil
Căldărar (*T: 0764 109 693*) or his brother Culiță Căldărar (*T: 0763 368 565
or 762 290 721*). Their house is right at the Mediaș end of the village on
the left-hand side. Note that everyone will demand payment if you take
photographs of them and that if you are visiting to see the architecture, it
is important to agree a price prior to the visit.

The main road becomes increasingly built up between Brateiu and Mediaș.
The valley is wide here with more sophisticated farming.

MEDIAȘ

Mediaș (Mediasch/Medgyes) is the main town of the western Târnava Valley and the economic driving force of the region. Arriving by train, from Vienna, Budapest or Bucharest, is a primitive experience—but it is improving. The journey is the only real way to sense the hugeness and thrill of old Austria-Hungary. I recommend it. The station and its surroundings, mixed with the aesthetics of Communism, tell of an industrial past that has seen better days. The station platforms are level with the tracks, so under a fall of fresh snow it is impossible to see the start or end of either.

The railway has been here since 1872. That and the early 19th-century foundations of colleges—technical, agricultural and, for the daughters of rich Saxon farmers, domestic science—meant a head start over the neighbours. This part of Transylvania exported expertise and goods into Austria-Hungary. The technical college still exists and offers courses in design. The shoe industry benefits from this, although today foreign shoe producers bring their designs to be made in Mediaș.

Wine production was also important. Then gas was discovered in Delenii (formerly Șaroșul Unguresc/Magyarsáros) and drilling began in 1907. Exploitation came relatively late to the region, as there is evidence as early as the 17th century that gas had been discovered, while the glass and chemical industries had been drilling for potash for some decades. Budapest had its first gas lights by 1856. It was not until 1909 that the Hungarian government began to exploit the gas fields of this eastern region, using German technology. In 1912, gas production became a state monopoly and a pipeline was developed through Transylvania. In 1923, Mediaș was chosen to be the headquarters of the Hungarian gas company, Ungarische Erdgas Gesellschaft. Mediaș continued in this role under the Communists, who in 1948 set up offices for the state gas company here. Today the Romanian Gas Company, Romgaz, has its headquarters in Mediaș, employing 3,000 people. There is also a college dedicated to training for the oil and gas industry, at graduate and postgraduate levels.

Crucifixion from the Mediaș high altarpiece.

In the 1980s Mediaş was the fourth most productive city in Romania. The chandeliers for Ceauşescu's gargantuan palace in Bucharest came from Mediaş and the town had the first glass factory in Romania to fire its kilns using gas. Even in those very difficult times, Mediaş was known as a place where much was available—excepting the famous glass (and salami), which were exported for hard currency only. Other goods, however, were readily available for lei: textiles, leatherware including shoes and harnesses, enamel work and ceramics. Now most of the factories have gone, apart from the enamel factory, which is still one of the most successful in Romania, and a little glass-making survives. Today a combination of industrialisation and ugly outskirts have made Mediaş less visited than many other towns in Transylvania, but it is a place that amply repays exploration.

The centre was built on a site inhabited since the 5th century BC by successions of Dacians, Romans, Goths and Slavs, for which archaeological evidence can be found in the Municipal Museum. Romanians will tell you that the town's name has a Latin origin. Hungarians say that it is Székely. Whatever the case, Mediaş was certainly inhabited by the Székleys, and when they moved east, the Saxons moved in, around 1267, which is the first documented date we have. In the 14th century it received its city charter. The Franciscans arrived in 1444, by which time the young city was of a size to make it worth their while. The remains of the walls, against which the Franciscan church nestles, give an idea of its original scale. The building of the walls was instigated at the command of the King of Hungary, Matthias Corvinus (r. 1458–90), who ordered every resident to contribute to their construction. They gradually went up between 1489 and 1534. After the Battle of Mohács (1526), Saxon Mediasch supported the claims of Ferdinand of Habsburg against Zapolya. The Venetian adventurer Alvise Gritti came here at the head of a band of mercenaries to defeat Zapolya in 1534. The resulting siege was immense, the city was overrun and Gritti was beheaded. The Saxons took refuge behind their finally competed walls and from this fastness attempted to withstand the slings and arrows of later centuries, as Hungarians and Habsburgs slugged it out during the Rákóczi wars and in the revolutionary year of 1848–9. Much is always made of the

Turkish menace, but in Transylvania just as much protection was needed against nearer neighbours. We know that in 1736 the walls of Mediaș had three large gates, four smaller ones and 19 bastions. The towers were all built by the guilds. In all there were some 33 guilds who contributed to the defence of the city. Stretches of walls and a few towers still survive today. Outside the walls are the barracks built under Empress Maria Theresa to garrison imperial troops.

AROUND THE MAIN SQUARE

The main square, **Piața Regele Ferdinand I** (a Hohenzollern, and the first king of Romania to rule over the vastly enlarged country that resulted from the division of the spoils after the First World War) is slightly shabby but in essence fine, an old market square surrounded by handsome houses with colourful façades and steep tiled roofs, their rooflines all at a pleasing low level. It contains restaurants and hotels, the theatre and a variety of shops. This was always the commercial centre. Seventeen thousand Saxons are recorded as coming for market day here before 1939. The central garden was planted after the Second World War but there is a move afoot among conservators to clear the space once more.

There are a few houses of note around the square. On the east side, no. 1 was the old Town Hall and is now the Library. Through the main entrance there is an attractive galleried interior. No. 3 was a seminary but is now a Montessori School. In the northeast corner of the square, close to the covered way to the citadel, is one of the oldest houses in Mediaș and perhaps once the residence of the donors of the high altarpiece in the citadel church. It is known as the **Schullerhaus** after the 16th-century mayor Johannes Literatus, or Schuller (the 'Schooled'), who built the house by uniting and adapting two earlier buildings.

Keeping the towers of St Margaret's and the citadel in front of you, walk straight ahead out of the northwest end of the main square, up Str. Johannes Honterus (named after the great Transylvanian Saxon cartographer). You will come into the small **Piața George Enescu**, where the Volksbank on the left has a useful ATM. The bank was originally founded as the Albina

(Bee) Bank in the early 20th century, for farmers and small businesses; note the hives decorating the roofline. Before the First World War there were several Austrian and Hungarian banks in the town. Nearby is a shop selling delicious fresh savoury and sweet pastries and there is a good bookshop serving also as the Tourist Information office (Razvan Ghica is most helpful; *T: 0740 498 343 www.mediasturism.ro*). The orange building opposite is a fine former Central European coffee house in Art Nouveau style. Its interior was removed in the '60s.

Before heading up into the citadel, look up to the far end of the square to see the **Liceul Teoretic Stephan Ludwig Roth**, the German-language secondary school, designed in 1909–12 by the Arts and Crafts architect Fritz Balthes (*see p. 75*). It is named after the teacher, reformer, Lutheran pastor and native of Mediaș who was put to death after the Hungarian revolution in 1849 (*see overleaf*). There is a small museum dedicated to him at Str. Johannes Honterus 10.

Nearby is the **market**, across the busy Strada Mihai Eminescu. It operates in two halves, with food produce and handicrafts to the left and to the right mass-manufactured goods. The market is held every day except Sunday, with the main market day having always been Thursday. Supermarkets have now begun to take custom from the stallholders but it is still worth shopping here: products on offer include local herbal remedies, honey, Roma skirts (mass produced, alas), simple doormats of woven straw and carved wooden spoons. On Thursdays in winter they have sellers of fur hats, including the jaunty astrakhan lookalikes, and jackets. The grapes and walnuts are delicious in season. The groups of Roma from nearby Brateiu make a colourful backdrop, especially the women in their long pleated plaid skirts, with contrasting floral-patterned blouses, headscarves and huge shoulder bags—as bold a mixture of design as a Rococo room. If you are buying meat, note that it is not hung, so beef and pork can look remarkably similar. You may be reduced to making animal noises to identify what is on offer. There is a Thursday **flea market** on the eastern outskirts, along the railway line from Brateiu on Strada Georghe Lazar, where you can find textiles.

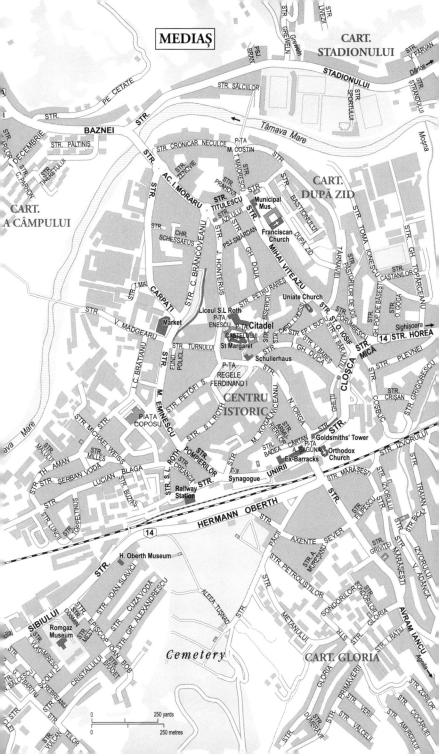

Stephan Ludwig Roth

The Lutheran pastor and teacher Stephan Ludwig Roth was born in Mediaș in 1796, the son of a Lutheran minister and schoolmaster. He won a scholarship to the University of Tübingen and from there went to Switzerland to study under the pedagogue J.H. Pestalozzi, until recalled home by his father. On his return, he took up a post as teacher in Mediaș. He entered the priesthood in 1835, becoming vicar of Nemșa in 1837 and of Moșna ten years later.

All his life, Roth was preoccupied with questions of reform. In Transylvanian schools he endeavoured to introduce physical education and music to a curriculum that concentrated exclusively on books and letters. Seeing how labour-intensive and inefficient was the agriculture of the Siebenbürgen, he put forward ideas on improved crop rotation and plant breeding. Most of his ideas fell of deaf ears and his life might have passed in peaceful failure had it not been for his involvement with the political future of his homeland. In the early 19th century the battle for influence in Transylvania was intense. Saxons did not want to cede their ancestral freedoms either to Hungarian or to Austrian interests. Hungarians in turn feared a too great dominance of Austria.

In 1841, in response to a move to make Hungarian the official language of the region, Roth wrote a famous, impassioned essay: *Der Sprachkampf in Siebenbürgen*. He ends with six points aimed at ensuring that all official business should be rendered intelligble to whichever people— German, Magyar or Wallachian (to use his terminology)—it most concerns. He recommends that correspondence between Tranyslvania and the throne in Vienna should continue to be in Latin. For day to day transactions, he asks that no language should lord it over another and that 'Madjarisch' should not be adopted as the national tongue. For the purposes of communication, there already is, he notes, a common language: Wallachian. Everyone has had to pick it up, since no Vlach speaks anything else. Roth was not suggesting that Wallachian should be enshrined in law as the official language of Transylvania. What he was hoping to demonstrate was the needlessness of giving such status to Hungarian. His aims were conciliatory, not malicious, but he had made enemies. Early in 1849, following a Hungarian victory in their battle against Austria, troops entered Mediaș and calls went out for Saxon rebels to be rounded up. Though an amnesty was announced after the Hungarians advanced to Sibiu, it was not respected and Roth was arrested for sedition and sentenced to death. He was executed by firing squad in Cluj prison in May of the same year.

Scholars have seen Roth's execution as a significant factor in the worsening of Saxon-Magyar relations in Transylvania and an important impetus in the turning of Saxon sympathies toward Vienna, a switch of allegiance which in the end was to prove disastrous to Hungary's hopes of retaining Transylvania. Romanians see him as a champion of their bid for rights, and while Roth certainly sympathised with the Wallachians' lack of protection and a voice, what mainly preoccupied him was the destiny of his own people. Espousing the cause of rights for Transylvanian Vlachs he saw as a way of combating the tide of Magyarisation, which he knew must inevitably negate the freedoms that Saxon Transylvania held so dear. He was a true child of his country: absolutism was anathema to him. Liberal Hungarians also joined their voices to those of the Vlachs, whom they viewed as allies against the Habsburg bulldozer. Neither the Hungarians nor the Saxons can ever have imagined that the Vlachs themselves would end up inheriting the ancestral homeland, uniting it to the Romanian provinces of Wallachia and Moldavia and turning it into a triumphant new nation of their own.

Roth was a humane man, a patriot and an idealist, unjustly done to death by a people in a panic. In a moving last letter to his children, he wrote, 'I did my best for my people, without ever meaning harm to any other'. Sadly his ideas could never have worked. He was pleading for plurality in an age when the clamouring of nationalism had made it impossible and in which, as he dreaded, *potior fit denominatio*. AB

THE CITADEL

Within the citadel walls lies the Saxons' church of St Margaret, surrounded by its own defences, the entry tunnel designed to put invaders at a disadvantage. The tall church tower, almost 70m high, is known as the **Trumpeter's Tower**, from the bugle player who would sound the watch from the top. Its base dates from the 13th century. In the 15th century it was raised to a height of five floors and in 1550 was heightened by three further storeys. In the following year the spire received its four corner turrets, a symbol that the city had the right of adjudication.

If not open, the key is held in the offices close to the east end of the church, which gives you a chance to visit the earliest house, the **Priest House** of 1515. Note too, the towers funded and defended by the guilds of ropemakers and tailors. There are other potent references to the power of the town guilds on the side pews in the church interior. The **church school** is here, within the walls, still teaching in German (this is the kindergarten). Towards the south side of the church is the **Tower of St Mary**, which preserves a vaulted chapel (where during times of plague it is thought that Masses for the dead were held). After the Reformation it was used by those who still clung to the old faith. It has good frescoes of the *Descent from the Cross*, with Mary holding the broken body of Christ. The vault contains the symbols of the Evangelists and around the walls are saints. The whole is decorated with *trompe-l'oeil* Gothic tracery. It is worth asking for the keys to see this example of open-mindedness.

There are also the remains of an interesting **fresco of the *Annunciation*** on the exterior north wall of the east end of the main church and the figure of Christ in a mandorla. This use of external painting is also found elsewhere in the region. It is still in the Western tradition and not influenced by the Eastern Orthodox Church and the painted monasteries of Moldavia.

The church of St Margaret
The interior of St Margaret's is stylistically lopsided, the result of successions of alterations and rebuildings. The nave and south aisle are late 15th century, built in the late Gothic manner of a German hall church; the north aisle is

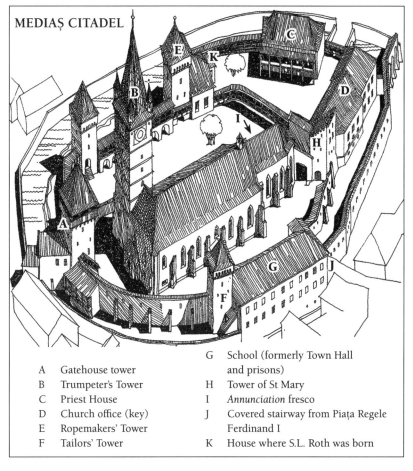

MEDIAȘ CITADEL

A	Gatehouse tower	G	School (formerly Town Hall and prisons)
B	Trumpeter's Tower	H	Tower of St Mary
C	Priest House	I	*Annunciation* fresco
D	Church office (key)	J	Covered stairway from Piața Regele Ferdinand I
E	Ropemakers' Tower		
F	Tailors' Tower	K	House where S.L. Roth was born

earlier and lower, dating to the end of the 14th century. The nave, south aisle and chancel are covered with a net vault, built between 1447 and 1488. Due to the wonderful collection of Anatolian carpets, the magnificent altarpiece of the 1480s, the fine fresco cycles and the memorials, both painted and sculpted, the effect is both sumptuous and interesting. As there is still a thriving Saxon community here, St Margaret's has become the repository of altarpieces and carpets from parishes where there are few, if any, Saxons remaining. Here too, at the east end, is the earliest bronze font in Transylvania, dating to the second half of the 14th century. Above,

Mediaș high altarpiece

Betrayal and arrest	Flagellation	Crowning with Thorns	Ecce Homo
Way to Calvary with St Veronica	Christ Resting while the Cross is made ready to receive Him	Crucifixion	Resurrection
	Last Supper		

in the vault, are the most charming bosses carved and painted with the Agnus Dei, the Virgin Mary and the symbols of the Evangelists.

The great **polyptych on the main altar** is of c. 1485, and is opened twice a year for the main Christian festivals of Christmas and Easter. When open, it displays the sculptured symbols of the Evangelists in quatrefoils on either side of a sculpted Crucifixion, below which are four standing statues of the Evangelists. There has been a suggestion that the quatrefoils came from a 14th-century Crucifix, possibly from the north aisle. The standing Evangelists are modern. The altarpiece when closed (its *Werktagsseite*) shows scenes of Christ's Passion (*diagram and illustration opposite*). The Passion cycle appears to have sat easily with the new Reformed religion, unlike images of saints, so many of which were destroyed in the iconoclasm that affected much of Europe at the time. Seven of the eight Mediaş panels may have been taken from copperplate engravings by Israhel van Meckenem from his large Passion cycle of the 1470/80s, though comparisons can also be drawn with the etchings of Martin Schongauer and with workshop pattern books connected with Vienna, where many artists went to study. It is possible that this altarpiece is by the same workshop as that of the masters who painted the altarpiece for the Schottenstift in Vienna. The Vienna Stephansdom appears in the background in two of the scenes (the *Crucifixion* and the *Christ Resting*). The two donor portraits underneath are beautifully drawn. Dr Emese Sarkadi has suggested that they are father and son, Georgius and Ladislaus Thabiassy, members of a rich patrician family of Mediaş. Georgius was *judex regius*, the royal administrator, in Mediaş, possibly living in the Schuller house. His son, on the left, was a clerk at the court of King Matthias Corvinus, and studied in Vienna.

There are further **pre-Reformation altarpieces** here, from Dupuş, Cenade and Nemşa (the latter may originally have come from Richiş). That from Dupuş is in the north aisle and is dated to 1522 but may be earlier. On either side of the *Crucifixion* are angels with symbols of the Passion. The other four panels show different feasts: the Last Supper, the Fall of Manna, the Passover and Abraham and Melchisedech. Below is a fine *Lamentation over the Dead Christ*. The frame is interesting, similar in style to the wonderful organ case which makes a journey to Dupuş so worthwhile (*see p. 136*). When the altar is closed there are representations of eight Passion scenes. In the sacristy, which has a fine net vault and aumbry cupboard, there is another early 16th-century altarpiece, once again with panels of the Passion and a fine predella. The altarpiece from Cenade, of 1520, is in the vestry.

The collection of **Anatolian rugs** in St Margaret's is one of the most important in Transylvania. They were discovered stored in the vestry in the last century and are therefore in relatively good condition. They consist of three Holbein rugs from the 16th century or possibly even earlier (*for more on rugs, see p. 203*). Along the side of the choir are hung a wonderful series of white-ground Selendi rugs with bird, çintamani and scorpion patterns. There are also a few Lotto rugs from the beginning of the 17th century. Some of the rugs have been brought here for safe-keeping from the church in Richiş. One of them, with a scorpion pattern, was included in a Budapest exhibition in 1914. Such items are a reminder that Transylvania was an important conduit for trade between Christian West and Islamic East.

There are some fine **funerary monuments** against the sanctuary walls, typical of Transylvania and in particular of the sculptors of Sibiu and Sighişoara. Note especially that of Barbara Theilesius (c. 1627) by the sculptor Elias Nicolai, who introduced a late Mannerist/early Baroque style to this artform (*for more on Elias, see p. 89*). There are also fine small painted memorial plaques on the walls of the church.

Most of the **frescoes** are in the north aisle or north wall of the nave. Some are faded and difficult to read. There is one of particular drama showing the *Ten Thousand Martyrs on Mt Ararat*, impaled on thorn trees and writhing with horrible contortions typical of the late Gothic period. In the spandrels is the *Betrayal of Christ* and Judas hanging himself. In the north aisle a splendidly attired lady with a seven-tiered crown is an allegory of Ecclesia, the Church, accompanied by the theological virtues, Faith, Hope and Charity. A *Tree of Jesse* covers two bays on the north wall of the nave. The early frescoes include a *Doubting Thomas* to the west.

The Baroque organ was restored in the 1920s and the pews have hinged backs so can face east or west. The pulpit baldachin is of the same period as the organ case.

OTHER SIGHTS OF MEDIAȘ

The Municipal Museum and its district

The museum (*Str. Mihai Viteazul 46, T: 0269 841 299; open Tues–Sun 9–5*) is housed in the 15th-century Franciscan cloisters. The friars were expelled at the Reformation in the 1530s but were invited to return under the Habsburgs in the 1720s as part of Charles VI's efforts to bring the last, late flowering of the Counter-Reformation to the eastern edges of his realm. The **Franciscan church** remains open for Catholic worship and has a simple Baroque interior.

The **Municipal Museum** itself needs a bit of refurbishment. Doubt over the ownership of the building has been resolved: it has now been returned to the Franciscan order and things are on the move, but it will take time, since until recently no one had either the money or the inclination to do anything. The museum presents three collections in one: ethnographical, archaeological and on the history of the town. There is a good model of the walled town, which gives an excellent sense of Mediaș as a great Saxon stronghold. It also has a collection of silver found in excavations in Șeica Mică. It is worth a visit but not a must.

Not far from the museum, on the corner of Str. Mihai Viteazul and Str. Cardinal Hossu, is the **Uniate church**. Uniate churches were typically the first places of worship permitted for Romanians within the walls of a Saxon town. The church is a charming late Neoclassical building of 1826 at the head of a wedge-shaped square planted with grass and shrubs. In the middle of these gardens is a bust of the influential Romanian poet, novelist and journalist Mihai Eminescu (1850–89). The Hungarian school is nearby. All around this area are some charming streets leading back to the citadel.

The Orthodox church and synagogue

Visit too the **Orthodox church**, built in 1929–35, well after Transylvania's unification with Romania, and dedicated to the archangels Michael and Gabriel. It sits defiantly opposite the Saxons' **Goldsmiths' Tower**, outside the walls on Strada Cloșca. It appears only to be open for services.

View of the interior of the Mediaș synagogue.

On the corner of Str. Unirii and Str. Mihail Kogălniceanu is the **synagogue**, built in the 1890s in an eclectic, faintly Moorish style typical of the period throughout the Austro-Hungarian Empire.

Jews played an important part in the Kingdom of Hungary and then in Transylvania. There has been a community in Mediaș since the 17th century, with many living in the neighbouring villages. After 1848, when Jews were given permission to live in the town, the community began to grow. The main patrons of the synagogue were the Czitron family and others, including the Kappels and the Bäumels. At the time of writing there were just four Jews left in Mediaș and the community had been dismantled. The synagogue is owned by the Jewish Federation. The interior is fine and restoration is starting with the archives, with assistance from the MET. There has been no rabbi here for 40 years and there has been difficulty raising funds but the synagogue has had an excellent response from volunteers from the local schools and the Rotary Club, amongst others. The archives are in German, Romanian and Yiddish. Most of these are upstairs in the women's gallery. All the archives are going to be digitised and there will be a small research centre here. The ritual bath and school await restoration. The baths were open to the public until the '60s but are now under separate ownership.

Although the Jews in Romania as a whole suffered the same devastating pogroms as elsewhere in Central and Eastern Europe, the community in Mediaș managed to escape the worst of the atrocities. That there are scarcely any Jews remaining here today is partly because, like the Saxons, they chose to go, in their case to Israel.

Around the railway station

One of the most interesting, inventive minds from Transylvania, whose impact was felt far beyond, was that of the physicist and engineer **Hermann Oberth** (1894–1989), who was born in Sibiu and lived in Sighișoara and Mediaș. His house is marked by a model of the rocket he invented. It stands in the garden of the modest bungalow overlooking the railway station. There is also a small museum in the house, though for some opaque reason, it is never open. There is a good account of his life and work in the museum in Sighișoara.

Set up away from the main road, near the cemetery and the Oberth house, is an elegant villa of the early 20th century. It served time as the maternity hospital and has now been restored by **Romgaz** as a museum. This has an interesting display on the history of gas discovery in Transylvania. It is well worth a visit even if this is not your subject (*www.muzeulgazelor.ro*).

On this road you will pass the **Vitrometan glass shop** (*Șos. Sibiului 31–3*) and you can continue to the remarkable church and village of Ighișu Nou (*see p. 162*).

It is always worth visiting the **cemetery** in a Transylvanian town, and Mediaș is no exception. It contains, within different sections, Saxons, Romanians, Hungarians and Roma.

Other shops offering made-in-Mediaș goods include one selling enamelled tinware (*Str. Carpați 19, www.emailul.ro*); a saddle maker (Velicea Constantin; *Str. Valea Adâncă 35, velicea-saddles.ro*); and the stove factory, one of the first of the private enterprises in Mediaș after 1990. It makes copies of Transylvanian stoves (Fabrica de Teracotă; *Str. Stadionului 55, www.teracota. ro*).

Goldsmiths in Transylvania

As you explore the towns and villages of the Târnava Mare Valley, you will notice some fine bronze bells and, in one or two places, bronze baptismal fonts of high quality. Raw materials, innovative craftsmen and willing patrons were all here in the Kingdom of Hungary. And bronze was not the only metal they worked. Today some of the finest examples of work made by Transylvanian goldsmiths, either Saxon or Hungarian, is found in the Esztergom Treasury in Hungary. One of the most photographed pieces of metalwork is the bronze equestrian statue of St George commissioned by the King of Bohemia for Prague Castle in 1373 from the two Kolozsvári brothers in Cluj. It shows an openness to international styles as well as revealing the standard of metalworking in Transylvania.

The mineral wealth in Transylvania is still rich. The Romans famously extracted gold from Roșia Montană, where their workings still survive. The Hungarian kingdom provided Europe with much of its precious metal before silver and gold were discovered in the New World.

Some of the finest metalworking in Europe was found in the Meuse area from the 12th century. The goldsmiths here were attempting to imitate Byzantine cloisonné enamels and from this they developed the technique of champlevé. It was from the Meuse region that many of the 'Saxons' came to Transylvania at the invitation of Géza II.

The first guilds are those of the German goldsmiths in Cluj from 1473. Until the mid-15th century goldsmithing in Transylvania was practised only by Saxons. From the middle of the 16th century Hungarian goldsmiths make their appearance at Cluj. Gradually goldsmiths grew in importance socially, sitting on town councils (one such is Sebastian Hann in Sibiu). Some were also ennobled. The first hallmarks were introduced in the 16th century. A special feature attributed to the Hungarian goldsmiths was *Drahtemail*, enamelled wire, and *Perlenfiligran*, pearl filigree, known as *modo transilvano*.

Gold cup with a relief of Solomon and the Queen of Sheba,
by the Transylvanian goldsmith Sebastian Hann (1644–1713).

Two towns in the Târnava Mare Valley, Sighișoara and Mediaș, and one very near it, Sibiu, were among the most important centres for precious metal processing. Their skilled production was highly sought after. Transylvania had to pay tribute to the Porte in such treasure. Craftsmen and miners were sent abroad to Russia and Vienna, Rome, Lviv and Augsburg. The courts of Gábor Bethlen and the Apafis had treasuries full of Transylvanian goldsmiths' work. In 1624 Gábor Bethlen ordered two gold tankards for his wedding feast from the goldsmiths of Mediaș. György Rákóczi I, another prince of Transylvania's golden age, was also a patron of the Mediaș guild.

When the Ottoman *serdar* Köse Ali Pasha invaded Transylvania in 1660, Sibiu had to pay protection money. It seems they found it impossible to mint coins fast enough from the vast quantity brought by 'noblemen who melted their gold and silver jewels, and by the bourgeois and peasants who melted their wives' belts and brooches.' (from Jenő Radisics: *Chefs-d'oeuvre d'art de la Hongrie*, Budapest 1901).

BAZNA & BOIAN

The two villages of Bazna (Baaßen/Bázna or Felsőbajom) and Boian (Bonnesdorf/Alsóbajom) are administratively linked but have had different histories and fortunes. One was a free village, the other feudal (*see box*). Both merit a visit.

BAZNA

Bazna was a 'free village', first documented in 1271 when it was given by the King of Hungary to the Saxon immigrants. In later years, this community was to benefit greatly from the development of the gas industry. In the 17th century (1671) it was reported that shepherds talked of seeing bubbling earth. In 1688 a pharmacist from Sibiu, Georg Wette, wrote a study of the phenomenon, which he called 'burning water': *De Aquis ardendibus*. Bazna was at last to capitalise on this when in 1913 it became the first village in Transylvania to get gas lighting, a tremendous coup for the community. Due to this head start the village still retains a sense of prosperity, being well laid-out and cared for. There is a 19th-century feel that still lingers here, with a sense that people used to promenade along the gaslit walks of the small park.

There are two main reasons to come here today: to visit the magnificent church and to enjoy the healing waters of the spa. The waters were well known in the 18th century and were analysed from 1762–79 by Andreas Gaspari. There is also an Orthodox Monastery. B&Bs are plentiful (*see p. 12*) and there is a good Tourist Information kiosk in the middle of the village, behind the chemist. Here is also a nice little bar selling locally-made țuică, plum brandy (you can visit the spa to work off the effects).

The church gateway is impressive. Helpful telephone numbers posted here are for Mr J. Eugen (*T: 0742 319 267*) or Albert Binder (*T: 0269 850 101*). Mr Binder is the churchwarden and can also, if given notice, organise lunch and a B&B.

Free Villages on Crown Land

The Saxon communities, due to the circumstances of their arrival in Transylvania and their relationship with the kings of Hungary, were in a position unlike that of the Szeklers or the Vlachs, as they were invited to settle on Crown Lands.

When Géza II (1141–61) invited 'hospites' from the Rhine/Meuse region and Flanders as settlers to strengthen the economy with their skills as farmers and craftsmen, he was following King Stephen's precept that 'a kingdom of one single language and with one single tradition is weak and frail, while a plurality of languages and traditions nurtures experience and contributes to the welfare of the country and the glory of the realm.' Instead of distributing land among the nobility, as was normal at the time, Géza gave it directly to the Saxons.

The yeoman *hospites* had self-governing status and were answerable only to the king. They had the right to elect their priests, to whom they paid tithes. They could also elect their judges. Their allegiance to the king was shown in the form of duties and liabilities such as military service and tax paid to the crown.

Until the 16th century these freedoms were continually challenged by the county elites, who attempted to grab feudal rights. Some succeeded, such as the Apafis. In the 13th and 14th centuries more than a quarter of the ethnic Saxons were hired by noblemen to settle on their estates, but with no guarantee of the freedoms that were given by law to their fellow settlers on Crown Land.

The **church** was rebuilt as a hall church at the beginning of the 16th century, with further defence in the heightened chancel. At the east end is a fine 1504 representation of the *Man of Sorrows* decorating the aumbry cupboard, which unusually retains its ironwork grille. The *Man of Sorrows* has been taken from the same pattern as that at Ighișu Nou, which is of 1491 (*see p. 162*). The choir stalls are early, dated to 1503, and are fine, with a Pelican in her Piety in the centre of the frieze. They are a version of those at Richiș and Biertan. The altar is late Baroque and the organ is by Johannes Hahn (1757). The pulpit is dated 1781, by Georgius Schuller, and painted by Stephan Valepagi (the latter Latinises his name). There are good Baroque galleries in the nave, which has a net vault. Unusually, the Second World War Roll of Honour is a photographic record of those who fought with the German army and those who died in Soviet Russia in the deportations. This emphasises, far more than the usual listings by house number, the tragedy of the Saxon population in the 20th century.

The **spa**, which is the only one at this end of the Târnava Valley, was opened in 1814 under the ownership of the Saxon community, giving the Saxons a good income. The water is renowned for its curative properties and runs off the sulphur springs that are so plentiful in the area. It is also known for its healing mud (I went out of season so I cannot give a report on the effects). There is one indoor pool (*open 10am–9pm*) and two outdoor pools and the staff are friendly and white-coated. There is also a bar and a restaurant open until 11pm. Some years ago the head of the Romanian Tourist Board in London suggested that if anyone wanted to invest in Romania, they should invest in a health spa. She might have been right. Spas were once a way of life in Central Europe and some of the buildings, especially the Art Nouveau baths of the early 20th century, are very fine. Waters rich in sulphur and mineral salts are plentiful. Alas, the buildings in Bazna are very utilitarian—but I would recommend a day spent here before the next part of your journey.

BOIAN

The key to the church in neighbouring Boian, 5km away, can be collected from the Tourist Information kiosk in Bazna. There is a rough road between the two, with remains of old and degenerate state farms; but do go: the church is such an interesting shape.

Boian has been grand but is so no longer. It appears to have no Saxons remaining, but the church, although crumbling, is interesting. It was given by King Matthias Corvinus as feudal property to the Moldavian prince

The church of Boian, down-at-heel but still proud behind its walls.

Stephen the Great (the Ștefan cel Mare after whom many streets and squares in Romania are named). His coat of arms, an ox head with the star, moon and sun, is mounted on the gate tower in the curtain wall. The original folding altar of the 14th century is now in the Brukenthal Museum in Sibiu. There is a remarkably-framed Baroque altar of 1772 in the choir. This was painted by Stephan Valepagi of Mediaş, whose work is also in Bazna. There is something most satisfactory about this stolid church and its well-preserved polygonal defensive wall, though the impact of it is now lessened by the ugly school building next door.

A good time to leave Boian is at the end of the day, in time to meet the herds of buffalo lumbering home to be milked. Most are going to individual houses, where their owners are waiting like parents for the school bus; and many to the state farm, which now belongs to the village. The Saxons have a saying, 'as dark as a buffalo', likening the all-surrounding blackness of a starless Transylvanian night to the buffalo's impenetrable hide. We got lost and drove onto an old track, meeting shepherds and deep ruts by the light of the moon. Then on to Bazna and so to Mediaş.

IGHIŞU NOU, MOŞNA, ALMA VII
& AN EXCURSION TO CINCU

The village of **Ighişu Nou (Eibesdorf/Szászivánfalva)** lies to the south of Mediaş off the main road between Blaj and Sighişoara. The road through Mediaş will take you past the house where the rocket science pioneer Hermann Oberth lived (*see p. 155*). The left turn to Ighişu Nou is in unattractive suburbs by a petrol station, Lukoil, and is signposted.

The land around the settlement, in the early 14th century, was owned by the Hungarian Apafi family (*see p. 100*), but it later gained the status of free village (*see p. 159*) and was given to the Saxon settlers.

The country road to the church runs alongside the town reservoir (really used for fishing) and past some new and expensive houses. The church key is held at house no. 41 in Strada Şcolii, just up from the church. The house courtyard itself is worth the visit. It is most picturesque, with many (largely friendly) dogs.

The church and its frescoes

Dedicated to the Blessed Virgin, the Gothic hall church can be dated to the late 14th or early 15th century. It is surrounded by its defending walls. The massive west tower was added later in the 15th century. It has two medieval bells and a third bell was added in 1929. There is a medieval granary. Recent restoration has left part of the sandstone wall without a lime wash, on the side of the entrance tower. This is presumably to illustrate building methods in the late Middle Ages. The sandstone, often from the Făgăraş Mountains, is typical of Saxon church buildings. Window embrasures are also of great blocks of sandstone. The west door is richly ornamented. There is a simple vault over the chancel, heightened in the late 15th century for further defence. The choir window tracery is good, with interesting sculpture. The aumbry cupboard is dated to 1491 (it is mirrored in the church at Bazna). There is a fine sedile in the south wall with a triangular pediment and late Gothic tracery. The altar is late

IGHIȘU NOU

Baroque. Johannes Hahn provided the organ in 1775 and a new pulpit was installed in 1863.

The current glory of this church, revealed in November 2014, are the frescoes on the north wall of the nave, in the chancel and on the chancel arch. There is no evidence of painting on the south wall. The top register on the north wall portrays the legend of St Ladislaus rescuing the maiden from the Cumans (*for the story, see p. 52*). The next register portrays scenes of martyrdom, including that of St Catherine, and possibly John the Baptist, with a table set reminiscent of a Last Supper. Below that are scenes of saints and the bottom section of the wall is a *trompe-l'oeil* dado of

On the way to the church at Ighișu Nou,
having successfully located the keeper of the key.

brightly painted architecture. The chancel arch has splendid angels with trumpets rousing the dead, on both sides. The chancel vault contains the Evangelists and Prophets. It is as yet unknown where the artists came from but the work is stylistically close to the cycle in the chancel at Mălâncrav (*see p. 92*), which was also held by the Apafi family. It would be a surprise if it were not by the same workshop.

The Monumenta organisation, run by chief restorers Pál Binder and Lóránt Kiss, was responsible for removing the layer of lime wash which covered this remarkable cycle of frescoes. The whole project, which also included the restoration of the church and tower, was funded by the EU.

MOȘNA

Moșna (Meschen/Muzsna) is on the back road from Mediaș near to Alma Vii and Pelișor. Even if you have already seen plenty of fortified churches and they are all beginning to merge into each other in your mind, you must still visit Moșna. The church has one of the most beautiful and sophisticated interiors in the valley.

Moșna is a large village. Employment is still mainly agricultural and there are few shops. Scarcely any of the original Saxon families remain. People from Mediaș are starting to buy houses here and commute. The old German *Gymnasium* (grammar school) and primary school remain. The former is named after Stephan Ludwig Roth (*see p. 146*).

The citadel

The size of the citadel and the elegance of the church speak volumes about past glory. The citadel, begun in 1520, is hugely dramatic. There is a sense here of the whole community being protected—but at the same time one cannot help wondering how much was to show off local wealth, as with the towers of San Gimignano. The wall defence system now contains a small museum with agricultural implements of the Saxon period as well as Romanian. The implements have been rescued from local dumps and the museum is used to show the local school children how land, religion and the state organisation worked together. The Saxons, in the main, left after

1990. The citadel is being restored, a huge project. A plaque at the church entrance commemorates the visit of HRH the Prince of Wales in 1991. This was his first visit to Transylvania and Moşna is proud of this. It is a timely reminder that Prince Charles was among the first to realise the importance and fragility of the Siebenbürgen region and to take steps to safeguard it.

Two of the citadel's towers have been restored, the Bacon Tower and City Hall Tower, and are now open to the public. It is also possible to have a meal in them. The local cheese and wines are delicious. There is village bacon hanging in the Bacon Tower and the temperature ensures that it keeps perfectly. Traditionally, every villager hung their smoked pork in the village's Bacon Tower and in times of trouble it provided a vital food supply. The sides of bacon were numbered according to the number of the village house that provided it, in case of theft, and there was a villager in charge of the tower who oversaw fair play.

Inside the church
The interior of this hall church looks to Bohemia and upper Hungary (modern Slovakia) for inspiration. It has a light elegance about it and an intimacy. It was developed c. 1485 by the stonemason known as Andreas Lapicida (lit. 'Andrew the Stone-cutter') on an earlier site (there are fragments of a 14th-century chapel in the north corner of the enceinte) and dedicated to the Virgin. He seems to have been responsible for the pulpit, the vestry portal, sedile and aumbry cupboard.

After the thunder of the defence system of the outer walls, the interior of the church, in contrast, is delicate and sophisticated. Beautiful alternating brick columns, some of them twisted, support the roof vault. The easternmost boss at the chancel end, representing the Virgin and Child, marks the end of the building campaign. The boss is dated 1525, which, 30 years or so after Lapicida, is hard to explain unless there was lack of money. But as Ciprian Firea points out, there was an earthquake between 1500 and 1536. The other shield on the ceiling boss has the letters AVID, perhaps standing for 'Alexander Vtrivsque Iuris Doctor', referring to a Dean Alexander, doctor of Canon Law. Firea suggests that this could be Alexander de Olczna, who donated a vineyard to finance a sung Mass for

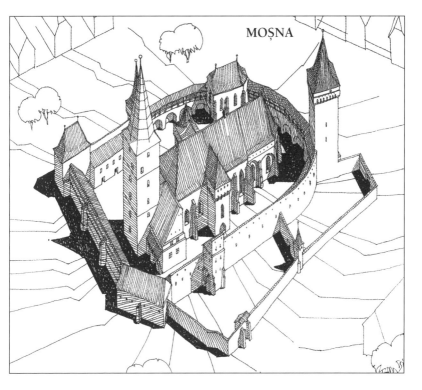

his family and uncle, Johannes de Olczna, also a priest of Moșna and Sibiu.

There is a beautiful tester over the pulpit topped by St Michael, made in 1703 by Johann Folbarth from Sighișoara. (Research needs to be done on his workshop as attributions to Folbarth cover a wide range of dates.) The organ is being restored. The high altarpiece of *Doubting Thomas* (1521), signed by Vincentius of Sibiu, is now in the church at Cincu (*see p. 175*).

Around the village

There is a very active mayor in Moșna (also in charge of Alma Vii and Nemșa) and under him the Town Hall has begun an imaginative Eco-tour. The **Town Hall** itself, dating from 1860, was built by a Saxon—with a deep wine cellar—and then given to the community. Tickets for the tour can be obtained in the **Eco Museum** in an old Saxon house, no. 524 in the main street (again restored with help from the MET). There are additions at the back of the farmyard for a small conference room and next to it a library with internet access. This has been supported by funding from the ASTRA Library in Sibiu. The children have chairs and the grown-ups sit on straw bales. There is even a village newspaper.

Walk around the village and visit the corn mill, cheese maker, etc. As part of the Eco-tour, visit the farm at no. 273 (Ioan Diac); the mill at no. 459 (Mihai Suciu); the 'House with Bee Hives' at no. 215 (Ana Popa); the 'Beam House' at no. 206 (Romulus Diac); you will find a bed at the Priest's House at no. 259 (Marianne Rempel; *T: 0744 624 776*).

On the way out of the village towards Richiş is the deconsecrated **Uniate church**, with a beautiful simple interior. Only a few hundred Uniates remained in the village in the 19th century. By 1946, the handful that remained were imprisoned. The priest was sent to certain death building the Danube Canal. Yet the village has not let this charming little church fall down and the mayor himself has been supportive. The Uniate

A white cabbage attired for the Moşna Festival.

Shepherd with his donkey.

community here was always poor. There are prints, not painted icons, on the iconostasis. The simple altar is covered in wooden crosses. Next door is the brand new **Orthodox church**, built on an earlier site.

Visit too Willie and Lavinia Schuster at Str. Cetății 543, who have blazed a trail with their cheeses and cheese tastings and wonderful rose-petal jam. Their opposition to fracking was featured on television and has brought many Romanian visitors to Moşna (*for contact details, see p. 13*).

The area around Moşna and Nemşa was important for wine-growing. The ground, it is said, is sweet, and produces cabbages as good as the grapes. There is a **Cabbage Festival** here each October. It began from necessity, as a way of promoting a vegetable that everyone needed to sell. But it proved such a success that it has been going for eight years. It is to be hoped that the revival of the narrow-gauge railway from Agnita to Sibiu will bring tourists to this area. Again, this is being assisted by the Mihai Eminescu Trust.

The workforce in the village boasts five carpenters, two blacksmiths, three masons and a tinsmith who will make your guttering. There are ten shepherds and each of the villages in the constituency has two foresters.

ALMA VII

Alma Vii (Almen/Szászalmád) is considered one of the most beautiful of the villages in the environs of Mediaş—and in this region, competition for such an accolade is fierce. It is first documented in 1289. Within living memory, the village was divided into a Saxon area around the church, a Romanian quarter around the Romanian school and a gypsy area on the fringes of the settlement. All this broke down in the 1990s after the Revolution. The Saxons, who planned the wide verges on either side of the stream and the grand flanking houses, have gone. Now there are some foreigners in the village but also many Romanians and perhaps, as in many other villages, the community spirit is not as strong as it was.

Taken as a whole, though, the wide verges, restored bridges, repainted houses, trees and waterfowl seem to present the perfect bucolic idyll and a lesson in good restoration. The MET has brought in Colin Richards MBE, head of Historical Environment at Shropshire Council (UK), to carry out training sessions for local apprentices in building restoration and furniture-making. He was involved in reconstructing the fine but simple wooden bridges across the stream running down the main street and in re-making the handsome courtyard doorways, which are such a feature of this village. Mr Richards has also started brick and tile kilns on the traditional model. The Romanian Schoolhouse has already been restored by the MET and now takes in guests, as do two further houses in the village. Beware: if you have problems getting into your lodging, it is because the locks are 'Saxon' and take some getting used to. Since this is a village which used to produce wine, grapes are once more a feature of the decoration of many façades.

The church and citadel
The 14th-century single-aisled church stands on the tallest hill, overlooking the main village street, and is reached by a path running up the side of

Interior of Alma Vii church. Left behind in the organ loft is the music for the Lutheran chorale *Gelobet seist du, Jesu Christ*: Praise to thee, O Christ.

the grand Priest House. Further defences and an encircling wall were added to the church in the 16th century. The asymmetry of the whole and the mixture of brick and sandstone enhance the picturesqueness of these fortifications. The entry tower of the citadel has protruding corner bastions on its four corners, echoing the tourelles of a Scottish keep. This is unique in Transylvania. The citadel is now the focus of one of the most impressive restoration projects in this region, being carried out under the supervision of the MET. The funding is from Iceland, Liechtenstein and Norway through the EEA and a private donation. As an example of the care given to authenticity of materials, the bricks and tiles are from kilns in Bățani and Sighișoara, all hand-made, and the woodwork throughout is constructed with the ancient technique of mortice and tenon joint. On one of the towers, storks have made their nest for generations. Since the

ALMA VII

Banners embroidered with verses from Scripture are common features of the Saxon churches in the Târnava Valley. Here at Alma Vii, the congregtion was exhorted to be 'Rejoicing in hope, patient in tribulation, instant in prayer' (Romans 12:12).

restoration of the roof, the nest has been put back. The storks' return is awaited. The church within the citadel is undergoing emergency repairs only for the foreseeable future.

Inside the church, much has changed from the medieval original. The organ is of 1791. In terms of the architecture, the original net vault and the choir ceiling were replaced and a gallery was built, possibly evidence of wealth and a growing population. There are no Saxons left in the village now and the restoration programme of the citadel complex as a whole involves wide-ranging plans for alternative future use. The four defensive towers, all different in form, size and original function, are to be museums. A guesthouse is planned and, as the kitchen in the citadel retains its baking oven, guests and villagers are to be invited to make their own bread. A performance area is also planned for the citadel (*for visits to the citadel, email contact@almavii.ro or go to www.almavii.ro*).

Excavations within the walls have discovered the remains of the village cemetery of the 14th century.

From Alma Vii you can take a beautiful walk to Richiş and on further to Biertan, through rolling open country and wonderful beech forests. There are orchards, once Saxon then state-owned, with apples, pears, plums and cherries. The soil around these parts, which can grow everything from grapes to cabbages, made a major impact on life here. In the area there are three main *stâne*, or sheepfolds.

Alternatively, if the missing original altarpiece from Moşna church has piqued your curiosity, you can make an excursion east and southeastwards across country to Cincu, where it is proudly displayed.

CINCU

Cincu (Großschenk/Nagysink) is not in the Târnava Valley. However, its wonderful altarpiece was painted for Moşna, which is.

Cincu, once a huge and commercially strong village, lies on the road to Făgăraş on the river Olt. Now the site of a large NATO exercise camp, it was, along with Sibiu and Nocrich, one of the earliest of the Saxon settlements of the end of the 12th century. Before the Second World War, the town had two banks and seven shops. The church community once numbered a thousand. Today, the defending walls around the church are largely demolished, the Saxon kindergarten and school are in a mixed state of repair and the roof of the Bacon Tower has fallen in. Press on, though. The church amply rewards a visit.

The church
The curator is Mrs Friderike Pall at house no. 272; T: 0268 244 192 or 0787 887 124 (mobile). The daughter of the caretaker speaks excellent English and is willing to guide around the church. A B&B is run from the Priest House.
The church, dedicated to the Virgin Mary, was an early foundation and has traces of Romanesque round-headed arches and scalloped capitals with incised decoration. In the gallery the round-headed arches were continued in later rebuilds. There is a date in the choir of 1522. The overall impression is one of grandeur. A fine net vault unifies the whole. Most of the original seating is retained and it is worth taking a moment to imagine how the

View of Cincu, with the church on its hill.

church would have looked when filled with men, women and children all seated in their ordained places according to their status and most in traditional costume. Some idea of how the priest looked is found in the Elias Nicolai (*see p. 89*) monument to Paulus Whonner (c. 1639) at the east end. An idea of the diversity of the guilds that once operated here can be gained from the insignia painted, unusually, on the hat stands on the walls above the pews. These include carpenters, metal workers, barrel makers, shoe makers and cloth workers.

There is a tunnel leading from the church crypt into the village. It is said that there are 7km of tunnels in Cincu. There is also a well near the base of the pulpit for supplies during a siege. The pulpit itself is of 1649. The church carpets are now in the Black Church in Brașov.

The altarpiece

In 1722, the citizens of Cincu decided to remove their Gothic altarpiece and replace it with the remarkable (if rather provincial) altarpiece of

The Virgin Mary (c. 1460) from the predella of the altarpiece at Cincu.

Doubting Thomas which they bought from the church in Moşna for 32 florins. It is a colourful work of the late Northern Renaissance and early Baroque, a confection of three parts assembled here in the 18th century. The parts are as follows: the central panel of *Doubting Thomas* with its lunette above and narrow predella below; a second predella below the first; and the frame.

The **lower predella**, showing the *Man of Sorrows* flanked by the Virgin and St John, is very fine. This must be of the late 15th century (it is dated by Dr Emese Sarkadi to 1460). Might this have been from the original Gothic altarpiece which the Moşna panel replaced? Above it is a narrow panel featuring the busts of 14 saints, as if in conversation, an unusual predella to the main panel of *Doubting Thomas*, which shows Christ thrusting Thomas' hand into his wound. Above, in a lunette, much more vigorous in style, is *St Christopher with the Christ Child* and at the side a possible donor, a monk. The main panel is signed 'Vincentius faciebat 1521'. Vincentius has been credited with painting the central panel, lunette and predella. It is assumed that he had a workshop in Sibiu, although he possibly trained in Vienna. He was influenced by Dürer and like some Mannerist painters, his style is characterised by the strange treatment of space and proportions. The altarpiece originally also incorporated a carved *Virgin and Child*, which Sigismund Kornis, Governor of Transylvania from 1713, took for his private collection in Cluj.

The frame dates from the time of the altarpiece's installation here, being of the 1720s. It cost the burghers of Cincu 100 florins. It is marvellous, with carved scrolling foliage surrounding roundels, perhaps of prophets, but these are now difficult to read.

The road into Cincu, if you are coming from the north, takes you through fine farming country and through **Agnita (Agnetheln/Szentágota)**, where there is an imposing Saxon church. There was also a narrow-gauge railway to Sighişoara which the MET, among others, have plans to reinstate. **Dealu Frumos (Schönberg/Lesses)** and **Merghindeal (Mergenthal/Morgonda)** also have fortified churches. Dealu Frumos has a Community Hall designed by the architect Fritz Balthes (*see p. 75*).

WESTWARDS TO VALEA VIILOR

As you wend your way westwards along the Târnava Valley from Mediaș to Blaj, numerous side roads offer opportunities for exploring. This chapter makes brief mention of some of the villages along those routes.

TÂRNAVA AND COPȘA MICĂ

The village of **Târnava (Großprobstdorf/Nagyekemező)** sits in a wide valley growing maize (the village's Hungarian name means 'Great Plough Field'). Its ploughshares were beaten into swords in March of 1849 during the Hungarian war of independence. The poet Sándor Petőfi, who fought here, dedicated a poem to the battle, in which he describes himself as intoxicated by smoke and the stench of blood, rushing heedlessly forward to live or die. Four months later he was killed in another battle at Albești (*see p. 59*). From the 1420s, the community paid its tithes to Sibiu. The road runs parallel to the railway line, which is set to be upgraded in 2017. The river has often burst its banks causing great destruction. Since the 1980s measures have been taken, including dams, to prevent this happening.

The area around **Copșa Mică (Kleinkopisch/Kiskapus)** was one of the first to be developed for gas. In fact, one of the wells blew in 1933 and continued to burn for seven years. It was said you could read a book in Mediaș at night by the flames from Copșa Mică. Under the Communists, Copșa Mică became home to a chemical plant and a blacking factory. It remained a byword for pollution until the 1990s. It was said that within five minutes of leaving the house your clothes were black, and respiratory problems were commonplace. In the early 1990s the factory was privatised and a filter fitted to the chimney. Copșa Mică is full of state housing now, in nice colours, but in the main it is still a testimony to the ill-conceived industrial plans that were foisted upon these beautiful valleys. The old factories may have been demolished but the ground is polluted. There have been several projects aimed at cleaning it up, including planting

Burning gas well at Copşa Mică in 1938.

special crops to extract the heavy metals. The idea is that the crops are then harvested and destroyed, but no one seems to be sure whether the plan was ever put into practice. It is rumoured, though, that a field of carrots is heavier around Copşa Mică than elsewhere.

Turn off in Copşa Mică down to the south, to Valea Viilor. The land on either side of the road in this broad valley is rather unkept at first, and then the beech forests appear again and some pastures with a state farm. There are vast hectares of strip farming on both sides with fruit and walnut trees lining the road. The fruits are free for anyone to collect.

VALEA VIILOR

Valea Viilor (Wurmloch/Nagybaromlak) is a mixture of Saxon and Romanian houses with a small Hungarian minority. The Romanian name means 'Valley of the Vineyards'. The Saxon name, literally 'Worm Hole', has been interpreted as deriving from 'Warm Hole' and thus as a reference to the gas, already noted by shepherds in the 17th century. In fact it is more likely to be a corruption of the Hungarian *baromlak* (rendered in early Romanian documents as *vorumloc*), which means 'Abode of Cattle'. Valea Viilor is altogether a more poetic compromise, although the past prosperity of the community was due to wine and agriculture in equal measure.

The village itself stretches out down the main road in typical linear fashion, but the church is attractive. (*The key is with Mrs Schneider at no. 211. The suggestion on the notice board is to go the Town Hall beside the church and they will telephone her. It is really worth going to the trouble to do this.*) There is a fine gallery in the church tower, which has been newly restored. Built on an earlier site, in the 14th century, the church was expanded in 1500 into a church-fortress: notice the great height of the defensive east end, rising high above the nave. Today it is listed by UNESCO and has received international funding as it was so affected by the pollution from Copşa Mică.

The church is fortified but alas has lost many of the surrounding storerooms within the walls. They were demolished in 1966–7. I recommend climbing to the top of the defensive east end of the church, where the wall walk has been restored. Note the portcullis of 1525 (in the defensive wall at the entrance). Inside the church, the choir has a net vault. There is an aumbry cupboard of 1504, choir stalls of 1528 and an altar

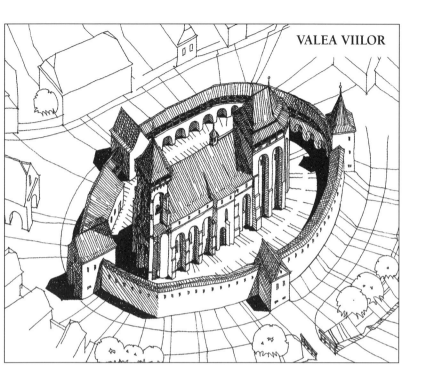

VALEA VIILOR

of 1779 by Stephan Folberth, who did much work in the neighbouring parishes. He came from Sighișoara. The pulpit is of 1746 and the organ of 1708.

It is difficult today to get a sense of the real importance and wealth of Valea Viilor before the last war. However, a young pastor from the Banat, Father Nagelbach, who had difficulties in the '30s because of his anti-Nazi sympathies, describes his life here, beginning with his election by the Saxons (he was a relative foreigner) and his welcome by all members of the community, including the Romanian churches, who did not speak to one another (one was Orthodox, the other Greek Catholic). Nagelbach writes of the close links the pastor had with the school, and mentions the fact that his job was for life and that he occupied the Priest House rent-free, noting also that his family were no longer paid tithes as the practice had ceased in 1870. The following is an extract:

'*There were mostly Saxon and a few Romanian houses on the street, as easily distinguishable by their colours and construction as were the people in front of them by their clothing. The Saxons looked down on the Romanians and the Romanians looked down on the gypsies and the gypsies looked down on everyone, as they lived on the hill.*

The pastor's land produced four railroad cars of potatoes every year (the potatoes were pulled by buffalo cart to Copşa Mică station), some hay, lots of apples, 800 gallons of wine, and grape, apple and prune brandy. We had 125 fruit trees and a huge fruit cellar to store as much of it as we wanted for our own use. The rest could be sold at the market in Mediasch. The young people in town traditionally made a party out of work for the pastor and church, including working the pastor's vineyards and orchard.'

Father Nagelbach's memoirs are one of the few English-language sources to cover the subject of the Saxons' relationship with the German Nazis from 1933. They acknowledged the success of Hitler's policies against inflation and high unemployment and believed that the party offered them a means of retaining their deeply ingrained customs and lifestyle, which, as a minority, they felt was under threat. They, like many in Romania, were deeply fearful of the Russian Communists (doubtless they had no knowledge of the Hitler-Stalin pact). With the coming of the Second World War, most Saxons were conscripted into the Wehrmacht or the Waffen SS. Germans were stationed in many of the Saxon villages until 1944, when Romania joined the Allies.

The Saxons were sorely punished for having joined the Axis forces. They were not expelled into post-war Europe as were the Sudetens or Silesians, but in January 1945, after the Russians had taken Romania, many were transported to the Ukraine and the Urals to a life of hard labour in the coal and uranium mines. Those that survived returned to find gypsies and Romanians occupying their homes and their land taken by the state. Many of the war memorials reflect this. The Saxons had established an extraordinarily flourishing society in Transylvania which had survived for 850 years; this wartime decision and its repercussions was one of the factors underlying their mass exodus in the early 1990s.

AXENTE SEVER & ȘEICA MARE

The drive to Axente Sever (Frauendorf/Asszonyfalva) takes you through a lovely valley that once belonged to the Hungarian Apafis (*see p. 100*). The village acquired free, non-feudal status in the early 14th century and was settled by Saxons. Since it lies in relative proximity to Copșa Mică and has had to deal with the problems of pollution, the village has benefited from EU money and expert advice on presentation and tourism. The church employs a good curatorial team of two sisters, Mrs Pelger and Mrs Depner. Dinner and lunch can be provided on request (*T: 0735 564 996 or email muzeulcetate@yahoo.com*). They have bikes for hire too.

The church and museum at Axente Sever

The church is small with its defensive walls outwardly intact. The strongly-built tower over the crossing gives this little bastion a charming if dumpy appearance. Jan Hülsemann, a specialist German architect working with the MET, and Ton van Rijn, a Dutch architect, restored the church and devised the small museum within the walls. Not only that, but a charming and simple *pensione* was inserted into the storerooms in the fortifications providing 14 beds with bathrooms, all done with simple style.

The **museum** is one of the best in the Târnava Valley, with not only an ethnographic collection of costumes, musical instruments from the brass band, exhibits on weaving, etc., but also information on why, and how, these churches were actually built. There are excellent maps of the endless past invasions that bedevilled early Transylvania and held it back until relative stability came in the late 16th and 17th centuries. All the information panels are very child-sympathetic—and illuminating also for adults.

The **interior of the church** is given its character by the sturdy piers supporting the tower above the crossing. Both nave and crossing are almost equally square and groin vaulted. There is a charming side chapel, again groin vaulted, to the south. The wall walk to the top of the bell-tower has been restored and the view is fine.

I met a Saxon from the village in the early '90s who (he did not realise at the time) had taken the last photos of the community in the church. He offered me some copies, which I accepted—charming young girls in their Sunday best among rather empty pews. Within months of the photos being taken these young women had probably left for Germany. The photographs are now in the museum.

The Naming of Places

To the German-speaking Saxons, Transylvania is the Siebenbürgen, the land of the 'seven seats', their ancient administrative regions. To the Hungarians it is Erdély and to the Romanians Ardeal. Towns and villages also have three distinct names, a Hungarian, a Saxon and a Romanian. In a large number of cases the Hungarian and the German names are simple translations of each other: Langenthal (Long Valley) = Hosszúaszó (Long Gully). The Romanian names are often phonetic approximations of these (Hosszúaszó is rendered Hususău; Neustadt is Noiştat; Frauendorf is Frâua). Romanian nationalism and its sense of identity, however, has brought with it changes in some of the place names. Hususău has become Valea Lungă, a direct Romanian translation of the German and Hungarian 'long valley'. Sometimes the change has gone further still. Frâua is no longer Frâua. In 1933 it was renamed, by decree, Axente Sever, after Ioan Axente Sever, the Romanian patriot and freedom fighter who was born here in 1821. Axente studied theology and philosophy at Blaj and attended the assemblies there in the revolutionary years of 1848 (*see p. 194*). He was also a prominent member of ASTRA, the movement for promoting Romanian literature and popular culture which was so instrumental in creating nationalist fervour in Transylvania.   AB

From Axente Sever there are lovely routes that can be taken in a four-wheel-drive car or by horse and cart, overland to Alma Vii (*though it is best to take a guide; ask in the museum).* Other recommended routes include heading back to the main road, turning right for Copşa Mică and so on towards Blaj (*described on p. 194*); or left to Agârbiciu and Şeica Mare (*described below*).

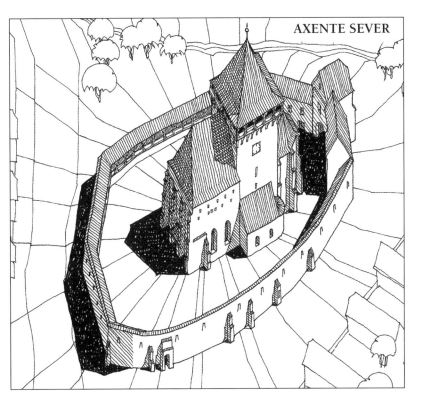

AXENTE SEVER

This drawing of the church and citadel at Axente Sever well illustrates the typical features of a Saxon fortified church. Thick defensive walls with storerooms in them surround the whole. The walled enclosure has a single fortified entrance (some Saxon citadels also have other covered entrances and even tunnels). The walls were often studded with turrets. One of these would have contained a meeting room for the town or village council, and also a prison or village lockup. Another building would have housed the school. There was also very often a Bacon Tower (*Speckturm*), where the village hams and cured meats were hung. Axente Sever church has the typical tall bell-tower with a walkway all around the top on which sentries could be posted so watch could be kept. Another common feature of Saxon fortified churches is the raised nave or chancel (in this case the nave) furnished with narrow windows and slits for firing and throwing missiles.

AGÂRBICIU AND ŞEICA MARE

Agârbiciu (Arbegen/Szászegerbegy) looks grand when seen from a distance, with its fine 18th-century church façade staring out across the wide, flat valley. This is a case, though, of imposing architecture being better seen from afar. From close quarters there is not much to detain the visitor. There was an early Gothic basilica here, built at the beginning of the 14th century, and the village is mentioned in documents of 1343. Much of the woodwork internally is Baroque. In the village there is a small, simple B&B.

The church at Şeica Mare (Markt-Schelken/Nagyselyk) dates from the 13th–16th centuries, at which last date the fortifications were added. It is in poor shape today and is hidden behind the rather fine Saxon school building on the side of the road. If you want to get in, ask at the small shop opposite the church entrance. I am not sure, though, with Şeica Mică so close by, that this little church is a priority. The addition of Mare (meaning large) and Mică (meaning small) to a place name is not an indication of the level of visitor interest offered. Always on a main transport route, Şeica Mare was the posting stop between Sibiu and Mediaş. As its German name, Markt-Schelken, reveals, it was a market town. But there is not a great deal to see today. Şeica Mică, on the other hand, *merita una visita*.

BOARTA, BUIA, MOARDĂŞ AND METIŞ

There is an attractive loop around to Boarta (Michelsdorf/Mihályfalva), which has a good altar of 1794 in its 19th-century church. Buia (Bell/Bólya) was once in the hands of Prince Michael the Brave, who was simultaneously Prince of Moldavia, Wallachia and Transylvania in 1600 (*see p. 23*). The church ceiling of 1710 was made by Thomas Viatoris and the Renaissance altar is of 1561. In 1693 the altar was given its typical Baroque-style framework. Late Gothic pews are found in the choir.

At Moardăş (Mardisch/Mardos) the church has a good interior for such an out-of-the-way village and a Baroque altar of 1789. At Metiş (Martinsdorf/Martonfalva) there is an organ of 1793 in the neo-Gothic church. There are remains of the medieval wall and vicarage.

ȘEICA MICĂ WITH AN EXCURSION TO VALEA LUNGĂ & SÂNMICLĂUȘ

The entry to Șeica Mică (Kleinschelken/Kisselyk) is not impressive: the houses are small and have been given the 'cement and triangle windows' makeover. There is a factory making curtains and all things to do with them on the right, which must bring employment. But what is so refreshing is that vines are being grown, vertically in rows going straight up the hillside, without terraces. This used be the tradition in all this wine-growing area. There has obviously been an active Saxon group here, who restored the interesting church in 2004 (*the key is held by Maria Pop at house no. 387; T: 0269 514 738*).

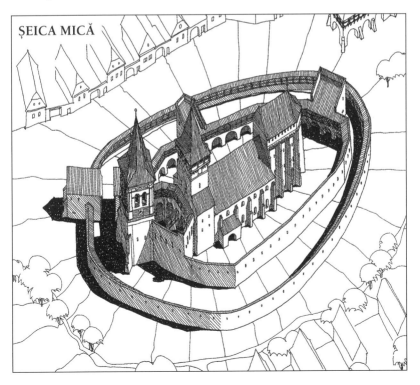

ȘEICA MICĂ

Before going into the church, it is worth taking the time to walk around the walls. From the east there is a gradual progression of roofs and towers until the last and latest in date at the west end (though photos may be ruined by looping telegraph wires). The defending walls of the church are like bits of Morse code: a gateway; a possible bacon tower and an old piece of wall. This and the church itself are encircled by a later brick enclosure which cannot really have offered much in the way of defence.

The most interesting part of the exterior is the **fortified enclosed well court** between the two steepled towers. The rather good label *in situ* calls it a well, though in fact it contains two lime pits; but nevertheless buttressed, galleried and open to the skies. Every church and house once had a dedicated lime pit for renewing the whitewash. From here you can climb the church tower to see a bell of the late Middle Ages and another of a later date. The climb, like many up towers and into roofs in this valley, is not for the faint-hearted.

The interior of the church is well ordered. There is a **monument to Michael Oltardt**, a prominent townsman and local pastor, who died in 1623. The inscription says he was priest here for 20 years. It is believed to be the original polychromy. The pews are charming and there are hymn books scattered. The good font of 1477 is now in Mediaş.

The short journey from Şeica Mică to the main road is good picnic country. The Târnava Mare Valley widens along this section, with hectares of maize, which is harvested in the middle of November. Carts bearing the grainless stalks are trundled off to have their loads processed into animal feed. From here you can make a short excursion to Ţapu and a charming small fortified church.

ŢAPU

Viewed from a distance from the road, Ţapu (Abtsdorf/Csicsóholdvilág) looks fine. The church was built in the 14th century and two centuries later it was fortified. It has additions of the 19th and 20th centuries and was in the ownership of the Hungarian Teleki family. The Târnava river is

Memorial to the priest Michael Oltardt (d. 1623), shown clutching a prayer book, with Bible and chalice at his shoulders and the Holy Dove on his head.

broad and sluggish at this point. There are generally fishermen to be seen, hopefully casting a line, which means the water must be clean enough. The route follows the railway line between Austria and Hungary and Bucharest. The railway upgrade should be completed by 2017. From both capitals there are usually good overnight trains. It was originally founded as a monastery (hence its German name of Abtsdorf).

VALEA LUNGĂ

Valea Lungă (Langenthal/Hosszuaszó) is 19km east of Blaj. It is tiny today but in 1848 there were 20 Hungarian families of minor aristocracy living here—which may explain the elegance of some of the houses, although none are large. There are shadows of the novels of Miklós Bánffy here. Bánffy conjures up a world at the turn of the 19th and 20th centuries when already many families, because of the divisions of the land holdings among the lesser aristocracy, were unable to make their estates pay for their way of life, though they still struggled to retain the veneer of ancient wealth. The Transylvanian Hungarians were never as wealthy as the families further west because of the nature of the land (hills not plains).

What is particularly interesting in Valea Lungă is the number of differing places of worship. The village boasts Roman Catholic, Uniate, Calvinist (donated by Baron Szentkereszty, whose family had holdings both here and in Mălâncrav) and Orthodox churches. Most are to be found off the main road to the north, in the direction signposted to Bălcaciu. The Saxons, in the 14th century, built a **Gothic hall church** which has a Baroque altar and pulpit of 1725. The coffered ceiling followed in 1729. There is an early font and fragments of late medieval frescoes. In the Valea Lungă of the 19th century, 15 percent of the population were Jewish and there was also, until after the Second World War, a synagogue.

The village was the home of the botanist Joseph Barth (1833–1915), who was pastor here. More importantly, it was the birthplace of Friedrich Müller (1884–1969), who was bishop of the Saxon communities. He was faced with the dreadful deportations of 1945 and their aftermath, when the returning Saxons found that gypsy families had moved into their houses and their land had been taken by the Communist regime. It was he who mediated with the Communists so that the Saxons had their houses returned. The land, which had been theirs for 800 years, remained sequestrated.

INTO THE VALLEY OF THE TÂRNAVA MICĂ

To reach the valley of the Târnava Mică, or Lesser Târnava, follow the main road through Valea Lungă (past a plethora of good picnic spots in the meadows beneath the beech forests) and continue north along an untarred road to the beautiful village of **Bălcaciu (Bulkesch/Bolkács)**. Wide open spaces are at the heart of this village and a fine Saxon church stands out on a mound (*the key is with Alexandra Zikeli in the Priest House below the church; T: 0748 895 425*). The church dates from 1319 though only the east end remains from the medieval original: it is tall and narrow with three tiers of defence floors and a timber-parapeted wall-walk. The Saxon community in Germany rallied to the rescue and the church is now finely restored, with the donors' plaques in the entry porch. Also in the porch is a fine Bethlen tomb of 1681, perhaps originally from elsewhere. The nave was rebuilt in 1807–10. The altar was carved with the figures of Sts John the Baptist and Evangelist by Michael Wolf in 1793.

Sânmiclăuş and Jidvei

North of Bălcaciu you come into the Târnava Mică valley. Along there, between Blaj and Jidvei, the houses change shape with the short sides to the road. The buildings then run back to the barns and are without the great gateways of the Saxons or indeed those of the Szeklers.

The Târnava Mică attracted a series of small castles belonging to the Hungarian aristocracy. The most important is the country house built by Miklós Bethlen. To reach it, follow the signposts to **Sânmiclăuş (Betelsdorf/Bethlenszentmiklós)**. In 1667 Bethlen started work on a new castle, which György Kelényi describes as 'one of the most significant 17th-century secular buildings in Transylvania.' You make your way through a very depressed old state farm to reach the house. It is worth the

detour to see its wonderful arcaded garden façade, now in need of urgent repair. In the state farmyard is the splendid ancient barn of the Bethlens, a pointer to the wealth of farming in this area. The Communist regime took malicious delight in the destruction of the past, especially that of the Transylvanian Hungarians.

From Sânmiclăuş, if you wish to follow the course of the Târnava Mică, continue upriver to **Jidvei (Seiden/Zsidve)**. To the south lie acres of vineyards. Wine was an important hard-currency export for Ceauşescu. The vineyards are now in private hands and there is a new winery open to the public where you can buy and taste a vast range of wines. Varieties include Pinot Grigio, Pinot Noir, Sauvignon Blanc, Muscat and the Romanian varieties of Fetească Albă and Fetească Regală.

Jidvei itself is quite attractive, with Saxon houses and a fortified church (*the key is to be found in the house adjacent to the church entrance and after the Town Hall*). There are two cash tills here and a public lavatory, the key to which can be obtained from the Town Hall.

From here you can do a round trip to Mediaş, along the 'wine' road to **Cetatea de Baltă (Kokelburg/Küküllővár)**, which stands out fortress-like: square with round towers on each corner. This is now a privately-owned winery. The road to Mediaş takes you through Boian and Bazna (*see p. 158*).

However, you may want to retrace your steps to complete the journey along the Tărnava Mare; if so, you will arrive in Blaj.

Opposite: Tombstone in the church porch of Bălcaciu commemorating Barbara Ostrosith de Giletincz, widow of Farkas Bethlen of Criş (*see p. 80*). Farkas, named here as 'Volffgang de Bethlen', was adviser to Prince Mihály Apafi, Chancellor of Transylvania and historian. He died in 1679 in Sânmiclăuş. Barbara died in 1681.

BLAJ

Blaj (Blasendorf/Balázsfalva) sits on an advantaged trade route, up from the old Transylvanian capital at Alba Iulia (Gyulafehérvár) and with the great wine-growing lands to the north. It is on the confluence of the rivers Târnava Mare and Mică, where several early Neolithic sites have been found. In more recent times it has been of historic importance for Romanians. Under Communism the town was best known for its dark, highly carved and heavy furniture. A suite of it would cost as much as a Dacia car.

On the face of it, Blaj has no reason to be a favoured stopover for the traveller. It is an ugly town, mainly modern and jumbled, and split in two by the railway. But it is the seat of a Uniate eparchy or bishopric, is important for the fame of its excellent education and for its fine Uniate cathedral founded under Maria Theresa. There are some handsome Austro-Hungarian buildings and (besides the cathedral) two things to visit that I would particularly recommend. Both shed light on why Blaj is seen as a shining beacon in the struggle for Romanian independence.

Before you enter the town on the Mediaş road (arriving from the east), up on a hillock to your right, marked by football stadium-type lights, is a huge **cross dedicated to Avram Iancu**, the great fighter for Romanian nationhood. It sets the tone for what you will find here. Blaj is filled with memorials to the independence movement, notably in **Câmpia Libertăţii**, now a park, where there were three mass rallies of Transylvanian Vlachs between April and September 1848. It is reported that 40,000 gathered here at the great *Adunarea* in May. These rallies were a product of growing Romanian nationalist feeling at a time when other nations within the Habsburg Empire, most notably here in Transylvania, the Hungarians, were also pressing for autonomy. In the middle of the traffic roundabout on Bulevardul Republicii is a **statue of the She-wolf of Rome suckling Romulus and Remus**, the unmistakable stamp of a Romanian town. Here at the west end of the Târnava Valley we are a world away from the Székely lands to the east.

The *Adunarea* or Assembly at Blaj of 15th May 1848.

The museum

1 Str. Doctor Vasile Suciu. Open Mon–Fri 8–4. Entry is free. There is parking behind the building.

A good way to pick up some background is to visit the museum, Muzeul de Istorie Augustin Bunea. Coming into the town on the main road from the east, there are two signs, right and left, to the centre. For the museum, keep right and follow the signs. It is housed in a 19th-century neo-Renaissance building. There are no labels in English but it does not matter. There is a lapidarium of fragmentary Roman finds from the area as well as finds from other ancient peoples who inhabited the Târnava Mică Valley. Archaeology is frequently used in Transylvania as a nationalist tool.

Some of the museum's most valuable items, including the gold finds, are now in the centre of the fortress of Alba Iulia, the old ecclesiastical and princely capital of Transylvania. Most interesting from the point of view of Romanian history is the information on the Şcoală Ardeleană (the 'Transylvanian School'), which encouraged the compilation and use of Romanian-language dictionaries and became influential in making Romanian a recognised literary language. There was a printing press in Blaj by 1747. The first public school teaching in the Romanian language was established here in 1754.

There is a small ethnographic section downstairs and a room with musty books: the archives. On the first floor there are some nice icons, from both the Orthodox and the Uniate churches. There is also a brief display on the First World War.

The Şcoală Ardeleană

Increasingly, in the first half of the 18th century, the Transylvanian Vlachs felt a growing sense of frustration and injustice that they and their culture were given no recognition and no power. Many, indeed, were still serfs. The union of nations that controlled Tranyslvania's affairs remained stubbornly three: Saxons, Székelys and Hungarians. The Vlachs felt that the time had come for the increasingly numerous fourth nation, themselves, to be represented. The Şcoală Ardeleană (Transylvanian School) grew out of developments in education and the ecclesiastical initiatives of Bishop Micu-Klein. Indeed his own nephew, Samuil, was one of its leading lights. Blaj was one of the centres of the school.

At around the same time, a group of priests began to research the origins of the Romanians, coming to the conclusion that they were descended from Dacian people conquered by the Romans in the 2nd century. The idea that the Vlachs of Transylvania were now not only the most numerous of the ethnic groups but also the people who had the longest history of habitation in the region, was to many minds inspiriational.

Some of the Şcoală's leading members, Samuil Micu-Klein, Gheorghe Şincai, Petru Maior and Ion Budai-Deleanu, presented their *Supplex Libellus Valachorum Transylvaniae*, pressing for rights equal to those of the three nations represented in the Diet, to the emperor Leopold II. At the same time they relinquished the Cyrillic in favour of the Latin script; they introduced the first dictionaries of the Romanian language (using Latin and French when lexical terms were lacking); produced the first written grammars and a translation of the Bible. Romanian-language schools were founded, many in rural areas. The Saxons had long realised the importance of education and from the time of the Reformation their schools had been a vital part of their communities. The Romanians wished for the same.

The philologist, journalist and professor of philosophy and theology Timotei Cipariu (1805–87) was born and educated in Blaj and in 1847 he founded one of the first Romanian newspapers in Transylvania, *Organul Luminării* ('*The Organ of Enlightenment*'). He was also vice-chairman of ASTRA, formed to preserve Romanian culture. There is a branch office of ASTRA in Blaj today, near the site of his house.

Piața 1848 and the Bishop's Palace

Among the museum's displays is an engraving of the square in front of the Cathedral of the Uniates. The square, now known as **Piața 1848**, has been little touched since the engraving was made. To reach it from the museum, cross the railway tracks by the bridge (you will see the Romulus and Remus statue if you come this way). The square is surrounded by buildings that are a roll call for the Romanian independence movement, including the Theological Academy and of course the cathedral itself. Southwest of the square, between it and the football ground, is the old the Apafi Castle, now the Uniate bishop's palace (**Castelul Mitropolitan Apafi**). The castle was originally given by King Sigismund to Balázs Cséry (the name Blaj in fact derives from Balázs) and finally ended up with the Apafis (*see p. 100*). The property was transferred to the Greek Catholic (Uniate) church by Charles VI, father of Maria Theresa, at which time it became the seat of the Uniate bishops. In 1687 a treaty was signed here between Habsburg Austria and Prince Mihály Apafi, in theory signalling Transylvania's continued independence—though it is a clear indication of the beginning of Habsburg interest in the region.

The Uniate Cathedral

the cathedral of the Holy Trinity (Catedrala Sfânta Treime), built of a lovely honey-coloured stone, is well worth a visit. It was part of a grand plan by Inocențiu Micu-Klein (*see p. 200*), who from 1737 planned the city to encompass the schools and church. The foundation stone was laid in 1741 and the cathedral was consecrated in 1765. The twin towers were added in

The Uniate Cathedral of the Holy Trinity in Blaj.

1838, and in fact the exterior appears completely Catholic, with theatrical cut-out figures in the niches of the façade. This is the first Baroque church façade in Transylvania based on the designs of the Viennese architect Anton Erhard Martinelli (1684–1747).

In the interior is a spectacular **iconostasis**, installed in 1765, believed to have been carved from lime wood by Aldea from Târgu Mureş and with icons painted by the master Stephen Tenetzky of Arad. The iconostasis is considered the most important in Romania because of its size and the richness of its décor. The **frescoes in the dome** were painted between 1748 and 1749 by Iacov 'Zugravul' ('the painter'), a Serbian. They depict scenes from the life of Christ, the heavenly liturgy and, in the upper register, portraits of nine popes. A large **carpet**, woven in 1900 in Maramureș by Octavian Smigelschi, is on display for special events. It depicts a large eagle with its wings spread over the city and the background colours of red, yellow and blue representing the Romanian flag. It was from the **pulpit** here that Simion Bărnuțiu, a leader of the 1848 revolutionary movement, preached, and the sparks of Romanian national feeling were lit. The **relics of Micu-Klein** were bought here from Rome and are to the right of the iconostasis. Cardinal Alexandru Todea (1912–2002) is buried on left on the iconostasis.

Byzantinesque dome frescoes by Iacov 'Zugravul', Blaj cathedral.

The Uniate Church and Bishop Micu-Klein

At the Synod of Alba Iulia, convoked in 1698, the Eastern Christians of the provinces that are now Romania forged a union with Rome that protected them from harassment by Protestants (Lutheran Saxons, Calvinist Hungarians) and also won for them the protection of the Catholic Habsburgs. This union became known as the Uniate or Greek Catholic Church. Its adherents acknowledge the pope as their head but hold services according to the Eastern Christian rite, not in Slavonic but in the vernacular. A second synod in 1700 ratified the first. The seat of the Uniate eparchy moved from Alba Iulia to Făgăraș in 1721. In Transylvania, the Uniates took on the mantle of a proto-independence movement.

Bishop Inocențiu Micu-Klein (1692–1768) was Primate of the Romanian Greek Catholic Church from 1730 until his resignation in 1751. A remarkable leader, he was at once bishop, monk, intellectual, politician and nationalist for the Romanian cause. Intelligent and ambitious, he studied philosophy in Cluj under the Jesuit Franz Fasching, who himself was a supporter of the Romanisation of the Romanian people. Micu-Klein was appointed Bishop of Alba Iulia and Făgăraș by Emperor Charles VI. He was confirmed by Pope Clement XII as a monk of the Congregation of St Basil (a Roman Catholic order). The same year he became a member of the Transylvanian Diet and was ordained bishop by the Eparch of Mukachevo (Ruthenian Catholic). His bases, one might say, were well covered.

In 1737 he moved the seat of the eparchy to Blaj and in the following year laid the foundation stone of its first Romanian-language school. He preached tirelessly on behalf of the Transylvanian Vlachs, pointing out that they were numerically the largest ethnic group, had been in the region longer than anyone else (according to the theory of descent from the Dacians) and had the right to be recognised as a nation alongside Hungarians, Saxons and Szeklers. Micu-Klein threw the full weight of his learning, as well as the prestige of the Church, behind the Romanian national movement. This was not at all what Vienna had planned when the emperor had first encouraged the Uniate Church (in what is now the Ukraine), seeing it as a canny way to limit the power of Russia. Its clever blend of Orthodox rite and papal supremacy was now gaining support from all sides and the Transylvanian Vlachs claimed descent from the Romans—with all that such a kinship suggested about being heirs to the Enlightenment.

In 1741, Micu-Klein laid another foundation stone: that of the Cathedral of the Holy Trinity in Blaj, which was completed in 1747. Even more importantly, he gained, from Maria Theresa, an agreement giving serfs (the status of most Transylvanian Vlachs at this time) the right to receive education and to hold public office. His ceaseless pressing for more rights for his people, as well as for the Uniate Church to hold equivalent status to the Catholic, finally exasperated Maria Theresa and he was summoned to Vienna under a cloud. He escaped to exile in Rome, where he died in 1768 and was buried in the church of the Madonna del Pascolo (now the Ukrainian Greek Catholic Church). In his writings, however, he had expressed a wish to be buried in Blaj and in October 1997 that wish was finally granted when his remains were reinterred here.

Inocenţiu's nephew Samuil was another prominent figure of the independence movement, a student of history, theology and language and editor of a number of books in Romanian.

After the collapse of Austria-Hungary at the end of the First World War, the Uniates were keen for Tranyslvania to join Romania. After World War Two they suffered greatly under Communism. While the Ceauşescu regime was loosely supportive of the Romanian Orthodox church, which he saw as a useful nationalist ally in his power struggles with the Soviet Union, his persecution of Uniates was unrelenting. The church only began to flourish again after 1989, though many cases of restitution remain unresolved.

Detail of a 16th/17th-century western Anatolian white-ground Selendi bird rug in Biertan church. Bird rugs feature in a few European paintings from 1557–1625.

ANATOLIAN RUGS/TRANYSLVANIAN CARPETS

When visiting the Protestant, Lutheran churches in Transylvania, you will experience one of the finest collections of Ottoman rugs from Anatolia outside the museums in Budapest and Istanbul. These rugs are known generically as 'Transylvanian' carpets though they were mainly made in Western Anatolia from the 15th–19th centuries but preserved in Saxon churches here as objects of great value. They fall into various categories depending on pattern and where it is thought they were made: major centres were Gördes, Kula, Selendi and Uşak in western Anatolia.

The rugs are of wool pile, knotted onto the warp with the double Turkish or Gördes knot. They are dyed with natural dyes (madder, indigo, walnut, etc.) and multiple dipping was used to vary the colours. The vast majority of surviving rugs are from the 17th century, but there are many from the 18th and a few from the 19th centuries too. The 19th century saw a shift in taste at the Ottoman court, which was looking to the West for inspiration. But taste, habits and politics had changed in Transylvania too. The years 1848 and 1849 were hardly conducive to trade, as the country was immersed in a virtual civil war.

Many of the 'Transylvanian' carpet styles are classified under the names of 16th-century Western artists who used them as props in their studios to reflect their sitters' wealth and status or to give a sense of the exotic. Lorenzo Lotto used an Uşak rug, henceforth named a 'Lotto'. A 'Holbein' is of the type used in his famous painting of *The Ambassadors*. 'Crivelli', 'Ghirlandaio' and 'Memling' rugs are also found in the pattern types. From Selendi come the beautiful 'bird' and 'scorpion' rugs, so named from the stylised motifs on them which resemble scorpions with upturned tail or birds in flight. It has been suggested that some of these carpets might equally have been made in the Balkans. Of great beauty too are the Çintamani rugs, with a motif of three balls and wavy lines, derived from Buddhist symbolism. This probably entered along the Silk Route and spread in Anatolia through inspiration from Chinese fabrics.

The Charity of St Antoninus (1542) by Lorenzo Lotto, altarpiece in the
church of Santi Giovanni e Paolo in Venice, prominently featuring an
Oriental rug of the type that now bears the artist's name.

A high proportion of the rugs found in Transylvania are of a type
originally conceived as Muslim prayer mats. They are often decorated
with the stylised outline of a mihrab (prayer niche), which would have
been placed facing Mecca when the rug was in use. Some have designs
of elegant slender columns or hanging mosque lamps. However, the
original religious significance of such rugs was no hindrance to their use
as decoration or as votive offerings in the Protestant churches, many of
which, ironically enough, had been fortified to keep out the Infidel. Even
in times of war the carpets found their way, possibly via Turkish-controlled
towns such as Buda or Oradea, into the Principality of Transylvania. The
peace treaty between Sultan Beyazit II (r. 1481–1512) and the King of
Hungary, Matthias Corvinus (r. 1458–90) stated that 'the merchants of
the said Hungarian King…shall come and go in my victorious lands,
shall do business, their persons and riches shall not suffer damage by the
inhabitants of my lands. My merchants shall likewise come and go and

shall not suffer ill-treatment and damage from anybody.' On the occasion of his marriage to Beatrice of Aragon in 1476, Matthias was presented with '*tapetti*', amongst which it can be assumed that there was a Turkish rug. We know that in 1503, a total of 500 carpets reached the city of Brașov in only ten months through commercial channels (the church still has a fine collection). Brașov had no special concession but, uniquely, its customs books survive. The dealers were Turks, Greeks, Armenians and Jews. It is tempting to see Dumbrăveni, with its Armenian population from the second half of the 17th century (*see p. 96*), as an important source for local rugs. Alas, there is no proof.

There are descriptions by Hungarian travellers to Turkey in the 15th century describing the hanging and use of carpets in the djamis, and this might be a possible source of inspiration for the custom of decorating both Catholic and Protestant churches, where the carpets were hung on the walls and over furniture. However, the Oriental carpet was also an indispensable adornment of Hungarian royal castles and nobles' country houses, with records going back to the 15th century. There are numerous accounts of Prince Gábor Bethlen, and others in the 17th century, buying from Constantinople for their personal use.

During the long intermittent wars which lasted until the end of the 17th century, carpets were the main sources of warmth and colour and the easiest means of signalling evident wealth. They could also be quickly packed and removed from danger. In the Magyar interior, therefore, chests were an important item of furniture. Carpets were also used in processions and progresses, as caparison for horses and in coaches. Most of the secular carpets have not survived, making the collections in the churches all the more valuable.

Many of these lovely rugs, made by women in Anatolian villages, were given by the Saxons and Hungarians to their church as gifts after a wedding or funeral, or as exotic votive offerings in token of thanksgiving. They could be given by a guild, or as payment for customs duty. They were draped over the seats of dignitaries such as the local judge or the priest's wife. They decorated the pulpit and were hung from the galleries. Many of the carpets are hung sideways, making them more difficult to 'read'. Rugs were also used to adorn the Catholic churches but were placed on the floor before the altar, which caused wear and tear. Those in the Protestant churches have fared better, still retaining their *kilim*, the selvage or band of flat weave at either end, used to hold the rugs together. Many retain too their fringe (the ends of the warp), frequently of delicate colours. According to Ferenc Batári in *The Collections of the Museum of Applied Arts, Budapest* (vol. 1), in 1920, when Hungary lost Transylvania, the Hungarian churches were forced to sell their carpets to meet overheads. Other church carpets were sold to collectors in the West and America at the turn of the last century, before the trade was halted when it was realised that the carpets are an integral part of church decoration and culture. Many of the Saxon churches in villages where few Saxons now remain have loaned their rugs to Mediaș, Sighișoara or Brașov for safe-keeping.

Anatolian rugs are vital evidence of a flourishing East–West trade and are witness to Transylvania's important part in this. Although the Reformation in Transylvania did not see large-scale removal of Catholic altarpieces or frescoes, as in other parts of Northern Europe (indeed there was a continuation of pre-Reformation decoration in this tolerant, culturally pragmatic society), the carpets add a blast of colour and glory to these great fortresses of faith on the outer borders of the Western Church.

BEE-KEEPING AROUND RICHIȘ

Bee-keeping is an important industry in Romania; it is also an acute barometer of changing land use and bio-diversity. Bees are a vital part of farming, and keeping them is a skill which most farmers down the Târnava Valley have taken for granted for centuries.

Wilhelm Untch, one of the few remaining Saxons in Richiș, saw his first swarm in a tree aged nine, while helping his parents spray the family vines. The copper sulphate solution had to be dragged up the hills by oxen. Each evening the Untchs were all green with the spray. Wilhelm's father worked in Mediaș so, as a boy, he had to help his mother with the farm. He went to the grammar school in Sighișoara and in the holidays worked on the land. Wilhelm himself is now retired, having worked for Romgaz. He has kept bees since he was nine years old and had five hives by the age of 14. He now has nearer 40, producing honey, wax and swarms, which he sells to other bee-keepers. Jars of his honey can be found for sale in the Tourist Information Centre in Richiș. There are two varieties, acacia and milleflora. Wilhelm Untch is also a trustee of Pro Richiș and works for the church in Mediaș. The following is his account of bee-keeping today:

'There are two types of hive used in the region. One, which is high and narrow, was invented by a priest, Father Gerstung, and is named after him, the Gerstung. The other, the Dadant, is broader and gives the bees more room. I favour the former as it keeps the bees warm, although swarming is inevitable.

I take two harvests of honey a season. The acacia in the first part of the season from May to July. The start of the season depends on the length of the winter but bee-keepers watch the temperatures from the beginning of February. The second crop is in late summer and has always been, traditionally, milleflora in an area so rich in wild flowers. Now, however, this has changed. We only have 40 cows in the village when we used to have 300 and we have many more sheep and goats. Hay is no longer made as much as it used to be. The grazing habits of the sheep prevent most of the flowers from blooming. This is affecting the run of honey.

Wilhelm Untch, at work with his bees.

Recently, around the villages, phacelia is being sown to increase foraging for the bees, who now return laden with blue/mauve pollen. Goldenrod has become invasive on the meadows but the bees love it in September. Beekeepers are increasingly interested in the rape harvest and in the Richiş area there is some wild rape. Lifting the hive lid I can smell the start of the rape harvest.

The hives in Transylvania are sited close together and are brightly coloured so that the bees can come home to the correct hive. The acacia is important and in a country as large as Romania the lorries carrying the hives head south in the spring and gradually work their way north at the end of the season. In my childhood the Saxons used to plant acacia, and in May the forests are white with the blossom. There is a monastery on the way to Sibiu where the nuns have planted much acacia for the bees.'

FLORA & FAUNA OF THE TÂRNAVA VALLEY

Romania's Saxon Transylvania is one of Europe's last surviving medieval landscapes. Its flowery hay-meadows, rolling pastures and wealth of wildlife have, like the unspoilt traditional villages and fortified churches, somehow survived in the modern world. The wildflower-rich grasslands in particular comprise a habitat and landscape feature that have not been seen in northern Europe for a generation, and the extensive oak-and-hornbeam woodland still hold roe deer, wild cat, wolves and bears.

Until recently, farming in this distinctive region remained largely traditional, with few agro-chemicals—a marvellously wildflower- and wildlife-friendly regime. Tractors are now gradually replacing horses but farming remains non-intensive. The main crops are maize (often inter-cropped like a Native American plot with climbing beans and squashes), wheat, oats, two-rowed barley and potatoes. Hops are making a comeback after a recent decline and there are still a few patches of hemp. Most vineyards were grubbed out in Communist times. Larkspur and poppies remain a conspicuous feature of some wheat fields, but in general the crops are surprisingly clean. In the villages, wayside weeds that are a living link with history include old medicinal herbs such as elecampane, marsh mallow and stinking goosefoot, which would have been widespread in 18th-century England but today are mostly extinct.

The most obvious richness of plant and animal diversity is, however, the traditionally managed grasslands that brighten and colour the spring and summer countryside with sheets of wildflowers. These are probably the best lowland hay-meadows and pastures left in Europe, still so extensive that you can walk through them for several hours. Their colourful and varied flora, an echo of our own lost meadows in western Europe, comprise a mixture of western and central European plants, but also many steppic and Mediterranean species. In early and mid-summer this 'meadow-steppe', which has retreated even in most parts of central and eastern Europe, is a scene of astonishing beauty and floral diversity. Wiry fescue grasses dominate the sward, with feather-grasses on drier slopes, alongside 20–30 or more legume species, notably pink sainfoin (*Onobrychis viciifolia*), yellow dwarf brooms and white, pink, purplish and yellow clovers (*Trifolium spp.*). Some places are yellow with massed hay rattles (*Rhinanthus spp.*), lady's bedstraw (*Galium verum*) and agrimony (*Agrimonia eupatorium*); and dropwort (*Filipendula vulgaris*) and Charterhouse pink (*Dianthus carthusianorum*) make splashes of white and rich purplish-red respectively.

On hot, dry, south-facing slopes the flora is distinctly steppic, with violet nodding sage (*Salvia nutans*) and early in the season clumps of yellow pheasant's-eye (*Adonis aestivalis*), scattered patches of purple Hungarian iris (*Iris aphylla*) and creamy mounds of Tartar cabbage (*Crambe tatarica*). Many of the wet places and damper grasslands have been badly damaged by drainage and over-grazing, especially under the Communist regime, but a few flower-rich damp meadows survive, often in remote valleys deep in the woods. In late spring they are dotted with the scented white flowers of narcissus (*Narcissus poeticus*), followed by the pink spikes of bistort (*Persicaria bistorta*) and yellow buttercup-like globeflower (*Trollius europaeus*) and in mid-summer by crimson marsh gladiolus (*Gladiolus palustris*). In September, damper pastures are tinged lilac with massed flowers of meadow saffron or autumn crocus (*Colchicum autumnale*). These often attract late-emerging silver-studded blue butterflies. Several summer flowers also persist into autumn, and in drier grassland it is worth looking out for the autumn-flowering fringed gentian (*Gentanopsis ciliata*).

Animals abound as well as wild flowers. Hares and deer run across the grassland, and lesser-spotted eagles and buzzards soar overhead. Storks stride among the cut grass in search of frogs and other food. Shrikes perch on scrub and telegraph wires. Lizards and slow-worms scuttle and wriggle in the grass. Fire-bellied toads (in Transylvania a variant intermediate to yellow-bellied toads) live in pools and flooded cart-ruts. Butterflies—blues, browns, coppers and fritillaries—and day-flying moths flutter everywhere over the flowers. Bees, flies, beetles and other insects crawl and fly among the grass-stems. Two birds with distinctive calls, the corncrake and the quail, both now rare over most of Europe, creep through the long grass.

Woodlands too, mostly of oak and hornbeam, with some beech, are flowery, especially in spring before the trees are in leaf. At winter's end, sometimes in grasslands as well, patches of purple hellebore (*Helleborus purpurascens*) are conspicuous. Later, white-flowered wood anemone (*Anemone nemorosa*) and greater stitchwort (*Stellaria holostea*), the purplish-pink heads of coral-root (*Cardaria bulbifera*), mauve soft lungwort (*Pulmonaria mollis*) and purple spring vetch (*Lathyrus vernus*) brighten glades. All-brown bird's-nest orchid (*Neottia nidus-avis*), which thrives in leaf-mould, lurks in shady spots. In summer the woodland margins have a fringe of brother-and-sister (*Melampyrum bihariense*), almost restricted to Transylvania, with spikes of yellow flowers set off by violet bracts. Another conspicuous plant of woodland margins is the big, bold, yellow daisy Telekia (*Telekia speciosa*), with heart-shaped leaves.

The fragile floral carpet and its wildlife survive precariously in the face of expanding modern agriculture, insensitive land management (for example, over-stocking of sheep) and urban development. For more than 15 years, conservationists have combined with the enthusiasm and enterprise of local people to conserve the fabric and style of the landscape, farming communities, the ancient churches and village farmhouses, promoting sustainable but innovative farming, access to markets for farm and garden produce, traditional building, crafts and products. If we are to save the wildflowers, an older way of life needs to remain relevant and viable at a time of change and uncertainty, combining traditional skills with the best of the modern world. Not only are EU funds available for grants to support sensitive management of grassland, but also there is farming technology available such as high-tech mowing machines with huge roller wheels that prevent soil compaction and allow grass cutting on steep slopes previously cut by scythe. Infrastructure projects such as building and restoring milk-collection points in villages, with associated facilities to ensure milk hygiene, are helping to keep small farmers on the land—the key to conservation of this rich floral landscape.

John Akeroyd

The following is a list of wild plants, by no means complete, noted over ten days in the villages of the Târnava Valley, in June. Not every species of plant seen was recorded, many being those familiar to us in the British Isles. Acknowledgement is due to the field guide *Wildpflanzen Siebenbürgens* by Elise Speta and László Rákosy, whose excellent colour photographs proved very helpful in identifying plants seen, plus the many plant lists provided in various forms by John Akeroyd. *Roy Lancaster*

RICHIŞ

Meadowland
Agrimonia eupatoria (agrimony)
Allium scorodoprasum (sand leek)
Astragalus onobrychis (milk vetch)
Carduus acanthoides (plumeless thistle)
Chamaecytisus banaticus
Coronilla varia (crown vetch)
Dorycnium herbaceum
Euphorbia cyparissias (cypress spurge)
Hypericum perforatum (perforate St John's-wort)
Inula ensifolia (narrow-leaved elecampane)
Jurinea mollis
Lavatera thuringiaca (tree-mallow)
Muscari comosum (tassel hyacinth)
Nonea pulla
Onobrychis viciifolia (pink sanfoin)
Salvia austriaca (Austrian sage)
Salvia pratensis (meadow clary)
Salvia verticillata (whorled clary)
Scabiosa ochroleuca (cream scabious)
Scabiosa columbaria (small scabious)
Sedum telephium (orpine)
Senecio carpaticus (Carpathian ragwort)
Silene vulgaris (bladder campion)
Teucrium chamaedrys (wall germander)
Thymus pulegioides (large thyme)
Verbascum phoenicium (purple mullein)

Roadsides and waste places
Anchusa azurea (Italian bugloss)
Arctium tomentosum (downy burdock)
Calamagrostis epigeios (feathertop reed-grass)
Carthamus lanatus (woolly distaff thistle)
Clematis vitalba (old-man's beard/traveller's joy)
Consolida regalis (field larkspur)

Cyanus segetum (*Centaurea cyanus*) cornflower
Datura stramonium (thorn-apple)
Echinochloa crus-galli (cockspur)
Echium vulgare (viper's bugloss)
Erigeron annuus (annual fleabane)
Euphorbia esula (leafy spurge)
Galinsoga parviflora (gallant soldier)
Galinsoga ciliata
Lactuca serriola (prickly lettuce)
Lavatera thuringiaca (tree-mallow)
Mentha longifolia (horse mint)
Thalictrum lucidum (meadow rue)
Xanthium spinosum (spiny cockle-bur/Bathurst burr)

Arable fields, meadow and woodland margins
Acer campestre (field maple)
Amaranthus retroflexus (amaranth/tumbleweed)
Arctium tomentosum (downy burdock)
Asclepias syriaca (common milk-weed)
Astragalus glycophyllos (wild liquorice)
Astrantia major (great masterwort)
Bunias orientalis (Turkish rocket)
Calamagrostis epigeios (feathertop reed-grass)
Campanula persicifolia (peachleaf bellflower)

Campanula rapunculoides (creeping bellflower)
Carpinus betulus (hornbeam)
Cephalaria radiata? (leaves only)
Chaerophyllum aromaticum (broad-leaved chervil)
Cichorium intybus (chicory)
Cornus sanguinea (dogwood)
Elymus hispidus (wheatgrass)
Eryngium campestre (field eryngo)
Euonymus europaeus (spindle)
Frangula alnus (alder buckthorn)
Fumaria schleicheri (fumitory)
Galium glaucum (waxy bedstraw)
Gymnadenia conopsea (fragrant orchid)
Helleborus purpurascens (purple hellebore)
Inula ensifolia (narrow-leaved elecampane)
Inula helenium (elecampane)
Lathyrus tuberosus (tuberous pea)
Linum austriacum/L. perenne (Asian flax)
Malus sylvestris (crab-apple)
Melampyrum bihariense (brother-and-sister)
Parnassia palustris (grass of Parnassus)
Plantago media (hoary plantain)
Polygala major (milkwort)
Polygonatum latifolium (broad-leaved Solomon's seal)
Polygonatum odoratum (angular

Solomon's seal)

Quercus robur (English oak/
pedunculate oak)

Rhinanthus rumelicus (rattle)

Salvia glutinosa (Jupiter's distaff/
sticky sage)

Sambucus ebulus (dwarf elder)

Saponaria officinalis (soapwort)

Senecio carpaticus (Carpathian
ragwort)

Sisymbrium strictissimum (perennial
rocket)

Stachys germanica (downy wound-
wort)

Stellaria aquatica (water stitchwort)

Thalictrum minus (lesser meadow
rue)

Trifolium ochroleucon (sulphur
clover)

Verbascum blattaria (moth mullein)

Verbascum lychnitis (white mullein)

Viburnum opulus (guelder rose)

Vicia angustifolia (narrow-leaved
vetch)

Vicia cracca (tufted vetch)

Vicia tetrasperma (smooth vetch)

Vincetoxicum hirundinaria
(swallow-wort)

Viola arvensis (field pansy)

Xanthium italicum (cocklebur)

Woodland

Amanita caesarea (Caesar's
mushroom: a large, orange-
capped toadstool said to be edible
and excellent in a genus known
for its poisonous, sometimes
deadly, species)

Campanula patula (spreading
bellflower)

Epipactis helleborine (broad-leaved
helleborine)

Fagus sylvatica (beech; dominant)

Galium odoratum (woodruff)

Geranium sylvaticum (wood crane's-
bill)

Helleborus purpurascens (purple
hellebore)

Hepatica europaea (liverwort)

Lamiastrum vulgare (yellow
archangel)

Lathyrus vernus (spring vetch; in
seed)

Melampyrum bihariense (brother-
and-sister)

Melittis melissophyllum (bastard
balm)

Platanthera bifolia? (lesser butterfly
orchid: no flowers)

Polygonatum latifolium (broad-
leaved Solomon's seal)

Polygonatum odoratum (angular
Solomon's seal)

Pulmonaria rubra? (red lungwort;
no flowers)

Tragopogon pratensis ssp. orientalis?
(goat's beard)

Grassy areas in village
Althaea officinalis (marsh mallow)

Acidic heathland
Achillea millefolium (yarrow)
Agrimonia eupatoria (agrimony)
Asperula cynanchica (squinancy-wort)
Campanula cervicaria (bristly bell-flower)
Campanula patula (spreading bellflower)
Carex distans (distant sedge)
Clinopodium vulgare (wild basil)
Cynodon dactylon (Bermuda grass; colonising ant-hills)
Deschampsia cespitosa (tussock grass)
Dianthus carthusianorum (Charterhouse pink)
Euphorbia cyparissias (cypress spurge)
Euphrasia minima? (eyebright)
Filago vulgaris (common cudweed)

Galium verum (lady's bedstraw)
Genista tinctoria (dyer's greenweed)
Geranium dissectum (cut-leaved crane's-bill)
Holcus mollis (creeping soft-grass)
Leonurus cardiaca (motherwort)
Linum catharticum (fairy flax)
Mentha longifolia (horse mint)
Onopordum acanthium (cotton thistle)
Polygala serpyllifolia (heath milk-wort)
Potentilla tormentilla (tormentil)
Potentilla reptans (creeping cinquefoil)
Prunella laciniata (cut-leaf self-heal)
Stachys germanica (downy wound-wort)
Thymus pulegioides (large thyme)
Trifolium medium (zigzag clover)
Verbena officinalis (vervain)
Verbascum thapsus (great mullein/Aaron's rod)

ȘAROȘ–BIERTAN ROAD

Agrimonia eupatoria (agrimony)
Anchusa azurea (Italian bugloss)
Asclepias syriaca (common milk-weed; large colonies)
Campanula sibirica
Cichorium intybus (chicory)
Coronilla varia (crown vetch)

Dianthus armeria (Deptford pink)
Dianthus carthusianorum (Charterhouse pink)
Dorycnium herbaceum
Echium vulgare (viper's bugloss)
Eryngium campestre (field eryngo)
Galium verum (lady's bedstraw)

Gentiana cruciata (star gentian)
Hypericum perforatum (perforate St John's-wort)
Lotus corniculatus (bird's-foot trefoil)
Melilotus officinalis (ribbed melilot)
Onobrychis viciifolia (pink sanfoin)
Ononis spinosa (spiny rest-harrow)
Origanum vulgare (wild marjoram/oregano)
Plantago media (hoary plantain)
Prunella grandiflora (large-flowered self-heal)

Scabiosa columbaria (small scabious)
Solidago virgaurea (goldenrod)
Tanacetum vulgare (tansy)
Teucrium chamaedrys (wall germander)
Trifolium ochroleucon (sulphur clover)
Tragopogon pratensis (meadow goat's beard)
Veronica spicata (spiked speedwell)
Vicia tetrasperma (smooth vetch)

COPȘA MARE AND ALMA VII

Meadowland

Agrimonia eupatoria (agrimony)
Amanita sp. (an all-white fungus not unlike *A. virosa*, the Destroying Angel
Ballota nigra (black horehound)
Galium verum (lady's bedstraw)
Gymnadenia conopsea (fragrant orchid)
Leucanthemum vulgare (oxeye daisy)
Lysimachia punctata (dotted loosestrife)
Lythrum salicaria (purple loosestrife)
Mentha spicata (spearmint)
Rhinanthus minor (yellow rattle)
Stachys officinalis (betony)

Stellaria graminea (lesser stitchwort)
Trifolium hybridum (alsike clover)
Trifolium purpureum (purple clover)

Woodland

Fagus sylvatica (beech)
Acer campestre (field maple)
Carpinus betulus (hornbeam)
Juglans major (walnut)
Polygonatum odoratum (angular Solomon's seal)
Pulmonaria rubra? (red lungwort; no flower)
Sanicula vulgaris (sanicle)

MĂLÂNCRAV

Acer campestre (field maple)

Ajuga genevensis (Geneva bugle)

Anchusa azurea (Italian bugloss)

Arctium tomentosum (downy burdock)

Astragalus glycophyllos (wild liquorice)

Brachypodium erectum

Brachypodium sylvaticum (false brome)

Brassica elongata ssp. integrifolia (long-stalked rape)

Briza media (quaking grass/totter grass)

Campanula patula (spreading bell-flower)

Cardamine bulbifera (coral-root)

Carduus crispus (welted thistle)

Chamaecytisus banaticus

Chrysopogon gryllus

Clematis vitalba (old-man's beard/traveller's joy)

Consolida regalis (field larkspur)

Crataegus monogyna (hawthorn)

Cruciata laevipes/Galium cruciatum (crosswort)

Cuscuta epithymum (dodder)

Cytisus nigricans (black broom)

Dianthus carthusianorum (Charterhouse pink)

Dorycnium herbaceum

Elymus hispidus (wheatgrass)

Epipactis palustris (marsh helleborine)

Equisetum telmateia (giant horse-tail)

Fagus sylvatica (beech)

Galeopsis tetrahit (common hemp-nettle)

Galium verum (lady's bedstraw)

Geranium dissectum (cut-leaved crane's-bill)

Geranium molle (doves-foot crane's-bill)

Geranium pratense (meadow crane's-bill)

Helleborus purpurascens (purple hellebore)

Jurinea mollis

Lathyrus niger (black pea/black bitter vetch)

Ligustrum vulgare (wild privet)

Medicago falcata (yellow alfalfa/sickle medick)

Oenothera biennis (evening primrose)

Onobrychis viciifolia (pink sanfoin)

Ononis spinosa ssp. austriaca (spiny rest-harrow)

Prunus spinosa (blackthorn)

Quercus pubescens (downy oak)

Quercus robur (English oak/pedunculate oak)

Rosa canina (dog-rose)

Salix purpurea (purple-barked willow)
Salvia transylvanica (Tranyslvanian sage)
Tilia cordata (small-leaved lime)
Trifolium medium (zigzag clover)
Trifolium montanum (mountain clover)
Trifolium pratense (red clover)
Trisetum flavescens (yellow oat-grass)
Xanthium italicum (cocklebur)

SIGHIȘOARA AND CRIȘ

Acer campestre (field maple)
Asperula cynanchica (squinancy-wort)
Cardamine impatiens (narrow-leaved bitter-cress)
Carpinus betulus (hornbeam)
Geum urbanum (wood avens/herb Bennet)
Geranium pratense (meadow crane's-bill)
Ginkgo biloba
Lysimachia punctata (dotted loosestrife)
Oenothera biennis (evening primrose)
Onopordum acanthium (cotton thistle)
Picea abies (Norway spruce)
Scirpus sylvaticus (wood club-rush)
Telekia speciosa (yellow oxeye)
Tilia cordata (small-leaved lime)
Trifolium pannonicum (Hungarian clover)
Trisetum flavescens (yellow oat-grass)
Polygonatum latifolium (broad-leaved Solomon's seal)
Vinca minor (lesser periwinkle)

SASCHIZ

Grassland and scrub
Bryonia dioica (white bryony)
Campanula persicifolia (peachleaf bellflower)
Campanula rapunculoides (creeping bellflower)
Campanula sibirica
Campanula trachelium (nettle-leaved bellflower/bats-in-the-belfry)
Cornus sanguinea (dogwood)
Cuscuta epithymum (dodder)
Elymus hispidus (wheatgrass)
Eryngium planum (flat sea-holly)
Lathyrus sylvestris (narrow-leaved everlasting pea)

Lathyrus tuberosus (tuberous pea)
Lavatera thuringiaca (tree-mallow)
Leonurus cardiaca (motherwort)
Ligustrum vulgare (wild privet)
Melilotus officinalis (ribbed melilot)
Onobrychis viciifolia (pink sanfoin)
Rhinanthus minor (yellow rattle)
Rhinanthus rumelicus (rattle)
Salvia nemorosa (Balkan clary)
Thalictrum minus (lesser meadow rue)
Viburnum lantana (wayfaring tree)

Woodland

Acer campestre (field maple)
Arabis hirsuta (hairy rock-cress)

Asarum europaeum (asarabacca)
Corylus avellana (hazel)
Daphne mezereum (mezereon)
Fagus sylvatica (beech)
Helleborus purpurascens (purple hellebore)
Mycelis muralis (wall lettuce)
Polygonatum latifolium (broad-leaved Solomon's seal)
Polypodium sp. (polypody)
Quercus robur (English oak/pedunculate oak)
Sanicula vulgaris (sanicle)
Tilia cordata (small-leaved lime)

BIRDS SEEN IN TRANSYLVANIA

The following sightings also occurred towards the end of June.

Barn swallow
Black redstart
Blackbird
Buzzard
Carrion crow
Common swift
Cuckoo (heard only)
Golden oriole (heard only)
Green woodpecker (heard only)
Hoopoe
House sparrow
Jay
Magpie

Red-backed shrike
Roller
Spotted flycatcher
Scops owl (heard at night)
Skylark
Southern grey shrike
Stonechat
White-backed woodpecker
White stork
White wagtail
Wryneck
Yellowhammer

THE ROMA IN TRANSYLVANIA

The migration of the gypsies into Europe from India started before the 13th century. First they came to Persia; then to the Byzantine Empire. In 1323 their presence is recorded in Crete; in 1348 they reached Serbia and in 1378 Bulgaria. By the beginning of the 15th century they were well spread throughout Europe. Their movements have been traced through their language. Unlike the Székely and Saxon peoples, the Roma did not arrive to settle land granted to them by the King of Hungary in the largely uninhabited parts of Central Europe: they are historically a nomadic race, and they simply arrived. Nor, when they got here, did they enjoy special privileges and freedoms in return for service as border guards or farmers. Their skills were certainly appreciated although in Wallachia and Moldavia during the Ottoman period they were used as slaves, a practice which came to an end under the Habsburgs. In Transylvania the Roma were serfs of the king, a status granted to them in the 15th century and which obliged them to perform tasks for the state: there are 16th-century records of Roma being required to provide certain services to the towns, such as repairing the gates, mending the roads and making weapons. They were used for menial work as cleaners, gravediggers, dog catchers and executioners. Access to more skilled employment was difficult as it brought them into conflict with the guilds, but Roma are often to be found as horse dealers or blacksmiths, nail-makers and gold-washers. At a later stage they took up agriculture, working with both Székelys and Saxons although as serfs, never owning their own land. The Roma who settled in the Saxon villages retained their free status but were second-class citizens, typically inhabiting the smaller houses on the village edges. With the mass exodus of Saxons in the 1990s, however, many Roma have moved into the vacated houses closer to the village centres. Brateiu is a good example of a once-Saxon village that is now mainly a village of Roma. Predominantly they are copper workers; their wares are spread out for sale along the roadside. They make stills and associated objects, forbidden under the Communist regime.

The Roma suffered during the Second World War. Under Antonescu, many were taken to Transnistria to concentration camps, along with Jews and political undesirables.

Today you can often recognise their houses from the simple cross that decorates so many of them. On the whole the Roma belong to the Orthodox communities.

Though emancipation of the Roma came in the middle years of the 19th century, as well as a programme to provide access to education and to settle them in communities, there are still a few groups who have doggedly clung to their nomadic existence. If you are lucky you will come across some of them: their movements are well planned as they migrate from summer to winter pastures. They can travel in conoys of 20 or so covered wagons. It is a sight in today's world to be treasured.

Below is a list of each tribe/family group according to their historical trade or speciality. Many of the crafts in which the Roma are involved have evolved over the years and many also have come about as a result of historic restrictions on their freedom to do other work. Grateful thanks to www.discoveromania.ro for permission to reproduce the list:

Căldărari (*căldăre* = pail): boiler makers, coppersmiths;

Carausi (*caraus* = carter): they used to transport a variety of goods, now they are drivers or furniture movers;

Cocalari: they make a variety of objects using bone (*kokala* means bone in Greek). Some of them are workers in abattoirs, scavengers, flayers, but also thieves or beggars;

Corturari (*cort* = tent): these used to be the nomad gypsies; now in Romania only two percent of the Roma population is nomadic;

Cositori/Spoitori: tinsmiths (*see also Gabori, below*);

Florari: florists;

Gabori: this group live especially in Transylvania, they used to be horse thieves, now they are traders or tinsmiths;

Gropari: grave diggers, workers in agriculture and traders;

Lovari: gypsies from Transylvania who practise horse-trading (*ló* = horse in Hungarian); the horse has a symbolic meaning, is considered a magical animal and is offered as a wedding gift (as symbol of fecundity) or as symbol of power (the place where the nomadic tents are put is marked initially by the horse circumambulating the area);

Lăutari: originally musicians; now they are often also artists and actors. They are considered the Roma elite;

Fierari: blacksmiths; today they are iron workers and mechanics;

Rotari: they also do metalwork but specialise in making cartwheels;

Rudari: they work in wood or as forest rangers. Initially they used to extract gold from rivers, especially in Transylvania. The word *ruda* comes from the Slavonic word for ore; in the gypsy language *rud* means metal;

Șelari: strap makers, leather cutters, belt makers;

Sobari: chimney sweepers and stove fitters;

Turcaleți: Muslims, former slaves of the Ottomans, they speak a combination of Romanes and Turkish and have different occupations, often working as traders or metalworkers;

Ursari: gypsies who travelled with their bears and made them dance to the tune of the fiddles, concertinas and bells; jugglers and magicians. They no longer exist;

Vatrasi: gypsies who have abandoned their traditional occupations and way of life and are now assimilated in Romanian society;

Zidari: masons and bricklayers, also known as cărămidarii;

Zlătari (*zlata* means gold in Slavonic) or Aurari (*aur* means gold in Romanian): jewellers in gold and silver, gold traders.

Căldărar gypsy with his wares by the roadside at Brateiu.

ROMANIAN GYPSY MUSIC

Sadly, nowadays, there are many fewer practising traditional Gypsy musicians, *lăutari*, in Romania than there were before the 1989 Revolution. This is partly because of the ready availability of recorded music and partly because of the great exodus of Romanians since the country joined the EU in 2007. You might be more likely to hear Gypsy musicians busking in Venice these days than in wedding processions or *crâşme* (pubs) in Romania.

On the other hand, modern Gypsy music, which is traditional in most respects, is thriving, and fashionable, not only among the Gypsies themselves but also among the young from Bucharest and other cities of Romania. The best modern Gypsy singers are Sandu Ciorbă, Nicolae Guță and Denisa. Sandu Ciorbă is the most in vogue at the moment, as he plays the wildly fast and energetic music called *țiganeasca*, to which Gypsy men love to dance and show off, clicking their fingers and slapping their thighs and heels in time with the music at astonishing speed. The girls prefer another form of Gypsy music, *manele*, which allows them to dance more provocatively. *Manele* is derived originally from Turkish music, via *mahala* music from the suburbs of Bucharest, and although popular, it is criticised in intellectual circles for its banal and often anti-social lyrics. Nowadays, however, at the dances in the villages, if there are live musicians they will play a mixture of traditional Romanian dances, the *învîrtite* and *sîrbi*, but there are likely also to be *manele* and *țiganeasca*, showing that, although it is looked down upon, *manele* is, whether people like it or not, a genuine part of popular culture. Occasionally as well there will be interludes for the slower and doleful *doine*.

Although traditional Gypsy music, *lăutareasca*, is less fashionable than it was, there are some notable *tarafuri* (bands), who play both in Romania and abroad. The most famous is the Taraf de Haïdouks (or Taraful Haiducilor, to give them their Romanian name) but there are others, less well known, including Suraj from Târnăveni, the Szászcsávás Band from the predominantly Hungarian village of Ceuaș, and the Nadara Gypsy Band, also from Ceuaș. 'Na dara!' in Romany means 'Be not afraid!'

In general the Romanian Gypsy music of today is a mixture of Turkish, Greek, Arabic, Bulgarian, Hungarian and Serbian influences, and probably others too. Gypsy musicians have always adapted to the music of whichever ethnic group they find themselves among, be they Romanians, Jews or Ukrainians in the Maramureș, Hungarians or Saxons in Transylvania, or Serbians in the Banat. Modern Western music has made few inroads into the Gypsy communities of Romania. Most Gypsies have not heard of any Western bands and singers, however famous they might be in the West.

William Blacker

CONSERVATION TRUSTS IN THE VALLEY

I have mentioned several times, during the writing of this guide, the work of the Mihai Eminescu Trust (the MET), Horizon and ADEPT. I thought it would be useful to outline what these, and other notable trusts at work in the area, do. A handful of those involved in these trusts were acquainted with the situation in Romania under the Communist regime. Jessica Douglas-Home, for example, the founder of the MET, set up an English-speaking branch to confront the threat of 'systematisation', the bulldozing by Ceaușescu's regime of historic towns and villages. Some chanced to be in Transylvania as the Saxons started their exodus and therefore were among the first to understand the full impact this would have on the landscape in the villages and towns. Some of the founders of the trusts were already working in conservation outside Romania. They, more than most, understood the unique quality of this part of Europe, its value and fragility. More importantly, all the trusts mentioned below have sufficient experience not only to recongise the challenges, but also to offer solutions.

The Mihai Eminescu Trust

This trust, commonly known as the MET, was founded in London in 1986. The organisation developed slowly, due to the inauspicious political climate of the times. The Trust is named after Romania's pre-eminent poet of the 20th century, a choice which relates to the initial purpose of the organisation, which was to open channels of communication between dissident Romanian philosophers, writers and artists and Western European universities, especially Oxford and Cambridge.

One of the first major interventions of the MET was a reaction to Ceaușescu's systematisation plan. The Trust brought the danger to the attention of HRH the Prince of Wales, who then gave a successfully influential speech to the London Civic Society on the tragedy of the planned destruction of Romania's historic villages.

As part of its unique 'Whole Village Project', the Trust started developing responsible tourism by renovating Saxon houses as guesthouses for small groups of visitors. So far, the Trust has arranged for the professional training as certified tour operators of 40 villagers throughout the Târnava Valley.

In developing tourist infrastructure, the MET takes into consideration the criteria of sustainable management, local community development, cultural heritage and the preservation of the natural environment. The MET, working closely with Horizon, is organised from its office in Sighişoara. *www.mihaieminescutrust.org*

Horizon

The Horizon Foundation has supported the Mihai Eminsecu Trust in a great many projects over the last fifteen years. The outcome is designed to bring greater prosperity to each village under its auspices as well as to foster a proper appreciation of the value of cultural heritage, both historically and economically, in order to encourage conservation as the natural order of things. Villages covered in this guide that are part of the Horizon programme are Mălâncrav, Richiş and Alma Vii.

Horizon has also supported individual projects of differing natures, including the restoration of the Mălâncrav church frescoes. There have been projects in Sighişoara to restore, repair and furnish towers in the defence wall of the citadel, with a view to finding contemporary uses for these. More recently, Horizon has provided the seed funding necessary for the archaeological and architecture studies of the citadel at Alma Vii which have enabled the MET to compete for—and eventually win—a very substantial EU grant for the conservation of its defence wall and towers. Other areas in which MET has been engaged, for example town planning, education, school summer camps and nature conservation, have been backed up by Horizon funding.
www.horizonfoundation.nl

ADEPT

ADEPT was founded in 2004 to protect the Transylvania landscape and its related communities. Created over centuries, these are nature-rich, farmed landscapes created and still managed today by traditional farming communities. Ecologically rich, these are natural habitats in balance with sustainable farming practices, intrinsically linked to the small-scale communities who work in them.

These landscapes are not just of historical and aesthetic interest, they also provide high productivity and local employment as well as being havens for many of Europe's endangered wild plants and animals.

In spite of these benefits, social and economic factors are threatening these landscapes and it is only in recent years that NGOs and policy-makers have come to recognise their value. ADEPT's work to support these traditional farming communities has helped contribute to this shift in vision and policy, and ADEPT is now an NGO with national and European influence.

ADEPT's office, a source of information and publications on the area, and its tourist information centre selling local products and a range of publications about the culture and natural history of the Saxon area, are in Saschiz, near Sighișoara. ADEPT can also arrange local accommodation, and tours showing visitors the lives of local farmers, and the wildlife linked with the landscapes.

www.fundatia-adept.org. ADEPT also have a website dedicated to the Târnava Mare area: www.discovertarnavamare.org

Prodan Romanian Cultural Foundation

The Prodan Romanian Cultural Foundation is a charity, based in England, which was formed to promote Romanian culture beyond Romania's borders. They particularly focus on the activities of the Romanian diaspora who fled their country to excape the two world wars and the Nazi and Communist regimes.

Alongside promoting and collecting works by Romanian artists of the past, they also translate into English and publish works by Romanian authors and have their own recording label, Brancusi Classics. The foundation has also paid for the restoration of Romania's oldest keyboard instrument, a clavichord of 1820 at Sighișoara, jointly with the MET.

www.romanianculture.org

Pro Richiș

Some villages have also started self-help associations, which cover conservation and also practical social issues such as funding school transport. They are also encouraging volunteering and tourist centres.

Pro Richiș is made up of members of the village, and supports tourism, communication and sporting activities. There is also a strong social and economic element and the newly-opened Tourist Information Centre plays a dual role in giving community advice and helping visitors.
www.prorichis.ro

The ASTRA Library

The ASTRA Library in Sibiu was set up as the Transylvanian Association for Romanian Literature and Culture in 1861. They campaigned for the rights of Romanians within the Habsburg empire and then under the Dual Monarchy of Austria-Hungary. It now concentrates on disseminating information on Romanian cultural history, with departments of restoration and conservation, as well as running a number of ethnographic museums in Transylvania. They have provided IT support to the villages of Moșna and Biertan.
www.bjastrasibiu.ro

Hosman Durabil

The Hosman Durabil (Sustainable Hosman) Association was founded in 2005 by four Hârtibaciu Valley immigrants: two from the Hungarian-speaking Székely area, one returning from Germany and one from the Baltic Sea. Thanks to help from the Mihai Eminescu Trust, the group purchased the ruined Moara Veche (Old Mill) in the village and started to restore the complex. The milling machinery alone is worth the visit. A bakery with a wood-fired oven was installed, public milling takes place each Tuesday for the villagers, and horseshoes and other needs are made at the smithy. The barn and garden offers a venue for events, such as the local crafts markets that take place in May and September every year. They also make delicious picnics in the barn.

Tourism is a vital to the association's survival. Hosman Durabil offers, for

example, guided tours of the Old Mill in English. You can ask book a meal of local cuisine (*T: 0740 959 389 or send an email to info@moara-veche.ro, preferably with two days' notice*).
www.hosman-durabil.org

Patrimonium Saxonicum

The Foundation was set up to help preserve Transylvanian Saxon heritage by promoting tourism to Saxon monuments and advising in conservation and related legal matters. The prime mover behind this is Professor Hermann Fabini, previously city architect of Mediaş and head of the construction department of the Lutheran Church in Romania. Professor Fabini has long been at the forefront of restoration initiatives targeting the most endangered of the fortified churches of Transylvania. He has written and published, first in German and subsequently in English, *The Church-Fortresses of the Transylvanian Saxons*, drawing the attention of a wider audience to this unique cultural phenomenon. Many of the superb line drawings from the book have been reproduced, with permission, in this guide.
www.patrimonium-saxonicum.ro

Fundaţia Prinţul de Wales

This is a new charity established by Charles, Prince of Wales to support his charitable work in Romania. The Foundation will develop a number of projects to support the preservation of architectural heritage and sustainable rural development. The Foundation is a subsidiary of The Prince of Wales's Charitable Foundation (UK). Aura Woodward, Executive Director (*aura.woodward@royal.gsx.gov.uk*).

Transilvania Card (Entdecke die Seele Siebenbürgens)

This is not strictly a trust but is an initiative by the Lutheran church community to save the fabric of the Saxon churches. The site sells visitor cards that give free entry to 41 of the most important churches in the region. It also offers discounts at selected hotels etc. For details, see www.transilvania-card.ro. See too *Entdecke die Seele Siebenbürgens*.

Hans Schaas.

WINEMAKING IN THE VALLEY

Richiş was once known as a rich village and images of grapes are found on many of its house façades. Until very recently the slopes all along its valley were under vine. Now this is all in the past, as the privatised winery at Jidvei has withdrawn from Richiş, making those involved in the wine industry redundant. Hans Schaas is one of the few remaining Saxons in the village. He has been involved in winemaking since he was a boy, although he was a wheelwright by trade. It is he and his wife, Hanne, who have kept the church going. His children are in Germany.

The following is an account, in Herr Schaas's own words, of the history and importance of winemaking in the Richiş area:

'Every man, woman and child was involved with wine growing in Reichesdorf, for several hundred years before phylloxera in 1890. When the disease hit the vines, 300 people from the village of Riechesdorf alone emigrated to the USA as here there was no work at all.

To prevent this happening again and because people did not want to give up, a wine school was set up in the village at house no. 123, which was owned by Simon Nemenz. They taught the next generation how to graft onto healthy stock and schooled them in the art of pruning so this great industry was reborn. Every family grew grapes, if they owned half a hectare or five hectares or more, they planted five or more varieties of grape altogether; the so-called royal varieties.

The success of the wine industry in Reichesdorf was due to the soil, which is slightly acidic. This gives the wine its edge. I worked for 30 years in Mediaş with the chemist Dr Bocianca, who brought wines from the south of Romania and mixed them with the Reichesdorf wine. I also worked at the winery in Biertan. Every seventh year we had a harvest that yielded 170 grams of sugar to the litre, making the wine very sweet. Buyers came from Constantinople, Bucharest and, nearer to home, from Făgăraş. The Hungarians also bought from us.

Many varieties were grown together on a single plot and included:

Mädchentraube (Fetească Albă)
Welschriesling
Gornesch (Grasă)
Gornesch x Mädchentraube (Fetească Regală)
Ruländer (Pinot Gris)
Neuburger
Muscat Ottonel
Sauvignon Blanc

Of these, the Pinot Gris was the longest established here and the sweetest. Our soil is very productive. Just the quantity that was taken by train from Dumbrăveni to Bucharesti is interesting. At the time it was normal to transport six waggons each, full of 400-litre barrels. Directly after the war, when there was nothing in Bucharest, 20 or 25 waggons, each full of wine in 400-litre barrels, went to the capital. We had not been able to sell our wine during the war.

The grapes in Reichesdorf were harvested on the 15th of October each year and we had to get help from the surrounding villages, from Agnita and other places, and people were paid in grapes. Every house in Reichesdorf has its own cellar, some of them very large, such as the one in the Priest House, which can take barrels large enough to stand in. Each family had their own wine press in their barn, with a wooden channel from the press through the wall and into the cellar.

The barrels were first opened in Reichesdorf in January and tested for clarity. Then the buyers came. One year a friend's father managed to buy his house on the proceeds from a single year's grape harvest. At other times the vintages were poor but there was someone in the village who mixed the good with the bad in 1934.

The '50s were very good wine years. However, the Communists took everything. They confiscated every litre. My parents could not believe that the harvests were so good because the Communists, unlike the Saxons, had no history of winemaking; they were more used to herding sheep. They took all our wine and destroyed our vine stocks. They introduced grape varieties like Isabella and Nova—we make schnapps out of them.

When the Saxons were here, every piece of land was cultivated. In the valleys, anywhere that would take a plough was put to use to grow crops such as maize and potatoes—anything. The hills were used for vines. The problem was getting the water and the copper sulphate up to the top. It had to be taken by ox carts with the oxen on their knees up the last ten metres.

It was the Communists who built the terraces around Richiș and Biertan between 1958 and 1960. The Communist Youth did that. Previously we grew our vines, as do the Germans, straight up the hillside (as can be seen in paintings of the village of c. 1950 in the Village Hall). Every five years we had to rebuild the eroded soils. The Communists thought that terracing would stop erosion but it has not. Now all the vineyards have gone, although we had a wonderful year in 2009. We need to start producing wine again here. The Communists took everything but they cannot take the soil. We need someone to start producing wine again here.'

BIBLIOGRAPHY

ART, ACHITECTURE AND CHURCH FURNISHINGS

Batári, Ferenc: *Ottoman Turkish Carpets*. The Collections of the Museum of Applied Arts Budapest, 1994

Bielz, Julius: *The Craft of Saxon Goldsmiths of Transylvania*. Foreign Languages Publishing House, 1957

Cosnean Nistor, Letitia: *Reşedinţe nobiliare din Podişul Târnavelor în perioada secolelor XVI–XVII* [*Noble Residences of the Târnava Basin in the 16th–17th centuries*]. PhD thesis, Bucharest, 2014

Drăguţ, Vasile: *Arta gotică în România*. Bucharest, 1979

Drăguţ, Vasile: *Legenda 'eroului de frontieră' în pictura medievală din Transilvania*. BMI, 1974/2

Drăguţ, Vasile: *Pictura murală din Transilvania*. Bucharest, 1970

Fabini, Hermann: *The Church-Fortresses of the Transylvanian Saxons*. Monumenta Sibiu, 2010

Firea, Ciprian: *Art and Its Context. Late Medieval Transylvanian Altarpieces in their Original Setting*. New Europe College. GE-NEC Program 2004–7, pp. 317–60 (published 2010)

Firea, Ciprian: *Artă şi patronaj artistic în Transilvania medievală: polipticul din Sibiu*. In *Ars* XII–XIII / 2002–3, pp. 123–38

Folberth, Otto: *Gotik in Siebenbürgen: Der Meister des Mediascher Altars und seine Zeit*. Vienna and Munich, 1973

Gündisch, Gustav: *Studien zur Siebenbürgischen Kunstgeschichte*. Cologne: Böhlau, 1976 (includes a section on the life and work of Elias Nicolai)

Ionescu, Stefano et al: *Antique Ottoman Rugs in Transylvania*. Verduci Editore Rome, 2005 (2007)

Karczag, Ákos and Szabó, Tibor: *Erdély, Partium és a Bánság erődített helyei* (*Fortified Places of Transylvania, Partium and the Banat*),. Semmelweis Kiadó, Budapest, 2012

King, Donald and Sylvester, David: *The Eastern Carpet in the Western*

World from the 15th to the 17th centuries. Hayward Gallery London, 1983

Kovács, András: *La civiltà ungherese e il cristianesimo.* From the 4th International Hungarian Studies Conference (information on the organ and pulpit ordered by Prince Gábor Bethlen for Alba Iulia), József Jankovics, István Monok, Judit Nyerges and Péter Sárközy eds. Budapest-Szeged, Nemzetközi Magyar Filológiai Társaság, Scriptum Rt., 1998

Lángi, József and Mihály, Ferenc: *Erdélyi falképek és festett faberendezések (Wall paintings and painted wooden furnishings in Transylvania).* Budapest, 2002, 2004, 2006

Machat, Christoph: *Die Bergkirche zu Schäßburg und die mittelalterliche Baukunst in Siebenbürgen.* Munich 1977

Melzer, Roland: *Die Grabsteine in der Bergkirche von Schäßburg.* Siebenbürgisch-Sächsischer Hauskalender, Jahrbuch, 1980

Mérai, Dóra: *Apafi György síremléke (The funeral monument of György Apafi). Credo 11*, no. 1–2, 2005

Mérai, Dóra: *Memory from the Past, Display for the Future. Funeral Monuments from the Transylvanian Principality (16th–17th centuries).* PhD thesis, Department of Medieval Studies, Central European University, Budapest, in progress

Richter, Gisela and Otmar: *Siebenbürgische Flügelaltäre.* Innsbruck, 1992. Used for the diagrams of the altarpieces in this guide.

Sarkadi Nagy, Emese: *Local Workshops–Foreign Connections: Late Medieval Altarpieces from Transylvania.* Studia Jagellonica Lipsiensia, 2012

Servatius, Gustav: *Das Mediascher 'Kastell', die Stadtkirchenburg* (digital version at http://members.aon.at/fresh/literatur/kastell.htm)

Szilágyi, András: *Hungary's Heritage, Princely Treasures from the Esterházy Collection.* Catalogue, London, 2004

FLORA AND FAUNA

Akeroyd, John: *The Historic Countryside of the Saxon Villages of Southern Transylvania/Peisajul Istoric al Satelor Saseşti din Sudul Transilvaniei.* Fundaţia ADEPT, Saschiz, Romania, 2006

Rákosy, László: *Fluturii diurni din România–Cunoaştere, protecţie, conservare.* Editura MEGA Cluj-Napoca, 2013. Text in Romanian. Best book on butterflies.

Speta, Elise and Rákosy, László: *Wildpflanzen Siebenbürgens.* Austria, 2010. Excellent botanical source book.

HISTORY AND MEMOIR

Achim, Viorel: *The Roma in Romanian History.* New York, 2004

Bassett Richard: *For God and Kaiser, the Imperial Austrian Army.* Yale, 2016. One of the best descriptions in English of the reign of Maria Theresa especially amidst the other Habsburgs.

Bethlen, Gladys: *Visszaemlékezése elhunyt férje családtörténetére és életútjára* (*Memoir of her late husband's family history and career*). Korunk, 2002

Bodea, Cornelia and Cândea, Virgil: *Tranyslvania in the History of the Romanians.*East European Monographs, Boulder, Colorado, 1982

Cartledge, Bryan: *The Peace Conferences of 1919–23 and their Aftermath: Mihály Károlyi and István Bethlen: Hungary.* London, 2009

Czernetzky, Günter: *Lager Lyrik–Gedenkbuch 70 Jahre seit der Deportation der Deutschen aus Südosteuropa in die Sowjetunion.* Schiller. Sibiu, 2015. A book of photos, drawings and verse from the camps of the deportees.

Finkel, Caroline: *Osman's Dream. The Story of the Ottoman Empire 1300–1923.* John Murray, 2005

Köpeczi, Béla et al eds.: *Erdély története* (*History of Transylvania*). Akadémiai Kiadó, Budapest, 1986

Nagelbach, Michael A.: *Heil! and Farewell A Life in Romania 1913–1946.* Chicago, 1986. One of the few sources looking at the Saxon communities under the Germans.

Philippi, Paul: *Transylvania, a Short History of the Region, the Hungarian and German Minorities.* Schiller Publishing House, Sibiu, 2016

Porter, Ivor: *Michael of Romania: The King and the Country.* Sutton Publishing, 2005. One of the best biographies of the 20th century.

Roth, Stephan Ludwig: *Der Sprachkampf in Siebenbürgen.* Kronstadt (Cluj), 1842. Digital version from the Bayerische Staatsbibliothek.

Scholten, Jaap: *Comrade Baron*. Helena History Press, 2016. The Transylvanian artistocracy under Communism.

Shaw, Stanford: *History of the Ottoman Empire and Modern Turkey*. Cambridge University Press, 1977

Szabó, Attila M.: *Medgyes történeti kronológiája* (*Chronological History of Mediaș*). On www.medgyes.ro.

Wittmann, Anna M. and Umbrich, Friedrich: *Balkan Nightmare: a Transylvanian Saxon in World War II*. Columbia University Press, 2001.

TRAVEL AND GENERAL BACKGROUND

Akeroyd, John and Forescu, Bogdan: *Harta turistica-Tourist map, Sighișoara-Târnava Mare*. Descopera Eco-Romania no. 1–2 (2007, 2009). 1:50,000 map of the Târnava Mare area.

Bánffy, Miklós: *The Transylvanian Trilogy*. Arcadia Books, 2011 or Everyman's Library, 2013

Beudant, François-Sulpice: *Voyage mineralique et géologique en Hongrie*. Paris, 1822

Born, Ignaz: *Briefe über die mineralogische Gegenstände auf seiner Reise durch das temesvarer Banat, Siebenbürgen, Ober- und Niederungarn*. Frankfurt and Leipzig, 1774

Brown, Edward: *A Brief Account of Several Travels in Hungaria, Servia...* (1669–70), London, 1673

Carnell, Maureen and Redman, Tony: *A Taste of Transylvania–Food and Drink from the Heart of Transylvania*. Hospices of Hope, 2009

Dootz, Sara: *Mit der Sonne steh ich auf*. Landwirtschaftsvlg Münster, 2010

Esmark, Jens: *Kurze Beschreibung einer mineralogischen Reise durch Ungarn, Siebenbürgen und das Banat*. Freiberg, 1798

Hall, Donald: *Romanian Furrow: Colourful Experiences of Village Life*. Bene Factum Publishing, 2007

Ogden, Alan: *Winds of Sorrow: Travels in and around Transylvania*. Orchid Press, 2007

Paget, John: *Hungary and Transylvania*. London, 1850

Riley, Bronwen: *Transylvania*. Frances Lincoln Limited, 2007

Schaas, Johann: *Das Leben ist so schön, wenn man darüber lächeln kann!*
  Eminescu, 2013
Shakespeare, Nigel: *Times New Romanian.* Matador, 2014.

VILLAGE HISTORY

There is a selection of village histories which came out in the 1880s and
  more recently. They include:
Saschiz. Monografia Localității 2011, Târgu Mureș
Dumbrăveni. Translated from Hungarian into Romanian by Ion Calinescu
Reichesdorf, eine Ortschaft im Weinland Siebenbürgens. Compiled by
  Andreas Nemenz, Munich, 1999

Although not directly related to the Târnava Mare Valley, there are two
interesting sources on ancient farming practices in Romania: a charming
booklet, *Povestea fânului–The Way of Hay* (Google the title and download
a pdf) and an upcoming documentary on transhumance, still practised in
the hills above Copșa Mare. Visit www.transhumance.ro to watch a trailer
for this fascinating film.

INDEX

Major references are given in bold. References in italics denote illustrations.

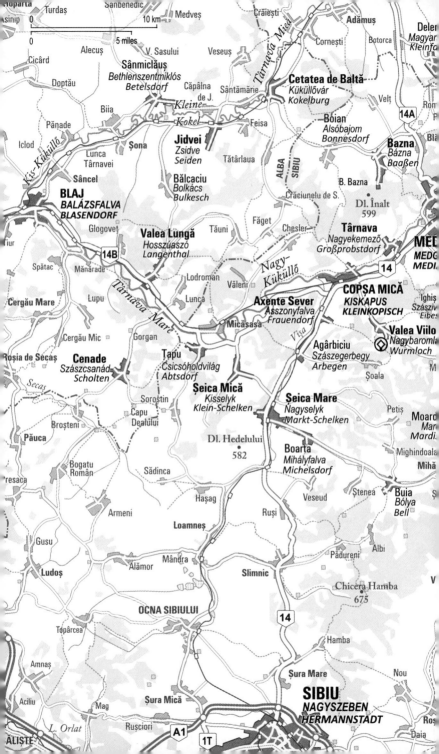